What Is Iran?

CW00821470

What is Iran? What are its domestic politics? Its history? Its international relations? Here, Arshin Adib-Moghaddam sheds fresh light on these questions, offering a general introduction to everything there is to know about this country. Uniquely, he uses musical pieces as a way to offer a holistic understanding of the full spectrum of Iranian affairs.

As a result, even the general reader is invited to traverse a wide array of topics in an interactive format which merges approaches from the social sciences with philosophy, poetry and art. These topics include a variety of themes, issues and personalities: from Trump, Khomeini, the shah, Saddam Hussein and Qasem Soleimani, to Israel, Syria, Latin America, China and the Gulf monarchies.

Ultimately, this book demonstrates in clear and accessible prose the impact of Iranian politics on a global scale, and offers solutions to the various crises enveloping the country in the region and beyond.

ARSHIN ADIB-MOGHADDAM is Professor in Global Thought and Comparative Philosophies at SOAS, University of London, and By-Fellow at Hughes Hall, University of Cambridge. He is the author and editor of seven influential books including *A Critical Introduction to Khomeini* (2014) and *On the Arab Revolts and the Iranian Revolution: Power and Resistance Today* (2013). A double graduate of Cambridge University, he received his Professorship at SOAS as one of the youngest academics in his field. Since then he has been elected to several honorary positions all over the world, some of them with royal seal and including at the Harvard University and Yunnan Academy of Social Sciences in Kunming, China. @Adib_Moghaddam

The Global Middle East

The Global Middle East series seeks to broaden and deconstruct the geographical boundaries of the 'Middle East' as a concept to include North Africa, Central and South Asia, and diaspora communities in Western Europe and North America. The series features fresh scholarship that employs theoretically rigorous and innovative methodological frameworks resonating across relevant disciplines in the humanities and the social sciences. In particular, the general editors welcome approaches that focus on mobility, the erosion of nation-state structures, travelling ideas and theories, transcendental techno-politics, the decentralisation of grand narratives, and the dislocation of ideologies inspired by popular movements. The series will also consider translations of works by authors in these regions whose ideas are salient to global scholarly trends but have yet to be introduced to the Anglophone academy.

Books in the series:

1. *Transnationalism in Iranian Political Thought: The Life and Times of Ahmad Fardid*, Ali Mirsepassi
2. *Psycho-nationalism: Global Thought, Iranian Imaginations*, Arshin Adib-Moghaddam
3. *Iranian Cosmopolitanism: A Cinematic History*, Golbarg Rekabtalaei
4. *Money, Markets and Monarchies: The Gulf Cooperation Council and the Political Economy of the Contemporary Middle East*, Adam Hanieh

What Is Iran?

Domestic Politics and International
Relations in Five Musical Pieces

ARSHIN ADIB-MOGHADDAM
SOAS, University of London

CAMBRIDGE
UNIVERSITY PRESS

CAMBRIDGE
UNIVERSITY PRESS

University Printing House, Cambridge CB2 8BS, United Kingdom

One Liberty Plaza, 20th Floor, New York, NY 10006, USA

477 Williamstown Road, Port Melbourne, VIC 3207, Australia

314–321, 3rd Floor, Plot 3, Splendor Forum, Jasola District Centre,
New Delhi – 110025, India

79 Anson Road, #06–04/06, Singapore 079906

Cambridge University Press is part of the University of Cambridge.

It furthers the University's mission by disseminating knowledge in the pursuit of
education, learning, and research at the highest international levels of excellence.

www.cambridge.org
Information on this title: www.cambridge.org/9781108844703
DOI: 10.1017/9781108953351

First published 2021

A catalogue record for this publication is available from the British Library.

ISBN 978-1-108-84470-3 Hardback
ISBN 978-1-108-94876-0 Paperback

To my students

@SOAS

#Globally

(With special thanks to Lida Sherafatmand for painting the cover for this book during the worst pandemic in recent human history)

Contents

What Is Iran?: *A Playlist*

Music to Read By:

Richard Strauss, 'Also sprach Zarathustra' (1896)
Reza Rooygari, 'Iran, Iran, Ragbar-e Mosalsalha' (1979)
Alireza Assar and Foad Hejazi, 'Vatan' (2005)
Hichkas, 'Ye Mosht Sarbaz' (2008)
Julia Boutros, 'Moqawem' (2017)

Prologue: Iran in the New World Order

'World War III?' or 'A nuclear holocaust?'. These are among the favourite questions of journalists when they ask about the endgame of Iran's recurrent confrontations with the United States. 'Only fools rush in' tends to be my answer, but unfortunately there is plenty of foolishness about, both in Washington DC and among decision-makers in Tehran. The signposts of the dangerous situation that this book addresses with alternatives for peace and understanding are indeed a threat to the whole world.[1] This is the main reason why Iran is 'shocking' so many people. The present book looks at palliative therapies to smooth out some of these emotional reactions that our topic provokes. To that end, the book was intensely reviewed and scrutinised like no other of my previous attempts to address the Iranian presence in world politics and global history.[2] No one is indifferent about Iran and Iranians, or so it seems.

As I write these lines, the outgoing Trump administration has pursued a self-declared policy of 'maximum pressure' on Iran, which includes the enforcement of a devastating sanctions regime which has contributed to the deaths of some of the most vulnerable members of Iranian society including children and cancer patients. In a ruling by the International Court of Justice, the principal judicial organ of the United Nations, the United States was ordered to lift some of the economic sanctions it had imposed on Iran, because they hindered the importation of humanitarian goods and products, as well as imperilling the safety of civilian aircraft. As a reaction, US Secretary of State Michael Pompeo announced that the United States was

---

[1] See among others my interview with Ciaran McGrath of the *Daily Express*, 'World War 3: Trump's strategy will just unite people behind Iran's leadership, warns academic', *Daily Express*, 25 July 2018.

[2] I would like to thank the reviewers for their genuine dedication to scholarly integrity, and their wide-ranging comments on and engagement with the manuscript.

1

'terminating' the 1955 Treaty of Amity with Iran, upon which the ruling was premised.[3] Any president of the United States, including the incoming Biden presidency, will face this deeply entrenched political culture that preaches hostility to Iran, and will be affected by it, as I will argue more comprehensively in Chapter 4.

Even during the worst pandemic in recent human history (which was seriously mishandled in Iran by the government of Hassan Rouhani), the Trump administration increased sanctions against Iran (and Venezuela). In common with other countries, Iran faced a devastating crisis due to the novel Coronavirus or Covid-19 outbreak. Yet the Trump administration continued its maximum pressure policies, which many Iranians saw as a form of warfare by other means that increased the death toll in the country.[4] 'The American sanctions have 100 percent and absolutely played a role,' an oncologist in Iran said at the height of the crisis in March 2020: 'We are dealing with a shortage of basic supplies, like masks, because there is an embargo on paper materials ... As a result, nurses and physicians are forgoing wearing masks to give theirs to patients.'[5] A physician interviewed for this study added that the sanctions exacerbated the situation 'at every level of the medical chain' and that innocent 'Iranians are dying because of them.'[6] Several humanitarian non-governmental organisations (NGOs) confirmed this verdict. For instance Relief International issued a stark warning at an early stage of the Covid-19 outbreak in Iran: 'There is an extreme shortage of these supplies in-country, where stock is often low due to the steep price of medicines and medical equipment – a consequence of US sanctions.'[7] Other countries faced similar shortages, certainly the United States itself which recorded the highest number of Covid-19-related deaths in the world. But these countries didn't face sanctions to make matters worse.

[3] 'Top UN judicial body orders US to ease Iran sanctions', UN News, 3 October 2018.
[4] See further Esfandyar Batmanghelidj and Abbas Kebriaeezadeh, 'As Coronavirus spreads, Iranian doctors fear the worst', Foreign Policy, 3 March 2020, available at https://foreignpolicy.com/2020/03/03/iran-coronavirus-spreads-sanctions-covid19-iranian-doctors-fear-worst/, accessed 16 March 2020.
[5] Keyvan Shafiei, 'How US sanctions intensify the spread of the coronavirus in Iran', American Prospect, 17 March 2020.
[6] Anonymous, telephone interview, 19 March 2020.
[7] See further Sarah Lazare, 'US sanctions on Iran are increasing Coronavirus deaths. They need to be stopped now', In These Times, 17 March 2020, available at https://inthesetimes.com/article/22387/iran-sanctions-coronavirus-deaths-democrats-trump-nuclear-deal-medicine, accessed 18 March 2020.

There has also been a military component to the 'maximum pressure' campaign: On 3 January 2020, Donald Trump oversaw the assassinations of one of the highest-ranking generals in the Iranian military establishment and a top commander of the Iraqi Kataib Hezbollah paramilitary force, which is closely allied to Iran. The killings brought the world near to the brink of war, when the Islamic Revolution Guard Corps (IRGC)[8] retaliated with limited intercontinental ballistic missile strikes on the US military base Ain al-Assad in Iraq, though these were carefully calibrated to avoid casualities but ensure a deterrent effect at the same time. This train of events was foreseeable, as the Iranian state had built up General Soleimani as the operational figurehead and charismatic symbol of Iran's push into Syria and Iraq which has been geared to three interdependent dynamics. First, there was the need to prevent a 'Saddam Hussein effect', i.e. minimise the threat posed by a leader or movement that would invade Iran as Saddam Hussein did in 1980. Secondly, Iran has an interest in fighting terror groups such as al-Qaeda and Daesh, and the battle with these groups constitutes Soleimani's legacy for the many Iranians who mourned his death amid a massive outpouring of grief. That the Trump administration referred to Soleimani as a 'terrorist' contradicted his status among many Iranians, by whom he was considered a war hero, also because of his role in the liberation from Saddam Hussein's forces of the Iranian town of Khorramshahr in 1983, a symbolic event celebrated in Iran to this day. There are many other Iranians for whom Soleimani represented everything that Iran should overcome: its martyrdom complex, the abiding memory of war and destruction, the pain and sorrow of the war generation, and the self-righteous and cloistered appropriation of everyday life in Iran being some of them. Thus, the killing of Soleimani and al-Muhandis unleashed a subliminal set of highly emotive imagery and symbols that speak to Shia notions of sacrifice for a higher cause that is considered to be 'just', but that many Iranians consider detrimental to pacifying the political process in Iran, including the country's international relations.

And thirdly, the adversarial policies of the Trump administration and the historical memory of US interference in Iranian affairs reaffirmed the attitude of those Iranians of Soleimani's generation whose worldview was formed by the Iran–Iraq War, that Iran needed

---

[8] I have used the literal translation of 'Sepah-e Pasdaran-e Enghelab-e Eslami' here. In the following text I use Revolutionary Guards synonymously.

to reduce the military footprint of the United States in the region come what may, as all the leaders of Iran reiterated after the killings. Certainly, the Soleimanis of this world thrive within a context of conflict. Baptised in the bloodied battlefields of the region and traumatised in recurrent periods of war, their biography is geared very closely to confrontation, which is one of the dilemmas of the contemporary history of this region. The Trump administration served this framework perfectly, to the detriment of stability in West Asia and domestic politics in Iran itself, which has been securitised even further for the time being, hampering much-needed reforms that Iranians have been dying for since the inception of the Islamic Republic in 1979.

The state of Israel is a part of this dialectic of violence. As I write these lines, Israeli prime minister, Binyamin Netanyahu, has ordered another round of strikes against 'Iranian allies' in Syria, who are well entrenched and are considered to be complicit in some of the war crimes committed during the devastating civil war in the country, as I will discuss in Chapter 5. It is symptomatic that neither the US Congress nor European allies were alerted about the imminent killing of General Soleimani and Commander al-Muhandis, when it was decided, but the Israeli state was.

The very fact that Iran has built up military assets so close to the Israeli border is, of course, in itself an indicator for the expansion of Iran's sphere of influence in the region, which is problematic from the perspective of Iranians who would like to see the country as an incubator of regional peace, rather than complicit in a never-ending cycle of violence. Iran is certainly not a military threat to Israel. But with southern Lebanon firmly secured by Iran's allies Hezbollah and with pro-Iranian forces in Syria close to the occupied Golan Heights, Israel is swiftly losing its ability to dominate this strategic theatre by sheer force, while Iran's seeming over-expansion has provoked its own backlash in terms of public opinion in some quarters of the Arab world which speaks of 'Persian imperialism'. None of this is conducive to regional peace, but it explains why Iran is targeted with sanctions and threats of war.[9]

---

[9] On Syria and Iran see further Anoushiravan Ehteshami and Raymond Hinnebusch, *Syria and Iran: Middle Powers in a Penetrated Regional System*, London: Routledge, 2002; and Jubin Goodarzi, *Syria and Iran: Diplomatic Alliance and Power Politics in the Middle East*, London: Bloomsbury, 2006.

In this way we are witnessing a momentous change of the regional order with profound consequences for the international system. Afghanistan and Iraq, after the invasions in 2001 and 2003 respectively, are examplars of the impossibility of neo-imperial control. Both countries continue to be plagued by civil unrest and instability. Hundreds of thousands of civilians have been killed as a result. Such policy failures and their devastating humanitarian consequences for the people of that region are always also precipitated by a lack of knowledge and education. These 'wars on terror' were sold to us as 'just', but brought about some of the greatest injustices of recent human history: torture, death, displacement, famine, disease, forced migration, civil war. The peoples of the region have paid a heavy price for such obvious policy failures, now firmly inscribed in the historical record by critical scholars.[10] Hundreds of students each year are taught about these human tragedies, certainly in my own courses at SOAS, in order to encourage a better understanding of this part of the world, and hopefully lead to better policy-making in the future.

The fact that the wars in Iraq and Afghanistan were won militarily but did not deliver strategic gains (Iraq is closer to Iran than at any time in current history; the Taliban continues to control most of Afghanistan) accelerated the emergence of the current order in West Asia, a process that was precipitated by the Iranian revolution of 1979. Tremors of independence were already felt when the Nassirs and Mossadeghs of this world confronted colonial structures and pursued nationalisation campaigns in the 1950s, complementing the anti-colonial projects in Latin America, Africa and Southeast Asia. But the decisive shift away from an essentially US-administered imperial order has come in the last four decades. After Southeast Asia and Latin America, West Asia and North Africa (or WANA) is the third area of the world that is painstakingly moving towards independence from US hegemony. The ideational kernel for this counter-hegemonic project and its political realisation on a global scale can be situated in the revolutions of Nicaragua and Cuba (for Latin America), China and Vietnam (for Southeast Asia) and Iran (for West Asia and North Africa). All of these revolutions were also about national independence. With mixed results, they have largely contained US hegemony in

---

[10] See among others John Hagan, Joshua Kaiser and Anna Hanson, *Iraq and the Crimes of Aggressive War*, Cambridge: Cambridge University Press, 2015.

the non-Western world, a trend acknowledged and increasingly theorised even by 'realist' scholars of international relations, such as John Mearsheimer.[11] I will return to this transnational radiance of Iran throughout the book, including its violent manifestations and the challenges this version of Iran faces within the country itself.

At least at this stage of global history, no one could fathom *coups d'état* engineered by the US Central Intelligence Agency (CIA) which brought to power dictatorial regimes such as Pinochet's in Chile after 1973 and Shah Mohammad Reza Pahlavi's in Iran in 1953. In this respect, the revolutions in Cuba and Iran have succeeded in terms of the relative independence that they promoted, even if they failed to hold to their lofty promises in terms of political freedoms and the manifest independence of the individual from the state, certainly in Iran, albeit less so in Cuba where there have been decisive strides towards democratisation. In Central and South America, the Bolivarian Alliance for the Peoples of our America (ALBA), spearheaded by the late president of Venezuela, Hugo Chavez, and the late Fidel Castro, is a counter-movement to the faltering North American Free Trade Area (NAFTA) led by the United States, if not in economic terms then certainly in terms of ALBA's emancipatory political rationale. Repeated efforts to unseat presidents, for instance in Venezuela in 2019 and again in May 2020, have failed precisely because in Latin America the mainstream political culture is geared towards independence from foreign interference. In West Asia and North Africa, such sentiments have been repeatedly expressed, in Iran in 1979 and during the 'Arab Spring' in 2010.

What is missing to complete the revolutionary ethos underlying such movements is to complement independence from foreign interference with individual, civic independence from the arbitrariness of the state. Such pluralist momentum is behind the repeated demonstrations for reform in Iran – these are efforts to make independence tangible. Without freedom from state brutality, the slogans in support of the 'oppressed' and against 'imperialism' propounded by the Iranian state ring hollow. In fact, they reveal an ugly hypocrisy that has threatened to undermine even the relative independence that the Khomeinists have demanded with such uncompromising stealth. In fact, if Islam is the

---

[11] John J. Mearsheimer, *The Great Delusion: Liberal Dreams and International Realities*, New Haven: Yale University Press, 2018.

answer, as the system in Iran continues to advocate, then failing to put forward a version of Islam that is all-inclusive doesn't merely strike at the foundational myths of the Islamic Republic, it questions the political promise of Islam at its religious roots, too. The enemies of Iran know this dynamic very well, which is why every Islamophobe joins the equally bigoted Iranophobe to automatically hate the Islamic Republic of Iran, not merely as a state, but as an idea, a bit like the innate hatred of every anti-Semite for the idea behind Israel, with no acknowledgement of its ideational contradictions and internal differentiation. General Soleimani was absolutely right about this challenge to Islam that he expressed in his will/testament. He didn't acknowledge, however, that the violence that sustains the Islamic Republic as it is has been an unnecessary threat to the security of the country including the religious precepts that the state stands for:

The basis of the enmity against the Islamic Republic throughout the world, is for burning and destroying this tent [of the *velayat-e faqih*]. You should circle around it (like the circumambulation of the Ka'bah). I swear to Allah, I swear to Allah, I swear to Allah, if this tent is harmed, there will be no sign of God's House (Ka'bah), Madinah – where the shrine of the Holy Prophet is located – Najaf, Karbala, Kadhimiya, Samarra or Mashhad, and the Holy Qur'an will be damaged as well.[12]

Such circular tension between the claim of the revolution, its discontents and reinterpretation within Iran, from a regional perspective and globally, is a central theme of the present book.

Undoubtedly, Iran has contributed to a new order in the region, and Soleimani was the poster boy of the new realities which are decisively geared to regional dynamics in a way that this part of the world has not experienced since the demise of the Ottoman Empire. The administration of Barack Obama understood these new realities after the US debacles in Afghanistan and Iraq (and to a lesser extent in Libya) which gave impetus to the new dynamics that I will explore in the following chapters. The Obama interlude testified to an increasingly non-US-centric world order and the fact that military victories do not bring about strategic gains anymore (if they ever did).

[12] 'The Spiritual-Political Will and Testament of the Martyr Major-General Qasem Soleimani', available at https://soleimany-vasiatnameh.com/en, accessed 12 May 2020.

Diplomacy had to be cultivated as 'smart power' in order to galvanise waning US influence.

A comparable worldview is characteristic of President Joe Biden's approach to world politics. As he wrote in a lead article in *Foreign Affairs*: 'The triumph of democracy and liberalism over fascism and autocracy created the free world. But this contest does not just define our past. It will define our future, as well.'[13] Biden, too, sees the United States at the heart of a cosmic battle that is global. His strategy may differ, but the hegemonic approach to the rest of the world remains. The nuances are important, though. Biden is not Trump. His instinct as a decision-maker is driven by strategy carried by diplomacy, not the short-term reactionary posturing that is so typical of Trumpism. On Iran, Biden reinvigorates the prospect of rekindling the nuclear agreement that he helped to negotiate as Obama's vice president: 'America stands alone. Trump's policies have pushed Russia and China closer to Iran, while reducing transatlantic relations to their lowest point in decades,' he wrote for CNN. 'We will continue to use targeted sanctions against Iran ... But, I am ready to walk the path of diplomacy if Iran takes steps to show it is ready too.'[14]

This relative emphasis on diplomacy is one of the reasons why the Obama administration successfully pursued the Joint Comprehensive Plan of Action (JCPOA) which resolved the dispute over Iran's nuclear energy programme. Undoubtedly, this was an historic deal. On the one side, President Obama was a leader who understood the merits of diplomacy. On the other side, the departure of Iran's reckless and politically amateurish President Mahmoud Ahmadinejad in 2013 opened up the opportunity for rapprochement. The pragmatic presidency of Hasan Rouhani, flanked by his agile and eloquent foreign minister Javad Zarif, provided an opportunity that many experts had not anticipated due to a lack of knowledge of both Iranian politics and the positive role that US civil society plays in supervising a recurrently reckless state.

---

[13] Joseph R. Biden Jr, 'Why America must lead again: rescuing US foreign policy after Trump', *Foreign Affairs*, March/April 2020, available at www.foreignaffairs.com/articles/united-states/2020-01-23/why-america-must-lead-again, accessed 7 November 2020.

[14] Joe Biden, 'There is a smarter way to be tough on Iran', *CNN*, 13 September 2020, available at https://edition.cnn.com/2020/09/13/opinions/smarter-way-to-be-tough-on-iran-joe-biden/index.html, accessed 7 November 2020.

The JCPOA showed that Iran reacts to diplomacy, as many of us had argued for a long time. The 'mad Mullah' narrative was marginalised and Iran demonstrated that the country adheres to such international agreements, albeit under duress. In the United States, William Beeman had been the most consistent advocate of a better and empathetic understanding of the country and, based on that, more diplomatic engagement.[15] Scholars like him were vindicated when Iran and the United States signed the JCPOA, against all odds.

One can only reiterate that within the context of relations between Iran and the United States, after all that had happened between the two countries, this agreement was truly historic. The JCPOA was the outcome of a moment in history that elevated the language of diplomacy over the language of war and threats. Better Iranian–American relations required a discursive shift, as I argued in an article published in a special edition of the British journal *Critical Terrorism Studies*, which was inaugurated by my spirited colleague Richard Jackson.[16] Language is important in global politics. Once the Obama administration distanced itself from the rhetoric of 'regime change' characteristic of the George W. Bush administration (and Donald Trump today), diplomacy became possible.

However, this diplomatic opening was only short-lived, because a dominant part of the political culture in the United States is driven by right-wing thinking of the most extreme kind. After the withdrawal of the United States from the JCPOA initiated by the administration of President Donald Trump and the recurrent military operations of the Israeli army against Iranian targets in Syria between 2018 and 2019, the discursive field shifted towards war again.

The US withdrawal from the JCPOA became part of a wider strategy to provoke Iran into recurrent conflict, a stand-off that repeatedly emboldened the most radical elements of the Iranian state, to the detriment of reformists and civil society. The big analytical pointers have been there: With the appointment of John Bolton, Michael Pompeo, Rudi Giuliani and others, Donald Trump surrounded himself

---

[15] See further William O. Beeman: *The Great Satan versus. the Mad Mullahs: How the United States and Iran Demonize Each Other*, Chicago: Chicago University Press, 2008.

[16] See Arshin Adib-Moghaddam, 'Discourse and violence: the friend–enemy conjunction in contemporary Iranian–American relations', *Critical Studies on Terrorism*, Vol. 2, No. 3 (2009), pp. 512–526.

with personnel whose anti-Iranian agenda goes back decades. Trump himself was enraged about the Iranian alliances in Iraq, Lebanon, Syria, the Persian Gulf and beyond. Saudi Arabia and Israel have fed this anger and the Trump administration repeatedly promised to deal with the 'Iranian threat'. Iran thus continues to be targeted by the 'right wing', previously in the form of the neo-conservatives and then of the Trump administration. The institutions of war that are created on the basis of this ideology outlast presidencies and will continue to promote a policy of confrontation, which could quickly escalate into a prolonged war.

So I have explained the first, rather more strategic effect of the withdrawal from the JCPOA, not least in order to position this study in its historical context. In simple terms, the book is written during a period when the language of war is recurrently used to confront Iran, certainly by Trump's erstwhile national security advisor John Bolton and James Mattis when he was the US secretary of defence. No serious scholar is in doubt that Bolton in particular would have ordered full-scale military strikes against Iran if he could have, whether in Syria or, if push came to shove, in Iran itself. We are living through an era of global history which is beset, even dominated, by the global right wing and their dichotomies, by a politics of confrontation which is geared to war. This is an important component of the historical context surrounding this book, as it will affect, if not determine, its reception around the world.

So in the end, the US withdrawal from the JCPOA must be seen as more than a breach of an important multilateral agreement, one that was hailed as exemplary for the future of the global non-proliferation regime: First, the US withdrawal has already caused even more military escalations in the region, as we have witnessed in Syria, where the Iranian military presence in strategic areas such as Deir ez-Zur has provoked air strikes by Israel. Second, this instability has radicalised the international politics of West Asia and North Africa. In turn, this process of radicalisation increases the likelihood of international terror attacks and erodes the sovereignty of states that are hard-pressed to police their borders against intrusions from outside powers and non-state actors such as Daesh and al-Qaeda.

In many ways, all of this is simple political science. We witnessed this violent dialectic before and after the US invasions of Afghanistan and Iraq in 2001 and 2003 respectively, when al-Qaeda and later so-called

Islamic State unleashed a campaign of unimaginable terror. Such movements lodge into polities where the central sovereignty has been eroded by external intervention. The US/UK-led campaigns against Afghanistan (2001), Iraq (1990 and 2001) and Libya (2011) are good examples. They left behind 'rump states' and eventually destroyed the ability of the central institutions of governance to act against external interferences, either by powerful regional actors (e.g. Iran, Turkey, Saudi Arabia), global powers (increasingly China and Russia) or non-state movements (e.g. al-Qaeda, Daesh etc.). This is the new world order that the recent US/UK-led wars created, and the blowback has devastated the lives of many, both here and more profoundly in West Asia.

Third, the so-called resistance. or *muqawama*. axis has been entrenched, in particular after the killing of General Soleimani and Commander al-Muhandis which galvanised the Iraqi–Iranian alliances, exactly because it fed into emotive narratives of sacrifice and 'martyrdom for a higher cause' around the *muqawama* nodal point, in this case resistance to the United States and its role in the region. Even before the killings, Hezbollah and its allies won more seats in the 2018 elections in Lebanon, factions allied to Iran continued to play a major role in Iraqi affairs, Bashir al-Assad remained in power and those movements and states opposing US hegemony saw Iran at the forefront of the battle, once again. A radicalisation of this strategic theatre in favour of such actors that are entrenched in their own antagonistic agendas is not what this area of the world needs.

Whenever the United States chooses confrontation over diplomacy, movements for democracy are crushed with ever more righteous force. All countries in the region have experienced massive demonstrations in support of social empowerment, human rights, accountability and democracy, in recurrent waves. But democracy needs peace. Human rights cannot be cultivated in an atmosphere of constant securitisation because of the real threat of external intervention. As Mehran Kamrava highlighted in his important research into the dynamics of security in West Asia, the neglect of human dimensions of security and the recurrent policies of confrontation (rather than agonism) between regional actors and global powers are causes of the long-term volatility of this part of the world, to the detriment of everyone concerned.[17]

---

[17] See further Mehran Kamrava, *Troubled Waters: Insecurity in the Persian Gulf*, London: Cornell University Press, 2018.

The present book will demonstrate that US foreign policy has been a major impediment to democracy in West Asia, and certainly in Iran.

Fourth, with the US sanctions regime exacerbating the socio-economic plight of the most vulnerable members of Iranian society, many ordinary Iranians are reminded of the long history of anti-Iranian measures by successive US governments, from the 1953 *coup d'état* that deposed the country's elected prime minister, Mohammad Mossadegh, and which reinstated the dictatorship of the shah, to the massive US support to Saddam Hussein during the Iran–Iraq War (1980–1988), and lastly the killing of General Soleimani, which has been added to this long list of US interference in Iranian affairs. In this way, a one-sided narrative of endemic enmity between the United States and Iran can be written more easily, especially by those hard-line factions in both countries that want to make any kind of rapprochement impossible.

Finally, many Iranians in civil society point to the North Korean case as a good reason for an Iranian nuclear bomb. North Korea, the argument goes, is not threatened militarily or with 'regime change' precisely because it possesses nuclear weapons. Iran's top generals echoed this view as the influential *Tehran Times* in Iran reported. For example, Major General Mohammad Jafari, the former chief of the IRGC, welcomed the US withdrawal from the JCPOA. According to him, the United States wasn't 'credible' in the first place. 'This is not a new incident', Jafari added, 'and it will not have a decisive impact against our national interests in any field.'[18] Public opinion in Iran tilted against the JCPOA, too. According to a representative poll conducted at the Center for International and Security Studies of the University of Maryland, published in February 2020:

Iranians want their government to push back against foreign pressure, not cave to it, or turn the other cheek. After US withdrawal from the JCPOA, 60 percent said in May 2019 that Iran should withdraw, too, rather than remain committed along with the other P5+1 countries ... Despite economic unhappiness, public support for additional nuclear concessions remains low. In October 2019, after a series of more stringent US sanctions had taken effect, only 4 percent of survey Iranians said Iran

[18] 'Top Iranian generals welcome US exit from JCPOA', *Tehran Times*, 9 May 2018, available at www.tehrantimes.com/news/423392/Top-Iranian-generals-welcome-U-S-exit-from-JCPOA, accessed 16 May 2019.

should accept US demands for a longer-duration agreement, only 35 percent approved of that in return for greater sanctions relief than the JCPOA
offered, and 58 percent remained unconditionally opposed to a longer
agreement.[19]

Policies of confrontation always strengthen militancy, as the diplomats
are obviously sidelined. Certainly, in political terms the rather more
hard-line wing of the IRGC is more comfortable with a situation that
reinscribes the war narrative into the US–Israel–Iran triangle. This is the
common mindset of the right wing that I mentioned above. It is geared
to binaries, confrontation, whether in DC, Tel Aviv or Tehran. To be
more precise with reference to the situation in Iran: demonstrations in
support of more democracy, even social empowerment and equality,
most recently in November 2019, are crushed more easily and with
more self-righteous violence when the demonstrators can be dehuman-
ised as 'traitors' or collaborators with the enemy. This is the real tragedy
of Iranians, that affects the current context of the present book. Such
'spasms' of violence do not yield a democratic dividend for Iranian
society. But they do turn the political arena into a battlefield. It is only
natural that a military institution such as the IRGC is rather more
comfortable in a situation that is militarised, even if the Revolutionary
Guard has metamorphosed into a polymorphic institution with its own
contradictions and internal debates, especially in the last two decades as
the detailed research of Bayram Sinkaya shows.[20]

Due to the recurrence of conflict within and about Iran, this book
about the institutional, cultural and material foundations of Iranian
domestic politics and foreign affairs seems to be as timely as ever. This
position towards representations of Iran in the global media, among
some politicians and the armada of think-tank analysts who have made
a career out of pretending to know Iran, has been an important factor
in preventing military confrontation with the country. Therefore, 'critical Iranian studies' continues to be a prophylaxis against war because

[19] Nancy Gallagher, 'Iranian public opinion highlights need to redouble efforts to
save the JCPOA', *European Leadership Network*, 27 February 2020, available
at www.europeanleadershipnetwork.org/commentary/iranian-public-opinion-
highlights-need-to-redouble-efforts-to-save-the-jcpoa/, accessed 3 March 2020.
[20] See Bahram Sinkaya, *The Revolutionary Guards in Iranian Politics: Elites and
Shifting Relations*, London: Routledge, 2017. See also Hesam Forozan, *The
Military in Post-revolutionary Iran: The Evolution and Roles of the
Revolutionary Guards*, London: Routledge, 2016.

it fosters a truer understanding of the realities in contemporary Iran. In support of peace with Iran, I delivered dozens of lectures and held many meetings at Whitehall in London, in the United States, and with high ranking decision-makers all over the world. From New Delhi, Tokyo, Doha, Kyoto, Dubai, Yerevan, Istanbul, Berlin, Brussels etc., whenever I spoke about Iran, I made a case for peace, not just out of principle, but out of analytical necessity. I am mentioning this in order to show that a counter-discourse is possible, and to encourage the new generation of peace activists and critical scholars to move beyond the ivory tower and to show presence in that battlefield of truth. There are many policy institutions, and alternative news outlets, that are now staffed with individuals whose views about Iran are better informed than those of previous generations. At the same time, these colleagues operate within the confines of the interests of their respective institutions which are tied to power configurations, sometimes even the politics of the day. So the battle for truth continues, but it is the university that remains one of the last bastions of society where this struggle can be scrutinised, if increasingly under duress.

Critical Iranian Studies Today

In an age of deception, the truth has to be told. In order to meet the standards of truth, research needs to be revised. There is no study that remains unchanged and unaffected by time. Therefore, renewal is inevitable and necessary to any intellectual endeavour, even if all of this seems retroactive in an age of fast-food knowledge in this corporatised, techno-society of ours. In this spirit of renewal, a spring cleaning of sorts, the present book distils my research about Iran, that I have been gathering for over a decade now. The book was written with new impetus after reassessing dozens of book reviews about my previous work about the country, which this study substitutes.

I have long considered my previous research about Iran as rather abstract – mission statements more than anything else. The books that I hastily finished at the beginning of my 'career' were written at a time when I was an inexperienced 'kid scholar' who was advised to publish or perish by many of his peers. Hence my brushstrokes were heavy and at times convoluted, at least from my perspective today. Academia can be a merciless and intimidating trade, and at that point of my scholarly existence I almost felt coerced to produce, so I closed my eyes, wielded the pen and published. The books were well received, but I remained dissatisfied with some of the analysis. Research on a contested topic such as Iran, in particular, has to be modified in accordance with new primary material and novel concepts in order to meet the scrutiny of critical scholarship. Maybe I have failed on this occasion as well, but the solution could only be to keep trying.

So I thought it a good moment to build on this previous research in order to paint a fuller picture of contemporary Iran, both in terms of the controversial international relations of the country and the tumultuous domestic politics. The ideas behind the books were legitimate, but the execution was incomplete. This is an opportunity to refine and recalibrate and to experiment with new methods and primary material that I have been gathering over the past decade. Ultimately, Iran continues to mesmerise, shock and challenge many people around the world, so the time is right to talk about the country from a fresh perspective. I have kept the ambition to a rather more balanced and truer analysis of the drivers that make contemporary Persia what it 'is'. It continues to be necessary to fill the huge parenthesis that opens up behind the meaning of Iran. In this ambition, I connect to the distinctive work of many colleagues.[21] I called this approach to studying the country 'critical Iranian studies', and the term has been discussed in several international symposia ever since I toyed with it.

But critical Iranian studies can't merely mean correcting the misperceptions of many people about the cultural, political and socioeconomic realities of Iran. Some of these Iran watchers, we all know by now, have rather insidious and destructive political agendas.[22] Therefore, this criticism must continue to be systematic. In the last decade or so it has been extended to a wide range of stakeholders in the Iran story, both within the country and outside, not least in order to foster a better understanding of the past, present and future of the Persian presence in global history among Iranians themselves.

---

[21] See among many others quoted in the main chapters Mohammad Tavakoli Targhi, *Refashioning Iran: Orientalism, Occidentalism and Historiography*, London: Palgrave, 2001; and more recently Narges Bajoghli, *Iran Reframed: Anxieties of Power in the Islamic Republic*, Stanford: Stanford University Press, 2019.

[22] For the wider context of 'Islamophobia', including the Iranian case, see very recently Zafar Iqbal, *Islamophobia: History, Context and Deconstruction*, London: Sage, 2020.

Iran continues to elicit many reactions. I continue to contend that these representations are too often ideological and quite simply false. Responsible scholarship remains the only way to reach a better understanding of the Islamic Republic and Iranian history and politics more generally. The administration of US President Donald Trump rehashed, in a typically brute manner, some of the 'regime change' slogans of the George W. Bush presidency which motivated me to write about misperceptions of Iran in the first place. Politics can be the art of mass deception, and contemporary politicians such as Donald Trump have an overtly inflated sense of their capabilities to bend the truth and undermine history, which doesn't make the task of approaching the topic of Iran any easier, certainly not for many citizens of the United States who are exposed to a constant barrage of carefully packaged falsehoods on a daily basis.[23]

Fortunately there are limits to the way reality can be manipulated. As I have maintained for years against many detractors, including angry and patronising ex-Mossad officials,[24] there is a very well organised lobby out there which is against everything and everyone that questions US foreign policies and/or Israeli ambitions in the region: 'Iranophobia' is the poignant word of Haggai Ram, who used the term to dissect how some of the fears about Iran in the Israeli public sphere can be interpreted as projections of perceived domestic threats to the prevalent order in Israel itself.[25] This highly charged context makes it that much more difficult to speak about countries such as Iran without being 'targeted' by all sides, including by elements of the Iranian state, and their equally problematic representation of contemporary Persia. I am writing these lines when several of my colleagues are incarcerated in Iran for no good reason. Most of us don't dare to enter the country under such circumstances. One stands up for the

---

[23] For the dialectic of this social construction of 'identities' see among others Penelope Kinch, *The US–Iran Relationship: The Impact of Political Identity on Foreign Policy*, London: I.B. Tauris, 2016.

[24] See Michael Ross, a former 'deep-cover officer with the Israel Secret Intelligence Service Mossad' as the *National Post* in Canada described him. 'Michael Ross: Iran leaves subtlety out of assassination plot', *National Post*, 22 February 2012, available at https://nationalpost.com/opinion/michael-ross-iran-leaves-subtlety-out-of-assassination-bids, accessed 12 March 2013.

[25] Haggai Ram, *Iranophobia: The Logic of an Israeli Obsession*, Stanford: Stanford University Press, 2009.

truth, speaks truth to power as the late Edward Said famously put it, and one is immediately without cover between the trenches.[26]

But to try to speak the truth is the precarious, exhausting yet ultimately highly rewarding job of today's embattled intellectuals. On social networking sites, important as they sometimes are to stay connected beyond the ivory tower, everyone expresses an opinion. Yet, opinions fall short of the standards of scholarship and research that we uphold. A tweet is exactly that – a chirp, a high-pitched soundbite chattered in the moment. It is not scholarship. There is a truth to battle for, despite some of the self-defeating postmodern musings that I have been accused of myself. If this battlefield of truth is left empty, right-wing activists enter with their destructive and patronising agendas. For them the platform of social media sites such as Twitter and Facebook is perfect because vulgarities are by definition crass, mnemonic and hasty.

Being 'right-wing' is an attitude, a way of thinking in terms of strict boundaries between self and other, us and them, friend and foe, black and white. We certainly don't need any more of that. In the face of this system of anti-knowledge, critical scholarship that makes people think in terms of complexities and interdependencies, rather than binaries, is more important than ever as democracies can only be sustained by informed citizens. Promoting such self-education through reading, then, is a contribution to a tolerant and pluralistic society which is the backbone of any strong democracy.

In strict opposition to the new and resurgent right wing, the present book starts with the premise, and then demonstrates, that the revolution of 1979 achieved something unique in contemporary global history: it firmly put a formerly dependent people, in this case Iranians, in charge of their destiny. Whatever happens in Iran today is largely determined by Iranians themselves, including the crimes of some elements of the state. No foreign government is in a position to guide politics in Iran. This is a very important analytical factor in a region where military interference from non-regional powers has been endemic.

On a deeper intellectual level, my ambition to bring Iran closer as a topic continues to be steeped in philosophy. I want to be more explicit about this philosophical angle in this study. To that end, I tell the story

---

[26] See further Edward Said, *Representations of the Intellectual*, London: Vintage, 1996.

of Iran's international affairs and domestic politics with the help of five musical pieces that I found emblematic of the subject matter and my argument. I term this approach loosely 'discursive musicology', even if this is likely to be deemed jargonistic by some of my esteemed colleagues. The music framing the chapters is meant to speak to the other senses of the reader, not 'merely' the intellect. *What Is Iran?* is the first book of its kind to employ such a multisensory approach.

Sometimes emotive themes and terms can't be expressed within the confines of language, especially when they are taken from complex cultural settings. For instance, how can we translate and understand the sentiments of the revolutionary generation merely in words? How can one fully capture the visceral horrors of the Iran–Iraq War (1980–1988) with mere discursive descriptions? Introducing the following chapters with the five musical pieces that I have chosen may make it easier to 'feel' Iran from different angles as a dense, mesmerising and rather beautiful mosaic of global human history which defies any psycho-nationalist containment, exactly because of that multicultural radiance. To that end, the translations of the lyrics are adaptive and interpretive, and the musical pieces are embedded in a wider empirical and conceptual analysis.[27] There is no pretension here that the discussion of the musical pieces is exhaustive. But they appeared to me to add to our understanding of contemporary Iran, even if the reader merely listens to the flow of the music or reads through the lyrics. To make this link between discourse and music possible, the book is the first of its kind in this field that comes with a playlist. Ideally, the reader would listen to the musical pieces, lyrics at hand, before reading the chapters. It is an experiment and I hope the reader will excuse its shortcomings.

Almost all classical philosophers of the East, certainly Farabi (872–950) and Ibn Sina (980–1037) (Avicenna), experimented with interdisciplinary methods. I take my inspiration from some of their views on music and their wider philosophy. Farabi established an early form of musical therapy in *The Philosophy of Music* and in *Meanings of the Intellect* which reiterated the therapeutic effects of music on individuals.[28] Avicenna, probably one of the biggest minds in human

---

[27] I would like to thank my colleague and friend Seyed Ali Alavi and Naghmeh Esmaeilpour for their feedback on the translations.

[28] See further Amber Haque, 'Psychology from Islamic perspective: contributions of early Muslim scholars and challenges to contemporary Muslim perspective', *Journal of Religion and Health*, Vol. 43, No. 4 (2004), pp. 357–377.

history, picked up this theme and refined it in his monumental *The Canon of Medicine* which laid the foundation for contemporary pharmacology and medical studies. Both Farabi and Avicenna had something one rarely finds these days, especially in mainstream academia: an intellectual mind willing to say no to established rules and systems of thought. They were sceptics, both in their life and in their intellectualism.

Inspired by such approaches, my own ambition to attempt to pluralise the meaning of Iran evolved out of a passage in Avicenna's *Mantiq al-mashraqiyyin* (The Logic of the Orientals) written in the eleventh century AD, out of his self-criticism that questioned, as I read the passage, all the familiar certitudes of my own understanding of history and theory when I started to think about the social sciences over a decade ago. In this particular passage Avicenna describes how the narrative of the Greek Peripatetics determined how he viewed the world and that he would now like to distance himself from that system of thought. It was a critical departure, then, for his own intellectual development: 'Since those who were the people of learning were strongly in favour of the Greek Peripatetics,' Avicenna admits, 'we did not find it appropriate to separate ourselves and speak differently from everyone else.' He thus felt compelled to follow their lead, lamenting that 'with those philosophers who were more fanatical than any of the Greek sects' he too became fanatical. To simplify: Avicenna criticised himself for overlooking the faults of established schools of knowledge (the Greek Peripatetics) while he was 'aware of their errors'. To his mind, it was disingenuous that he only revealed some opposition to the guild philosophers 'in matters in which no patience was possible'.[29] He caught himself bandwagoning with orthodoxy and he was genuine enough to admit to his intellectual omissions and to correct them. One's own conduct, after all, must be the first object of criticism.

As such, Avicenna was ready to dismiss his own position (including his vast corpus of earlier writings) in order to distance himself from the system of thought dominating his 'discipline' and historical period. He was not afraid to take on the incertitude of 'anti-foundational' knowledge, unafraid of leaving the solitudes of a familiar territory, ready to

---

[29] Ibn Sina, 'Mantiq al-mashriqiyyin', in Seyyed Hossein Nasr with Mehdi Aminrazavi, *An Anthology of Philosophy in Persian*, vol. 1, Oxford: Oxford University Press, p. 269. The translation is based on *Mantiq al-mashriqiyyin*, Cairo: Salafiyyah Press, 1910, pp. 2–4.

sacrifice his reputation amongst his peers in order to question the status quo. Such intellectual 'migration' always precipitates the advancement of new ideas. In this case they travelled from eleventh-century Isfahan and Balkh, to twenty-first-century London and Cambridge. This self-awareness of Avicenna and his principled discipline of mind connects to the way I have started this book and my emphasis on the renewal of one's own scholarship. This is the purpose here: to contribute to an understanding of Iran that appreciates the complexity of the country and the mechanisms that explain its dynamics. Only with an appreciation of this plurality of meanings can our use of the terms 'Iran' and 'Iranians', and the peoples, cultures, dialects, politics, ethics, morals and histories to which these vastly abstract words refer, be adequately explored.

That is the intellectual juncture at which I have positioned studying Iran in the past and in the present, the following chapters being at the same time an exercise in critical Iranian studies and an attempt to put central issues affecting contemporary Iran in context. The essays explore, more specifically, five topic areas of primary importance to contemporary Iran. The book starts with a discussion of Iran as a global object, a post-national approach that carves out the framework for my argument that Iran escapes stringent definitions and the authoritarian politics that they inspire. Chapter 2 conceptualises the dynamics of the country's domestic politics, followed by the strategic preferences of the Iranian state (Chapter 3), the impact of right-wing thinking on Iran's relationship with the United States and Israel (Chapter 4), and the Iranian dialectic with the region and Eurasia more widely (Chapter 5).

Critical Iranian studies is also about suggesting 'solutions' to problems, so each chapter includes ideas for reconciliation; humble analytical signposts to foster peace and more empathy, which is the ultimate normative goal of any concerned and democratic, socially conscious scholarship. There is no pretension here that the book is a manual for peace. But I contend that the ideas contained herein are helpful to think politics in less destructive and inhumane terms. My discursive musicology is meant to speak to, and inform, these analytical and normative themes from a different, syntactically freer vantage point. Iran as a journey, an explosion of meaning as the cover of this book implies. I submit the following pages as another effort at this renewal of critical Iranian studies. For a long time to come, this will be my last study of Iranian politics.

1 | Also sprach Zarathustra: *Persian Longitudes*

Musical Piece:[1]

'ALSO SPRACH ZARATHUSTRA' (Thus Spoke Zoroaster)
Composer: Richard Strauss (1864–1949)
Date: 1896
ORCHESTRAL (SYMPHONIC POEM)
No lyrics

Another Iran

Politics in Iran is not very different from politics anywhere else. The terms, idioms and metaphors differ, but the mechanisms are the same. The difference is not so much that Iran is a special case. The problem understanding the country stems from its *longue durée* in global history and the complexity that this brings about. After all, the meaning of Persia has been contested since antiquity, which has brought about layers upon layers of interpretations. The area that is today's Iran has been at the heart of civilisational and religious history since the beginning of time. Iran has produced and is a product of the world; there are few topics that have zigzagged throughout global history with such a pronounced trajectory. Therefore, to understand Iran always also means to understand the past and present of global history.

I have chosen the opening fanfare of Strauss's symphonic poem *Also sprach Zarathustra* (Thus spoke Zoroaster) as the musicological theme of this first chapter in order to underline the grandiosity of the topic. The piece, his opus 30, was created by the German composer Richard Strauss in 1896, and is one of the very creative experiments carried

---

[1] All musical pieces are readily available on the Internet and the reader is encouraged to listen to them before reading the chapters.

21

out by European romanticists, artists and composers with Oriental themes in general and Persian themes in particular. This deep and intense Iranian–European dialectic informed Thomas Arne's opera *Artaxerxes* which premiered in February 1762 at the Theatre Royal in London's Covent Garden, Georg Friedrich Handel's opera *Serse* (or Xerxes) which was commissioned in late 1737 by the King's Theatre in London, 'Der Persische Marsch' (The Persian March) performed by Johann Strauss in Vienna in the autumn of 1864 and Giacomo Puccini's opera *Turandot*, which was completed by Franco Alfano in 1926 and which was based on the poetry of the Persian (Sunni-) Muslim polymath Nizami (1141–1209). Some of these themes come out perfectly in the distinctive work of Asghar Seyed-Gohrab and Hamid Dabashi.[2]

The intense and riveting fanfare of *Also sprach Zarathustra* that I will describe below demonstrates the momentous impact on human history made by the Iranian presence. In addition, I chose this particular piece because it is a good musical metaphor to show how globally embedded the idea of Persia really is. Ideally, the reader should listen to the composition before reading this section of the book and do the same for the following chapters with the other musical selections, as indicated in the prologue.[3]

Of course, Zoroaster is an international celebrity who casts a gigantic shadow on global history and thought. He established the first religion of the book, which affected all subsequent monotheistic religions such as Judaism, Christianity and Islam. Zoroaster's Ahura Mazda transmuted, quite literally, into Hashem, God and Allah, which gives the topic of Iran a truly transcendental and metaphysical edge. This is a transnational explosion that escapes the material and ideational geography of what we associate with today's Iran – Shiism, for instance. A few examples of the broad canvas that I am trying to populate with meaning will illustrate this point further: the French

---

[2] See further Asghar Seyed-Gohrab, *Courtly Riddles: Enigmatic Embellishments in Early Persian Poetry*, West Lafayette, IN: Purdue University Press West, 2008; Asghar Seyed-Gohrab, *Laylī and Majnūn: Love, Madness and Mystic Longing in Nezāmi's Epic Romance*, Leiden: Brill Publishers, 2003; and Hamid Dabashi, *Persophilia: Persian Culture on the Global Scene*, Cambridge, MA: Harvard University Press, 2015.

[3] Richard Strauss, *Also sprach Zarathustra*, 1896.

Enlightenment thinker Voltaire referred to Zoroastrianism in order to challenge the strict interpretation of Christian scripture; the celebrated German philosopher Friedrich Nietzsche titled one of his seminal works *Also sprach Zarathustra* (Thus Spoke Zarathustra), a book that inspired generations of thinkers and poets including Michel Foucault in 1970s Paris and William Butler Yeats (1865–1939) in Ireland; and finally there are Zoroastrian deities as far afield as in the Zen temples of Japan and they are visited by the millions of 'Parsees' who live in today's India. Therefore, Iran's *longue durée* has had a longitudinal impact on the world that the composition of Strauss neatly captures.

Inspired by the groundbreaking book of the German philosopher Friedrich Nietzsche, Strauss called the opening fanfare of his composition *Sonnenaufgang* (sunrise). This is an unintended linkage to Zoroaster that Strauss himself probably was not really aware of. It provides a connection to the Zoroastrian divinity of the 'Radiant Sun' (*Hvare khshaeta* in Avestan Persian). From these beautifully spiritual beginnings the sunrise also became central to psycho-nationalist inventions in Iran when it was embedded by successive dynasties behind a lion holding a sword as the famous *shiro khorshid* (lion and the sun) symbol. The sunrise of Strauss appears purer, however. Despite its awesome radiance, the composition does not convey an ideological tension. To that end, Strauss very carefully pairs a sustainable double low C on the double basses, contrabassoon and organ, which transmutes into an explosion of the brass fanfare introducing the 'dawn' motif which includes three notes in intervals of a fifth and octave as C-G-C. This genius succession of notes simulates a spiritual sunrise that appears ideologically neutral. In this way, it is a useful musicological incentive to start understanding Iran from a perspective as far away as possible from antagonistic views presented in the global media or by the Iranian state. At base, these are merely platitudes superimposed on a term – Iran – which is meaningless and innocent at the birthplace of its etymological inception.

As such, *Sonnenaufgang* could be construed as a new awakening to understand Iran beyond strict definitions. Iran as an explosion in human history that escapes compartmentalisation along neat 'identity' categories. Only in this circular connectivity, which always also requires basic intellectual capability to be grasped, can we connect Iran to the composition of Strauss via Zoroaster. From there we can continue the line and connect the theme of Zoroaster to Stanley Kubrick's cult film *2001: A Space Odyssey* (released in 1968) and the concerts of Elvis Presley in the 1970s. Both Kubrick and Elvis used the opening fanfare of *Also sprach Zarathustra* for their artistic musings. In both settings, this powerful opus created an almost metaphysical showdown, as it set the stage for a supernatural experience: science fiction in the case of Kubrick and the related aura of superstardom in the case of Elvis. Then the show could start, carried by the power of the drum roll, which creates a sense of exultation and ecstasy which speaks to the overwhelming power of the occasion, as though it had been composed just for the moment that it frames with such breathtaking aesthetic. The complex beauty of our topic can be grasped better at this stage, now that we display it in the limelight of global history.

Another example binds the composition of Strauss more closely to my concern to free my subject matter, Iran, from the shackles of narrow identity politics and psycho-nationalist pretensions. The first historians such as Herodotus and Xenophon understood the gigantic importance of Persia very well. Amidst some 'Orientalist' myths, they wrote hymns both about the country and in particular about Cyrus (Koroush in Persian), the founder of the Achaemenid Empire. Xenophon said about him in rather exuberant prose that 'those who were subject to him, he treated with esteem and regard, as if they were his own children while his subjects themselves respected Cyrus as their "Father"'.[4] In turn 'Cyrus the Father' appears in the Bible as the great liberator of the Jews from Babylonian captivity, which gives him an exalted presence in Judaism. There is a Cyrus Street in Jerusalem; he was an inspiration to Thomas Jefferson; a seventeenth-century bust of him adorns a public building in Hamburg; there is a Cyrus statue in the Olympic Park in Sydney; and the Cyrus Cylinder – one of the first written proclamations of rights. including for persecuted Jews – is currently held in the British Museum in London (it was found in today's Iraq).[5] Certainly, there are few emperors in human history,

---

[4] Xenophon, *The Cyropaedia*, London: Henry G. Bohn, 1885, p. 281, available at https://books.google.com.au/books?id=IA4ohkXjeF4C&printsec=frontcover& source=gbs_ge_summary_r&cad=0#v=onepage&q&f=false, accessed 1 September 2019.

[5] 'Cyrus cylinder: How a Persian monarch inspired Jefferson', *BBC*, 11 March 2013, available at www.bbc.co.uk/news/world-us-canada-21747567, accessed 12 October 2018.

from Queen Victoria and Napoleon back to the Caesars of ancient Rome, who have had such a good press.

I have started with these personalities to show how high the stakes are when we speak about Iran. Emperors, philosophers, poets, saints, prophets, even God are enmeshed in the Iranian narrative and in the inventions about the meaning of the country. I could add many more examples from history. The polymaths Avicenna and Farabi who set the precedent for several modern sciences such as pharmacy and medicine and reinterpreted and preserved ancient Greek philosophy through their scholarship. Poets and philosophers of love and romance such as Rumi, Sa'adi, Khayyam and Hafiz, with their mesmerising verses, inspired a range of artists, from the German poet Goethe (an ardent admirer of Hafiz) to twentieth-century stars of popular music such as Madonna (who adores Rumi). And then there is the Iranian–Christian dialectic which continues to be lived by the Iranian-Armenian community in the country: one of the three kings who visited Jesus was represented by the Western church as the Persian scholar Melchior, and in Shia eschatology it is Jesus who would return with the so-called Hidden Imam, the twelfth direct descendant of the household of Muhammad to which the Twelver Shia branch in Iran adhere, to deliver a just world order. Iran, then, was 'there' at the birthplace of Christianity and it would deliver the resurgence of Christ, at least in the imagination of the pious.

These admittedly broad and abstract brushstrokes are helpful to understand the intense interconnectivity between Iran and global history and to demonstrate to those readers who are just beginning to be exposed to the topic the distance between these images and representations of Iran today. Now this is partially because after the revolution, the Iranian state tried to narrow down the meaning of the country along a set of Shia-Islamic precepts. I called this psycho-nationalism in my previous book.[6] I have explained in *Psycho-nationalism* why Iran has been seen as one of the 'few relatively permanent political entities' or 'historic nations' of the world.[7] The imagination of grandeur is deeply inscribed in Iranian nationalism, in particular in its modern

---

[6] Arshin Adib-Moghaddam, *Psycho-nationalism: Global Thought, Iranian Imaginations*, Cambridge: Cambridge University Press, 2017.

[7] Eric J. Hobsbawm, *Nations and Nationalism since 1780: Programme, Myth, Reality*, 2nd ed., Cambridge: Cambridge University Press, 1992, p. 137.

manifestations since the Safavid dynasty which established itself in the early sixteenth century.

Due to this historical continuity, Persia has repeatedly attracted the attention of thinkers, historians, poets and conquerors. Moreover, the discovery of the first commercially viable oil fields in Masjed-e Soleiman in 1908 profited imperial interests: commercial empires like the Reuters news agency and British Petroleum (BP) wouldn't exist without the profitable 'oil rent' extracted from Iranian oilfields under imperial duress. These factors are part of the historical consciousness of Iranians, and have been passionately discussed by them within and outside the country as part of Iran's interactions with Europe and later on with the United States. These memories include individual histories dotted with tragedy, as Iran battled for independence and against successive authoritarian states governing the country.

Several recent studies of contemporary Iran have outlined the recurrent clashes between the Iranian state and society in the twentieth century and beyond. The common theme among them is this tension about the meaning of the country, its self-construction as a 'nation'. Studies by Ali Mirsepassi and Eskandar Sadeghi-Boroujerdi, and also the thorough history of cosmopolitanism in the Iranian cinema by Golbarg Rekabtalaei, are excellent examples for these highly innovative theoretical and empirical movements in Iranian studies.[8] When Mirsepassi looks at Iran's quiet revolution, and the thought experiments to that end, he is also asking 'what is Iran?'. Is the country about Zoroaster, Cyrus the Great, the ancient seat of the Persian Empire in Persepolis? Or is Iran about Islam, Hussein, Shiism and the imamate? The tensions within and between these immensely complex ideas have never been resolved by the modern state in Iran, and presumably not even within society, which explains why none of the upheavals in the twentieth century merged into a social contract, that would pacify the politics of the country. The shah wanted an Iran geared to problematic notions of Aryanism and the pre-Islamic period. The Khomeinists protested and shifted Iran in the opposite direction, contracting the

---

[8] See Ali Mirsepassi, *Iran's Quiet Revolution: The Downfall of the Pahlavi State*, Cambridge: Cambridge University Press, 2019; Golbarg Rekabtalaei *Iranian Cosmopolitanism: A Cinematic History*, Cambridge: Cambridge University Press, 2019; and Eskandar Sadeghi-Boroujerdi, *Revolution and Its Discontents: Political Thought and Reform in Iran*, Cambridge: Cambridge University Press, 2019.

historical space to an equally unrepresentative Shia-Islamic temporality. To make matters worse, all of this happened amid constant external interventions, at the beginning of the twentieth century by Russia and Britain, and after the Second World War by the Soviet Union and the United States. And today, Iran is a diasporic nation that is appropriated by millions of Iranians from outside the country.

In turn, the revolution of 1979 exacerbated, rather than resolved, that Iranian dialectic with global history. What was presented by the revolutionaries was a fundamental metaphysical challenge to the way Iran was perceived. Nineteen-seventy-nine was an identity revolution; it radically questioned Iran's historical consciousness, the country's self-awareness and *jahanbini* (worldview). This new identity discourse centred around invented notions of a new form of Islam, with strong Persian-Shia connotations. Suddenly, for many outside the country and in Iran itself, this newly invented identity was more Semitic than Aryan, more Iran than Persia, more Oriental than Indo-European, more black than white, more third world than emerging economy, more Eastern than Western. Indeed, the historical consciousness on which analysts of Iran have prided themselves may be little more than a reflection of these invented images. Ultimately, it is possible to view that historical consciousness as a specific prejudice of a biased author (or an ayatollah or shah) who claims to know Iran and who artificially substantiates the presumed superiority of one specific image and understanding of Iran over another. We can do better – critical scholarship can get closer to the truth and it is this constant battle for the truth which acts as an incubator for a peaceful dialogue about Iran and the country's role in global history and politics.

So the task must be to refrain from putting forward a singular argument about Iran and to embrace the opening that Strauss offers with his liberating succession of notes in *Also sprach Zarathustra*. In this way we can try to contribute to a new way Iran is understood and studied. Alas, misrepresentations are not confined to the so-called Western media. Too often, such biases about faraway places have been successfully nurtured within a political habitat that acts as a superstructure to narratives of war. Good, critical scholarship, journalism and activism counters the movement towards confrontation based on false perceptions.

On Iran and other countries in Asia, Central/South America and Africa, such humanistic and empathetic dialogue with the 'other' is continuously confined and challenged. We can trace the signposts of this superstructure in US politics, from the past to the present, not least among supporters of the current president Donald Trump. Before him there were many anti-Iranian voices among the neo-conservative coterie surrounding George W. Bush, as I will explain in Chapter 4. These hostile sentiments towards other countries are not expressed in a vacuum. They are dependent on the historical context and the political agenda that they are meant to serve. So whenever there is a manufactured stand-off, initiated by a hawkish government in the United States, between it and *any* other country, this superstructure, artificially imbued with propaganda and ideology, will rear its ugly head. With regard to Iran, this institutionalised manufacturing of the country as a 'security threat' comes out perfectly in the research of Elham Kadkhodaee and Zeinab Ghasemi Tari, two young scholars at the Faculty of World Studies of the University of Tehran, who studied how the Islamic Republic of Iran is framed as a security threat in US congressional hearings.[9]

I hope that even the most sceptical reader will agree that the minimal argument that we can deduce from the discussion above is that the topic of Iran is highly contested. On the one side, there is the Iran whose 'cultural essence' is considered Persian, in which the country's ancient, pre-Islamic civilisation and the poetry of Hafiz, Rumi and Khayyam are artificially divorced from contemporary life in the country. This is the Iran favoured at cocktail parties of the right wing and by Iranian-Americans such as Ray Takeyh who talk about 'regime change' and the 'Iran threat' every now and then in order to be accepted into the echelons of power in Washington DC whenever there is a hawkish president occupying the White House. Takeyh made it onto the US Council of Foreign Relations despite predictions, such as in 2011, that 'in the next few years Iran will be in position to detonate a nuclear device'.[10]

Iran as a career – many individuals obsessed with Iran because of their own personal agendas, especially in North America, speak with that hostile attitude about a country that they have never really

---

[9] Elham Kadkhodaee and Zeinab Ghasemi Tari, 'Otherising Iran in American political discourse: case study of a post-JCPOA senate hearing on Iran sanctions', *Third World Quarterly*, Vol. 40, No. 1 (2019), pp. 109–128.

[10] Ray Takeyh, 'The march toward a nuclear Iran', *Washington Post*, 29 July 2011.

studied. This hostility and anger has transmuted into a vast landscape of 'exile' media conglomerates financed by the US State Department (e.g. Voice of America) or the Saudi State (e.g. Iran International), which are quite obviously partial and which feed into a self-induced historical amnesia that allows many Iranian exiles to live in a false reality that speaks to what they *want*, rather than informing what really *is*. This can be described as a culture of self-imposed collective detachment from reality, which is not conducive to a truer and rather more dispassionate understanding of Iran.

And then there is a rather more cultured and innocent version of Persia which continues to have a celebrated, if distorted, presence in mass culture, fed by Hollywood productions such as Robert Rossen's *Alexander the Great* or Oliver Stone's *Alexander*, Raoul Walsh's *Esther and the King*, international bestsellers such as Tom Holland's *Persian Fire*, Deepak Chopra's *The Love Poems of Rumi* and video/casino games such as The Prince of Persia. Conversely, there is the Iran whose Islamic and revolutionary identities are in conflict with those representations. This is 'Hussein's Iran', the revolutionary country that celebrates its foundational myths with a grandiose cultural claim, the place where Buddha, Maria, Muhammad, Jesus and Moses become revolutionary figures in an eternal struggle for justice and spiritual atavism. These emotive ideas, at least, are central to the way the revolutionaries in the Islamic Republic wished to portray their project.

Those cultural tensions between the self-perception of post-revolutionary Iran and the representation of the country from without are central to the following chapters. Even though the main theoretical claims and hypotheses will be obvious to the reader engaging with this book, a few underlying themes are worth re-emphasising at this stage. One of the arguments I make here is that there is an almost unbridge-able difference between the way Iran is translated to us by the international media, political functionaries and many think-tank activists and the reality on the ground, the complex existence of the post-revolutionary Iranian polity. In the current period when there is a resurgence of narratives of war and confrontation, intellectuals can hardly remain ignorant that an insidiously close relationship exists between power and knowledge – especially when it comes to such contested subjects as contemporary Iran.

Every war is precipitated by lies. It is not that truth is the first casualty of war anymore. We are now confronted with a perfectly staged and performed 'false truth' that is far more believable than reality. The reality of our surrounding world can only be sufficiently accessed in some harassed pockets of society, such as universities. The Marxists were right to highlight the perils of false consciousness, it is just that their own version of reality was not as ruthless and manipulative as the liberal-capitalist one. That is why they lost the culture war in the 1970s, which delivered the decadent, hyper-capitalist system out of which someone such as Donald Trump could emerge as the president of a profoundly well-connected country such as the United States.

One of the immediate consequences of the corruption of truth is that discourse on Iran is saturated with policy-relevant, think-tank type analyses, which are too often designed to reify the caricature of Iran as a monolithic, unchangeable, eternally problematic place. These types of analysis ignore, in many ways deliberately of course, the fact that contemporary Iran has been in the middle of a complex transformation process that affects the domestic politics and international relations of the country in an irregular fashion. Concepts and theory provide us with a helpful toolbox to explain this.

Yet until very recently, our understanding of the 'Middle East' and Iran has been shielded almost entirely from questions of theory. This discourse about Iran holds up well, owing no doubt to disciplinary and paradigmatic boundaries. For too long, most scholars of 'Middle Eastern' studies simply did not care about theory, and political theorists didn't do much to extend their empirical scope to non-Western contexts. Furthermore, the non-European world was there to be translated in 'easy' prose. Scholarship was needed as description tailored to short-fused and intellectually unequipped state officials. The situation has shifted in the last decade or so (not so much in terms of the absence of intelligence in politics). New disciplines in the human sciences such as global history, global thought, critical geography and comparative philosophies have been helpful in opening up new thought patterns that are not merely local, but global. These are some of the approaches behind book series such as 'The Global Middle East' that I initiated in 2016, Adham Saouli's 'Disruptions: Studies on Political Activism, Social Movements, and Revolutions in the Middle East', published by Edinburgh University Press, or Bloomsbury's 'Suspensions: Contemporary Middle Eastern and Islamicate Thought', co-edited by two great colleagues of mine, Lucian Stone and Jason Mohaghegh. The Cambridge Global Middle East book series that I now co-edit with Ali Mirsepassi, one of the giants of Iranian studies, offers solutions to many conceptual dilemmas that the present book tries to disentangle. The series features fresh scholarship that focuses on mobility, the erosion of nation-state structures, travelling ideas and theories, transcendental techno-politics, the decentralisation of grand narratives, and the dislocation of ideologies inspired by popular movements. This is immediately pertinent, not only to the politics of this region of the world, but world politics more generally.

At the same time one has to admit with a good dose of frustration that such scholarly initiatives pale in comparison to some of the voluminous nonsense that is being written about Iran by an armada of 'Iran analysts' hard-wired to their Twitter accounts and Facebook pages. Undoubtedly, dumbed-down flash bites lodge far more neatly into many segments of society compared to reasoned analysis which requires some thinking beyond the consensus that Iranians or 'foreign'-looking people are always the bad guys. And then there are rather more sinister proponents of confrontation with Iran. For instance, in Britain there are journalists such as Con Coughlin who have been skewing the 'Iran story' for decades now.[11] Other countries have similar Orwellian ghosts to chase, as I will explain along the way. As a consequence, there is a scarce supply of good ideas about Iran. This is not necessarily because there is no demand for such approaches. Rather, it is because a plethora of think-tank pundits, journalists, political activists, writers and others have cashed in on the Iran business, lending their consumers the self-assurance that they have understood Iran, that they know the Islamic Republic, that they can explain the country, its ancient history, diverse peoples, powerful revolutions, indeed the collective reality of its over 85 million inhabitants, without at the same time intimating to the reader that a great deal in their analyses is based on political agendas.

There is money in being anti-Iranian; it's a real career path in Tel Aviv, Riyadh, Washington DC, Dubai, Manama and in many other places. Indeed, there have been at least two senior members of Donald Trump's team, his attorney Rudolph Giuliani and his former national security advisor, John Bolton, who received substantial amounts of money from the Mujahedin-e Khalgh (MKO) organisation, a fringe cult-movement somewhat reminiscent of the Manson Family. The MKO is despised by Iranians for its collusion with Saddam Hussein

---

[11] See further David Leigh, 'Britain's security services and journalists: the secret story', *British Journalism Review*, Vol. 11, No. 2 (2000), pp. 21–26.

during the Iran–Iraq War.[12] The organisation was responsible for several terrorist attacks in Iran including on US targets. Yet the aforementioned context allows the group to recruit interns among the student population of prominent academic institutions such as George Washington University in Washington DC. To many Iranians this would be comparable to al-Qaeda offering jolly internships to students at the University of Tehran – an unthinkable scenario.

The market for 'Iranian pop studies' allows some to become 'experts' on the country by writing a tweet, or an opinion piece without footnotes or with the citation of a few newspaper sources at best. Indeed, the quantitatively superior presence of these populist opinions about Iran, especially in North America and not so much in Europe, India, Japan and Russia, indicates that the putting into discourse of contemporary Iran, far from undergoing a process of rationalisation, on the contrary continues to be subjected to a mechanism of intransigent politico-emotional incitement. As one peace activist from the United States who visited Iran as a part of a delegation in March 2019 declared, 'We don't get a lot of information about [Iran] in the United States.'[13]

That the techniques of biased discourse exercised over Iran in some circles have not been subdued and that the will to know the complexities of Iran's post-revolutionary transformation has been compromised is, of course, primarily due to the repressive climate in the Islamic Republic itself. Iran's cultural revolution in 1981–1982 entailed a process of artificial 'monopolisation' of the academic curricula and media landscape under an Islamicised psycho-nationalist agenda that marginalised competing views to the extent that there continues to be a raft of artists, poets, writers, political analysts and philosophers who

---

[12] See further Rhys Dubin and Dan de Luce, 'Bolton's ascent gives Iranian group a new lease of life', *Foreign Policy*, 30 April 2018, available at https://foreignpolicy.com/2018/04/30/bolton-iran-mek-terrorism-trump/, accessed 12 June 2019; and Ambassador Daniel Benjami, 'Giuliani took money from a group that killed Americans. Does Trump care?', *Politico*, 23 November 2016, available at www.politico.com/magazine/story/2016/11/giuliani-mek-terrorist-group-money-bolton-iran-214479, accessed 12 November 2018. See also www.ft.com/content/cc6d5774-b23d-11e0-9d80-00144feabdc0; www.bloomberg.com/news/features/2019-04-05/where-rudy-giuliani-s-money-comes-from.

[13] See further 'US peace delegation to Iran welcome by foreign minister met by FBI agents on return', *The Real News Network*, 10 March 2019, available at https://therealnews.com/stories/u-s-peace-delegation-to-iran-welcomed-by-foreign-minister-met-by-fbi-agents-on-return, accessed 12 August 2019.

think about Iran either under duress within the country, in jail or from the confines of exile.

No contemporary state in Iran empowered its citizens to think freely. If there are breakthroughs, such as in the hard sciences and in Iran's world-class cinema, they are accomplished against some of the odds enforced by the security organs of the state.[14] These intransigent attempts to monopolise the interpretation of culture before and after the revolution in 1979 have hampered the establishment of decentralised, liberalised institutions which could compete on a global scale, as the cultural, philosophical and intellectual depth of the history of the country merits. Conversely, the immediate presence of the state pretty much everywhere has stymied the growth of human studies, especially with regard to the social and political sciences and philosophy. Most Iranian intellectuals, both in the diaspora and within Iran, agree that in the face of these intrusions into culture, the 'Reconquista' of Iran's vast cultural archives has remained unaccomplished.

Exploring the Iranian 'self' and its corresponding 'other' has been a constant theme in the modern intellectual discourse of Iran. The question *ma cheguneh ma shodim?* (How have we become who we are?), revisited in the post-revolutionary context by the Tehran University professor Sadeq Zibakalam,[15] has occupied the paradigms of most modern intellectual 'godfathers' of the country,[16] from Khalil Maleki (1901–1969) and Ahmad Kasravi (1890–1946) to Jalal Al-e Ahmad (1923–1969), Ali Shariati (1933–1977) and Ahmad Fardid (1909–1994), differences notwithstanding. As my brilliant colleague Ali Mirsepassi explained in a detailed study, it was Fardid who coined the term *Gharbzadegi* (or 'westtoxification') which was then picked up by al-e Ahmad and other Iranian revolutionaries including, at a far later stage, by Ayatollah Khomeini.[17] Modernity was experienced in

---

[14] On the allegorical 'method' of post-revolutionary Iranian cinema see Negar Mottahedeh, *Displaced Allegories: Post-revolutionary Iranian Cinema*, London: Duke University Press, 2008.

[15] See further Davood Gharayagh-Zandi, *Nahadha-ye madani va hoviyat dar Iran* [Civil groupings and identity in Iran], Tehran: Entesharat-e tamadon-e Iran, 1380 (2001).

[16] See also Negin Nabavi, 'The changing concept of the "intellectual" in Iran of the 1960s', *Iranian Studies*, Vol. 32, No. 3 (1999), pp. 333–350.

[17] See further Ali Mirsepassi, *Transnationalism in Iranian Political Thought: The Life and Times of Ahmad Fardid*, Cambridge: Cambridge University Press, 2017.

Iran as an onslaught on Iranian identity enforced by a stealthy, iron-fisted monarchy that ruled in the name of a pro-American (and secular), psycho-nationalist ideology. For the opponents of the shah, westtoxification denoted a national pathology, a state of cultural schizophrenia that divorced the true Iranian self from its wellspring of ideational purity. Such presumptions of origins fed into the belief that a total transformation of life can be achieved: revolution as an ode of love, as destiny, as refuge from an alienating world. This romanticism was at the heart of modern revolutions in Iran and elsewhere, for instance in Russia, China and Cuba. It was this promise of hope in a hopeless world that could turn everyone into a revolution-ary – if only you would believe in this utopia that would deliver the radical new order that is imagined with a good dose of intoxicating, positivistic certainty. In the twentieth century such idealism was still possible.

In revolutionary Iran, this oasis of hope was increasingly transfixed along loosely Islamic lines by the intelligentsia, in particular the legend-ary Ali Shariati who mixed powerful Islamic-Shia symbols with cosmo-politan themes that delivered an ideational Molotov cocktail that exploded with vehement force during the revolution of 1979. 'And then when I want to recognise my self,' said Shariati, 'I feel another culture's culture in place of my own. I complain of sufferings which are not even my own, and lament the pessimism that is not suited for my cultural, philosophical, and societal realities, and I discover aims, ideals and sufferings which are natural for that other society ... but which do not pertain to my society.'[18] Such highly passionate senti-ments, couched in terms of existentialist yearning that Shariati picked up in Paris, denote a spiritual and material call for a realistically non-existent 'pure' identity which was characteristic of the idealism of twentieth-century revolutionaries such as Shariati.[19] This had nothing to do with the Iran that we can transfix along the musical composition of *Also sprach Zarathustra*, of course. Strauss's composition evapor-ates stringent forms of 'identity politics'. Conversely, Shariati created

[18] Ali Shariati, 'Civilisation and modernisation', in Lloyd Ridgeon (ed.), *Religion and Politics in Modern Iran*, London: I.B. Tauris, 2005, p. 185.

[19] Arash Davari offers a fresh look at this issue here: 'A return to which self? Ali Shariati and Frantz Fanon on the political ethics of insurrectionary violence', *Comparative Studies of South Asia, Africa and the Middle East*, Vol. 34, No. 1 (2014), pp. 86–105.

an idea of Iran that was densely ideological. It was meant to serve the purpose of revolution, after all. In this sense, he was not very different from his contemporary Ernesto 'Che' Guevara, whom Shariati admired, and who was equally obsessed with re-engineering subjectivity. At heart, Shariati and Che were romantics – they were in love with the revolutionary promise and intoxicated by their moment in history. As Guevara famously said:

At the risk of seeming ridiculous, let me say that the true revolutionary is guided by great feelings of love. It is impossible to think of a genuine revolutionary lacking this quality. Perhaps it is one of the great dramas of the leader that he or she must combine a passionate spirit with a cold intelligence and make painful decisions without flinching. Our vanguard revolutionaries must idealize this love of the people, of the most sacred causes, and make it one and indivisible. They cannot descend, with small doses of daily affection, to the level where ordinary people put their love into practice.

The leaders of the revolution have children just beginning to talk, who are not learning to say 'daddy'; their wives, too, must be part of the general sacrifice of their lives in order to take the revolution to its destiny. The circle of their friends is limited strictly to the circle of comrades in the revolution. There is no life outside of it.[20]

In Cuba and in Iran such themes gained currency among the people exactly because they were so radically juxtaposed to the morbid politics of the *ancien régime*. Both Batista and Mohammad Reza Shah were seen as stooges of the United States, inauthentic, corrupt and with no real commitment to the people and their daily travails. In Iran, this impulse to flee the present reality in a disposition of romantic reverence for a new future (premised on a reinvented past) found its radical form in the narratives of *Bazgasht beh khish* (return to oneself) and *Gharbzadegi* which were central to intellectual life in 1960s and 1970s Iran. 'Iranian romanticism' condemned the materialism of the Pahlavi socio-economic doctrines and transplanted the intellectual

---

[20] Ernesto 'Che' Guevara, 'Socialism and Man in Cuba', available at www .marxists.org/archive/guevara/1965/03/man-socialism.htm, accessed 4 November 2020. See further Dierdra Reber, 'Love as politics: *Amores Perros*, and the emotional aesthetics of neo-liberalism', *Journal of Latin American Cultural Studies*, Vol. 19, No. 3 (2010), pp. 279–298.

himself into the struggle for the idealised future. Its agents advocated respect for 'authenticity'; Iranian romanticism placed a special value on the past, and reinvented idealised heroes of Muslim history, especially the persona of Imam Hussein, who was celebrated as the eponymous hero of the evolving revolutionary play. Hussein was the grandson of the prophet Muhammad and was killed in the iconic battle of Karbala in AS 680 by the forces of Yazid, an event commemorated during the month of Muharram. In the process of revolutionary ecstasy, this humble tale was turned into a cosmic play for justice which could wash away the sulphuric stench of Satan, once and for all.

Yet I have considered it a feature of Iran's *post*-revolutionary intellectual landscape that the very self of Iran's identity discourse, including that 'Hussein paradigm', appropriated and interrogated in the pre-revolutionary period, has been deconstructed and partially secularised all the way down to the 'traces' of the country's ideational archives: to the arcane fixed number of verses (*ghazzal*) permeating the poems of Jalaledin Rumi (Mowlana) and Hafiz; the epic tales of Rostam and Sohrab compiled in the *Shahnameh* of Ferdowsi; the esoteric mysticism of Omar Khayyam's *rubayyat* (quatrains); the political treatise of Abu Nasr Farabi; the *Avesta* (Fundamental Utterance) of Zoroaster; the dialectical musings of the *Mu'tazillah* and the Shia imamate. After the revolution, and in particular after the death of Ayatollah Khomeini in 1989, all of these themes have been up for incredibly inventive reinterpretation, under duress within Iran itself, but also from outside the country by the armada of scholars appropriating these vast intellectual archives from new perspectives.

This critical current, as indicated partially carried by a network of scholars and intellectuals who think about Iran from outside the country, has given impetus to an intellectual journey (*hejra*) away from the solitudes of imagining Iran within one authentic, exclusive metanarrative – Persian, Islamic or Shia. This process of reimagining the country is nurtured by two major institutions of Iran's heavy intellectual heritage: on the one side philosophy exemplified by the dialectic imperative intrinsic to the writings of Farabi, Tusi, Razes, Avicenna and others; and, on the other side, Persian poetry and art, the enduring relevance of Attar, Hafiz, Khayyam, Sa'adi and Rumi. It is in the art and poetry of these individuals that the meaning of Iran is purged of its psycho-nationalist venom. This is Iran painted on a canvas as a beautifully open and abstract space, rather than a portrait squeezed into a gilded frame. The composition of Strauss chosen for this chapter speaks to those sentiments which are imbued with a sense of love and care, without the revolutionary dictum that Che Guevara and Shariati called for. This is self-less love without a motif versus self-sacrificial love for a particular political agenda, in this case revolution. The former negates violence and antagonism, the latter demands it.

In a short introductory chapter like this, one can scarcely begin to cover all the ideas of Iranian thinkers and poets, nor, for that matter, can one expect to present an intellectual historiography of contemporary Iran. Suffice it to say that all social and political research, in a certain mimetic sense, is a reinterpretation of something; originality in our trade, as opposed to the natural sciences, is really to go beyond the *given*. Not only do intellectuals act within a given culture which shapes their thoughts, but they also work on the basis of pre-existing knowledge that can never really be discarded in total. We had better be honest about our own positionality then. This mixed cocktail, a cosmopolitan of sorts, is something that Iran's contemporary intelligentsia is painstakingly digesting. They are starting to think within an open ideational genealogy of Iran, conscious of its suspicion towards dry ontological certainties (*yaquin*), arrogant normative assent (*tasdiq*), hardened methodological conception (*tasawwur*) and stringent empirical definition (*hadd*).[21] Against the odds of oppressive governments before and after the revolution, Iranian intellectuals have been moving away from authority and towards individual freedom, away from self-objectification and towards an independent self, away from the secure fixities of the status quo and towards the drama of the secular, away from hierarchy and towards the sovereignty of the people, away from utilitarianism towards transcendence. In this sense, they have entered a post-structural zeitgeist that is increasingly divested of stringent systems of thought about what Iran 'is' and what it 'is' not.

---

[21] See further Shahrokh Haghighi, *Gozar az moderniteh? Nicheh, Fuko, Liotar, Derida* [Beyond modernity? Nietzsche, Foucault, Lyotard, Derrida], Tehran: Agah, 2001. See also Niku Sarchosh and Afshin Jahandideh's translation of Michel Foucault's *La Volonté de savoir, Eradeh beh danestan: Michel Fuku*, Tehran: Nashr-e Ney, 1383 (2004). For an overview see Afshin Matin-Asgari, 'Iranian postmodernity: the rhetoric of irrationality?', *Critique: Critical Middle Eastern Studies*, Vol. 13, No. 1 (1994), pp. 113–123.

This libertarian trajectory is central to the 'School of Love' and here especially Hafiz's poetry which gained him the title 'Tongue of the Unseen' (*lisan al-ghaib*), a translator of the other-worldly. This is to say that as students of Iran, it is important to be aware that contemporary debates between Iranian intellectuals cannot be detached from the overall ideational archives of the country. On the one side, many of the arguments that are floating around cannot be divorced from the philosophical engagements between *Akhbaris* and *Usulis*, *Asharites* and *Mu'tazillah*, *Kalam* and *Falsafah*, *Mashasha'i* and *Ishraqi*, *Urafa* and *Irfani*. On the other side, they cannot be analysed in isolation from the Iranian sensitivity to the transcendental, the propensity for poetic romanticism, which is embedded in the Persian language.

There is merit, then, in trying to attain to a higher level of critical historical consciousness, where the problem of bridging the gap between past and present is apprehended as a problem in itself, that is to say a problem whose solution is not to be found by pushing Iranian history into a confined space, Islamic, Persian, Shia or other. The more the governing elites in Iran have tried to narrow the meaning of the country down to platitudes, the more clearly they failed to escape the global currents of which Iran has always been a part. The formula for holding on to power in Iran is not to reduce the country to Shia-Islamic (the Islamic Republic) or Persian-Aryan (the shah) clichés. Iran is a global construct, embraced and blessed by a global consciousness. Governing Iran is not possible without an appreciation of that rapturous dialectic with the world to which the musical piece of this chapter speaks to so graciously.

The state in Iran has been recurrently reminded of that responsibility to divest governance in the country of its psycho-nationalist charge, most recently in the demonstrations of 2009, 2017 and 2019. It is true that these movements towards reform were about very concrete grievances. In 2009, the demonstrators rallied against the re-election of President Mahmoud Ahmadinejad, whose rather odd and amateurish tenure alienated many upper-middle class Iranians. In 2017 and 2019, the protests were about bread-and-butter issues, primarily in the provinces where the current president, Rouhani, failed to deliver upon his election promise to forge a rather more equitable economic order, not least because of the sanctions war unleashed by the Trump administration but also because of systemic failures in Iran itself that the government of Rouhani failed to address. These massive implosions must be analysed as surface effects of something profound: an emerging historical consciousness that arises in the impulse to create a new social contract between Iranian society and the state – Iran as a novel theatre production if you like. If this Iran can be understood as a performance, Iranians seem to say to their state, at least let's make sure we enjoy it. We have surely paid a heavy price to hang in there! These are some of the basic messages that Iranians have tried to convey to their leaders and they are all about keeping the broad contours of the libertarian/egalitarian message of the revolutions and revolts marking Iran's contemporary history, and adjusting their content to the realities of the present.

There is then a massive rupture here which is causing these recurrent earthquakes that have shaken the tectonic plates that hold this space called Iran together. This is comparable to the brass fanfare of *Also sprach Zarathustra* which is so immensely rapturous that it has opened this space to imagine Iran from a freer perspective. In her anti-foundational, relativist project, Iran's 'prototypical' post-revolutionary intellectual and activist may be positioned within a long tradition of such critical thought in Iran.

This rich philosophical tradition continuously chimes with the political culture of the country. Yet, whereas the narratives of *Bazgasht beh khish* and *Gharbzadegi*, which fuelled the revolution of 1979 with an immensely explosive identarian Juggernaut, were creative when they reminded Iranians of their past, they were counter-productive when they made of the 'fallen' present of Pahlavi Iran *nothing but* a consequence of deviance from Iran's idealised self. By contrast, interrogating that very self equips Iranian intellectuals in the period after the revolution with the power to penetrate the myths of a coherent past, to move away from universal certainty towards relative judgement as Farabi demanded. From that perspective the meaning of Iran is in the making: the historical archives of Iran are the a prioris of what can be expressed about the Islamic Republic. Here, the space of Iran is widened, more accommodating, less ideologically charged.

All of this means, in less conceptual terms, that the country hasn't stopped to reinvent the meaning of Iran. For sure, confining definitions of Iran to stringent themes is quite a futile endeavour, not least because fragments of Iran's heritage continue to be excavated in the vast archaeological sites of Iranian-Azerbaijan, Baluchistan,

Iranian-Kurdistan, Lorestan, Khorrasan, Khuzestan and Fars province almost on a monthly basis.[22] Imagine Britain discovering another ancient site every month. Archaeologists would have to question previous knowledge, historians would reinterpret the contours of 'national identity' in accordance with the new discoveries and the state would have to adjust its idea about being English or British, concepts that are under duress even without another major archaeological discovery that would challenge them. In Iran, this influx of history is increasingly accepted as an indicator that grand ideological experiments which proclaim one single meaning of Iran are simply wrong and untenable.

The salutary turn towards critical reflection on the contested, historically engineered meaning of Iran has been effected, certainly in the 1990s and early twenty-first century, amongst others by 'revisionist' clerics such as Mohsen Kadivar, Abdollah Nouri and Hasan Yousef Eshkevari and oppositional intellectuals such as Abdolkarim Soroush and Hashem Aghajari. Their stars have somewhat waned, not least because their paradigms display many of the contradictions of contemporary Iran, in particular an unnecessary commitment to 'Islam' as a political object of truth and source of identity. Islam can be left alone, given that the classical philosophers of the Muslim renaissance, polymaths such as Farabi, Avicenna and Averroes (Ibn Rushd), pursued different and more fruitful intellectual paths, even hundreds of years ago. For them being Muslim did not translate into a hysterical call for Islamicity for everyone. Their ideas did not lend themselves to the nefarious politics of identity, which is so typical of our current age.

But the rather more decisive push towards reinterpretation away from any type of authoritarian ideology comes from the many scholars and intellectuals who write about Iran with genuine dedication from outside the country. Although Iran's critical thinkers have no real methodological, theoretical or epistemological headquarter and only a few tolerated outlets for expressing their thoughts, their antifoundational ideas continue to extract themselves across the vast spaces of Iran's contemporary intellectual landscape which has always cast its shadows globally. They have thus created 'liberated territories' for intellectual activism, enabling a form of pluralism with regard to

---

[22] See further the website of Iran's Cultural Heritage Organisation at www.mcth.ir.

scholarly work and Iran's political status quo alike. We are now firmly placed in that space that Kubrick and Elvis appreciated about the composition of Strauss. Now our topic can be centre stage, carried on by the brass fanfare, to greet the reader in an open space which seems as though it has been composed with a nod to the infinity of meanings that our subject matter deserves.

2 | *God and Politics: Inside the Islamic Republic*

Musical Piece:

'IRAN, IRAN (RAGBAR-E MOSALSALHA)'
(Iran, Iran, a Storm Made of Automatic Rifles)
By: Reza Rooygari (1946–)
Release Date: 1979

Adaptive, free translation of lyrics:

Allah Allah Allah
There is no God but Allah
Iran, Iran, Iran, a storm (made) of automatic rifles (shooting on demonstrators)
Iran, Iran, Iran, (we) raise our fists and (we) declare from (the) roofs
There is no God but Allah
Allah Allah Allah, Allah o Akbar (God is the Greatest)
Iran, Iran, Iran, this spilt blood and the deaths from (our) uprising
Listen to the screams of our people
Look at us, a hurricane (of believers)
Iran, Iran, Iran the screams of our people, we, the hurricane
Allah Allah Allah
There is no God, but Allah
Allah Allah Allah, Allah o Akbar (God is the Greatest)
The tears of the orphans, the blood of the martyrs
When spring arrives, a hundred tulips (will) rain from heaven
The martyrs, their blood are (our) witness: A hundred tulips will rain from heaven
Allah Allah Allah
There is no God but Allah
Allah Allah, There is no God but Allah
Allah Allah Allah, Allah o Akbar (God is the Greatest)
Tomorrow when spring arrives, we will be free (only then) will we rest
Iran, Iran, Iran, Tomorrow when spring arrives, we will be free (only then) will we rest

No oppression, no chains, we are in the service of God
Iran, Iran, Iran, no oppression, no chains, we are in the service of God
Allah Allah Allah
There is no God but Allah
Allah Allah, There is no God but Allah
Allah Allah Allah, Allah o Akbar (God is the Greatest)
Those who say 'Allah' and have remained committed to their faith
Those who were not ready to accept disbelief (Kofr) and bow to a regime
which is against God
Those slain in the way of the Lord, May they be blessed with (the divine light)
Spread the message that there is no more fear, insecurity and worry
To the firm believers, May you be granted a divine reward which the
prophets promised you
Allah Allah Allah
There is no God but Allah
Allah Allah, There is no God but Allah
Allah, Allah, Allah (I am a witness, there is no God but Allah and
Mohammed is his messenger) Allaho Akbar
Allah, Allah, Allah (I am a witness, there is no God but Allah)

Islamised Revolution

Revolutions intoxicate. They are mind-altering like drugs or an aged bottle of Glenmorangie single malt whisky. Karl Marx, always also a bourgeois bohemian, must have thought about this effect of revolutions when he described religion as the opiate of the masses. Religions intoxicate too, Marx would agree, but like LSD, the Fata Morgana disappears into thin air, once the mind sobers up. In beautifully analytical German prose, Marx correctly analysed the powerful and enchanting romance with God and the world that any religion of the book so righteously promises. To his inquisitive mind, religion must be indicted for the illusions that it creates when it puts its objects on a 'high', as opium does. The gods need to be banished, Marx proclaimed, because they have failed to deliver the promise of a better tomorrow. Therefore, the criticism of religion is '*in embryo, the criticism of that vale of tears* of which religion is the *halo*'.[1]

---

[1] Karl Marx, 'Introduction', *A Contribution to the Critique of Hegel's Philosophy of Right*, 1843, available at www.marxists.org/archive/marx/works/1843/critique-hpr/intro.htm, accessed 12 December 2013, emphasis in original.

When the French philosopher Michel Foucault ventured into Tehran in 1978 in order to cover the revolution for the Italian newspaper *Corriere della sera*, he picked up that famous quote of Marx. Foucault was both a romantic and a sceptic, and certainly one of the great minds of the twentieth century. He too envisaged a better future for humanity, but he was less convinced than Marx that the communist utopia was the right one. In his commentary about Iran, he emphasised the point that Marx made about religion-as-spirituality, which was largely overlooked by materialists and hyper-realist interpreters of Marx's oeuvre. Given the lifelong interest of Foucault in forms of spirituality, he argued that the revolution in Iran was not an opiate for the masses. Instead, it constituted a new spirit for a spiritless world: Revolution as salvation.[2]

The explosive situation in Iran during those revolutionary weeks gave impetus to such exuberant statements by the world's leading intellectuals of the time. Against all odds, the Iranian revolution became one of the central events of contemporary global history. This is exactly because the utopian and romantic yearnings of the revolutionary generation in Iran were intermingled with a global zeitgeist prevalent among the combative "68 generation' everywhere. There was Woodstock, there was Jimi Hendrix, there was John Lennon, there were revolutionary movements popping up all over the world and the campuses of universities were brimming with calls for radical change especially from the left, but in particular from an increasingly successful anti-colonial movement anchored in Latin America, Africa and Asia (eastern and western). Foucault was certainly right about the Iranian contribution to these global calls for emancipation, even if he was wrong about the political momentum which delivered the Islamic Republic of today. Foucault would have been the first to admit that the empirical underpinnings of his philosophy were Eurocentric and that his initially positive take on the revolution in Iran was not informed by a close reading of Iranian history and politics. Like the revolutionaries themselves, Foucault was caught up in the momentary suspension of history that this exceptional event delivered in 1979. In the end, he never really

---

[2] See further Behrooz Ghamari-Tabrizi, *Foucault in Iran: Islamic Revolution after the Enlightenment*, Minneapolis: University of Minnesota Press, 2016.

recovered from the trembles that the Iranian revolution caused, not least within himself.[3]

In many ways Marx was right too. Religion as politics does intoxicate, in the Iranian case through a potent mix of Shia Islam and Persian nationalism with immense psychological power. Che Guevera could only liken revolution to love because there is this genuine feeling of exaltation in that very special moment, a sense of positive transcendence, even hubris, that makes this passage of time so exhilarating. In Iran this particular form of transcendental politics created the 'illusions' that Marx referred to. These dreams of a better tomorrow were necessary to bring about the downfall of the monarchy; for a revolution to happen people have to believe. In this way, the Iranian revolutionaries successfully forged a counterculture and its underlying critical discourse that was effective enough to dislodge the *ancien régime* of the shah.

The discourse of Shariati, al-e Ahmad, Fardid, but in particular the vigorous tropes that Khomeini propounded with such stern certainty and totalitarian vigour, had one thing in common: they all professed the possibility of the task. They were positivistic in the purest sense of the term. They delivered what the German philosopher Karl Mannheim termed a chiliastic utopia which promised to succeed de facto in the realisation of its projected content, i.e. revolution. 'Only those orientations transcending reality', Mannheim explains, 'will be referred to ... as utopian which, when they pass over into conduct, tend to shatter, either partially or wholly, the order of things prevailing at the time.'[4] Interestingly enough, Foucault used exactly this expression as well. To his mind, the Iranian revolution shattered the order of things, indeed the whole 'planetary system'.

Unrelated to the Iranian revolution yet with direct relevance for its analysis, Mannheim goes on to explain that such 'chiliastic' utopias are expressions of the ideal that is realisable in the here and now. 'For the real Chiliast', he elaborates, 'the present becomes the breach through which what was previously inward bursts out suddenly, takes hold of the outer world and transforms it.'[5] Paul Ricoeur argues in a similar

---

[3] See Arshin Adib-Moghaddam, *On the Arab Revolts and the Iranian Revolution: Power and Resistance Today*, New York: Bloomsbury, 2013.

[4] Karl Mannheim, *Ideology and Utopia: Collected Works of Karl Mannheim*, vol. 1, London: Routledge, 1936, p. 173.

[5] Ibid., p. 193.

vein, elaborating that chiliasm 'has the idea of a millennial kingdom coming from heaven ... [It] assumes a transcendent point of departure for a social revolution based on religious motives.'[6] Many Iranians believed in the metaphysics of such divine deliverance which made the emergence of clerical politics dominating the Iranian state possible in the first place. God was too involved in the political ideologies being invented here to prevent the emergence of theocratic structures which were institutionalised immediately after the revolution in 1979.

Khomeini was explicit about this inclusion of God, even when he was vague about the exact contours of his concept of the 'Supreme Jurisprudent' (*velayat-e faqih*), the leadership of a clerical philosopher-king, a concept so obviously affected by the Platonic tradition in Shia political philosophy: 'God has conferred upon government in the present age the same powers and authority that were held by the Most Noble Messenger and the Imams.' This is the deification of power in Iran that Khomeini perfected. 'Now, however, it is no longer a question of a particular person,' Khomeini proclaimed further, 'government devolves instead upon one who possesses the qualities of knowledge and justice.'[7] The 'Supreme Jurisprudent' as pope and Caesar who stands at the heart of the current constitution of Iran, as religious authority and head of state – this is what Foucault didn't anticipate and this is how the illusions that Marx wanted to set aside delivered a new political reality for Iranians and a major challenge to the prevailing world order.

Like the French, Russians, Chinese and Cubans before them, Iranians believed in the imminence of change, in the Iranian case brought about by a Muslim international that would shatter the status quo. Khomeini became the nodal point of this exceptional moment in global history and used it to institutionalise his version of an Islamic Republic. At the same time, he made it unmistakably clear that the revolution did not belong exclusively to Iran, when he declared that 'Islam [was] revealed for mankind and the Muslims ... An Islamic movement, therefore, cannot limit itself to any particular country, not

---

[6] Paul Ricoeur, *Lectures on Ideology and Utopia,* ed. George H. Taylor, New York: Columbia University Press, 1986, p. 276.
[7] Ruhollah Khomeini, *Islamic Government: Governance of the Jurist*, Qom: The Institute for Compilation and Publication of Imam Khomeini Works, 1379 (2000), p. 45.

even to the Islamic countries; it is the continuation of the revolution by the prophets.'[8]

The musical piece that I have used to frame this chapter speaks to those themes. The tropes of struggle, sacrifice, revolution, change, utopia, are central to Reza Rooygari's iconic song 'Iran Iran (Ragbar-e Mosalsalha)' which inspired a whole generation of revolutionaries in Iran. The emotive lyrics, which are set in tune with a repetitive, militant melody dominated by drum rolls, speak of the blood of the 'martyrs of the revolution' which would bring about a 'hundred tulips from heaven', an allegory to the respite from oppression that the revolution promised. The tulip became a symbol of sacrifice in revolutionary Iran much like the poppy which adorns the Tower of London and the attire of many British citizens on Remembrance Day, when the United Kingdom commemorates its fallen soldiers. Without the benefit of historical distance from the horrors of war, Iranians since the beginning of the Iran–Iraq War have thrown tulips at the caskets of the fallen veterans as a sign of respect. In the song of Rooygari, such metaphors are used to anthropomorphise Iran, to feminise, and to turn 'her' into a person with consciousness, feeling, personality and emotions. At the same time, the song has an eerie, in many ways tragic, yet defiant message – it is clearly steeped in the bloody struggles that the revolutionary generation fought to attain their utopia. My general analytical point being that periods of intense violence and rupture bring with them a set of tragedies, powerful enough to turn the beauty of flowers into memorable metaphors and seemingly contradictory tropes charged with pain, pride and heroism, and certainly nostalgia.

At Behesht-e Zahra, the national cemetery of Iran where most of the hundreds of thousands of Iranian war veterans are buried, a 'blood fountain' coloured in red was meant to symbolise these sacrifices made at the war front and during the revolution. The deep red colour of the tulip and the love that it symbolises in Iranian culture lent itself to these psycho-nationalist themes geared to problematic notions of blood and sacrifice for the nation (hence also the redness of the poppy which follows the same psycho-nationalist rationale). 'When spring arrives a

---

[8] Sermon delivered on 2 November 1979, in Farhang Rajaee, *Islamic Values and World View: Khomeyni on Man, the State and International Politics*, vol. XIII, London: University Press of America, 1983, p. 82.

hundred tulips rain from the heavens,' Rooygari sings with his penetrative voice. The humble tulip is turned here quite violently into a
transcendental connection between the revolution and its godly, metaphysical appeal to the heavens. The discourse and the political culture
of this revolution was exactly metaphysical, which is why God played
such an important role in the imagination of this generation of
Iranians. It also explains why the revolution delivered a state dominated by clerics who repeatedly used their power arbitrarily and with a
vehemence that was frightening and at times distinctly violent: Beware
of the righteous.

God as deliverance from tyranny. In Iran in 1979, Islam was thought
of as a liberation theology, which is why the Islamic Republic continues to be measured in accordance with that libertarian, freedom-
loving impetus behind the revolution. The song of Rooygari captures
this paradox perfectly. The other dominant themes of the lyrics of the
song, such as freedom, breaking away from the chains of tyranny and
putting oneself in the service of this godly revolution and its leader
Ayatollah Khomeini, are largely expressed in an allegorical, poetic
language which reveals both the melancholy and the intense sense of
euphoria that the revolutionaries felt. The voice of the singer is repeatedly interspersed with the chorus which is sung with immense intensity:
'There is no God but God, God is the greatest.' This is the chant that
Iranians shouted from the rooftops at night-time in the winter of 1978,
in defiance of the martial law proclaimed by the shah. Saying the
phrase is also the first requirement to become a Muslim and it is
repeated by the pious during their daily prayers towards Mecca.
'Spread the message that there is no more fear, insecurity, and worry' –
such intense idealism buttressed the hope that millions of Iranians
placed in the revolution and the Islamic Republic, exactly at the time
of its inception when this song was produced.

This is how strong, powerful, rigid yet highly emotive ideas under-
gird the *raison d'être* of states. At the time of its birth, the Islamic
Republic was sent out to the world as a project, almost a divine
mission. Even today, the ruling classes in Iran continue to believe in
the model that the Islamic Republic was meant to represent to the
'downtrodden' and 'dispossessed' of this world (*mostazafan* in
Persian), who were empowered to rule after the revolution.
Whereas the *ancien régime* adhered to the elitist representation of
the monarchy and Iran as the heir of pre-Islamic Persian empires at

the gates of reconstituting a 'great civilisation' (*tamadon-e bozorg*), the opposition to the metaphysics propagated by the Pahlavi state reverted to Shia-Islamic anti-colonial imageries as the dominant narrative of the Iranian self. The actual existing and ongoing order of the Pahlavi state (topia), was counteracted with 'wish-images' suitable to function as a counter-hegemonic rallying call for the opposition (utopias).[9]

Romanticising, yet frugal in their exaltations of the millenarian cause, erudite, yet bellicose in their manifestos for political emancipation, opprobrious, yet sanctimonious in their language of protest, and passionate, yet myopic in their promises about a better future, pre-revolutionary Iranian intellectuals managed to organise the Iranian population around powerful ideas, advocating not only revolutionary domestic change, but also the transformation of the identity of the Iranian state from a monarchic-nationalistic status quo power to a revolutionary-revisionist movement perceived to be in the vanguard of the fight for a new, equitable world order. This utopian-romantic, even hubristic self-perception (in the sense that the frail nation-state is elevated to the status of a vehicle of divine substance) constituted the nucleus of the political culture of revolutionary Iran. The following paragraphs investigate the cognitive reification of this political culture, followed by an exploration of its institutional manifestations. I have explained some of these dynamics in previous studies, so the reader will excuse the summarised approach taken here.

Trajectories of Revolutionary Political Thought

Carried by a cadre of revolutionary visionaries equipped with a range of counter-hegemonic utopias (Marxist, Communist, Maoist, Islamist etc.), the political culture of Iran experienced a radical change during the 1960s. In order to legitimate the monarchy, the Pahlavi state emphasised the ancient, pre-Islamic Persian heritage of Iran. Moreover, both Mohammad Reza Shah (r. 1941–1979) and his father, Reza Shah Pahlavi (r. 1925–1941) nurtured the idea of 'Persianism'. As a recent book by a colleague at the University of London demonstrates, The Pahlavis embedded the idea of 'identity' in Iran in the partially

---

[9] I have employed the terminology of Karl Mannheim here; see his *Ideology and Utopia*, p. 174.

racist discourse about a superior 'Aryan' nation (*mellat-e aryan*).[10] As with all such psycho-nationalist tropes, the nation was marked out in terms of language, in this case Persian which was presented in true 'Orientalist' fashion as Indo-European. One of the many titles of Mohammad Reza Shah included *Aryamehr*, which means 'light of Aryans' in Persian. His father, Reza Khan, who established the Pahlavi dynasty, promoted the name 'Iran' (or 'Land of Aryans') instead of Persia and supported the elimination of Arabic terms from the Persian language.

Golnar Mehran, a professor at Al-Zahra University in Tehran, argues in a similar vein: 'The self presented during the late Pahlavi period was mostly Aryan, taking pride in Iran's "superior" civilisation, language, and culture, and filled with a sense of supremacy toward neighbouring nations and cultures. What was important', she elaborates, 'was Iraniyat. Thus, government sponsored schoolbooks, especially history and Persian-language textbooks, instilled a sense of Iranianness, Iranian spirit, and Iranian identity among the young.' Conversely, in the textbooks of the Islamic Republic, there is a 'shift to the Irano-Islamic identity, as opposed to the solely Iranian one. The *national-religious* identity', in short, 'replaced the exclusive emphasis on *national* identity.'[11] In her examination of the image of Arabs in modern Persian literature, Joya Blondel Saad reaches a similar conclusion. She argues that for 'some Iranian nationalists, the Other has been not so much the West, but the Arabs and Islam'.[12]

At the heart of the revolutionary process was a relentless battle for the ideational fabric of modern Persia then. If the Pahlavi state attempted to externalise the Arab-Semitic other from the Iranian-Aryan self in order to position Iran more firmly in the 'Western' camp, oppositional intellectuals constructed the narrative of 'westtoxification' to protest this 'westernisation' of Iran. The term itself was introduced by a rather angry

[10] This has been fully discussed in the recent scholarship. See Reza Zia-Ebrahimi, *The Emergence of Iranian Nationalism: Race and the Politics of Dislocation*, New York: Columbia University Press, 2016.

[11] Golnar Mehran, 'The Presentation of the "Self" and the "Other" in Postrevolutionary Iranian School Textbooks', in Nikki R. Keddie and Rudi Matthee (eds.), *Iran and the Surrounding World: Interactions in Culture and Cultural Politics*, Seattle: University of Washington Press, 2002, p. 247, emphasis added.

[12] Joya Blondel Saad, *The Image of Arabs in Modern Persian Literature*, Lanham, MD: University Press of America, 1996, p. 134.

Iranian thinker by the name of Ahmad Fardid, as the research of Ali Mirsepassi shows, but it was popularised by the sensitive and intellectually eclectic Jalal Al-e Ahmad.[13] His influential book, which was published in the fall of 1962 under the Persian title *Gharbzadegi*, focused on dissonance, the articulation of an increasing gap between what was considered to be the authentic self of Iran and the 'distortions' caused by 'Western' modernity.

Employing a medical analogy, Al-e Ahmad deprecated the decadent, mediocre and inauthentic status of Pahlavi Iran. If left untreated, he argued, the spread of the disease-like present would lead to the demise of the country's cultural, political and economic independence, because society was made susceptible to 'Western' penetration.[14] Moving beyond the Iranian context, Al-e Ahmad saw the struggle against *Gharbzadegi* (westtoxification, occidentosis or westitis) in terms of a conflict between the 'Occidental West' and the 'Oriental East'. Reverting to the metaphor of 'the machine', he argued that while the 'West' had learned to master the 'technology of modernity', the mediocre 'East' was kept in a state of political and economic dependency. The definition of this milieu of subjugation and power was dramatised as a means to alert the 'Eastern mind' to the creeping intrusion of 'westtoxification' and its corrupting symptoms on societies programmed to be subservient to their imperialist masters.[15]

The second dominant narrative that had a determining impact on Iran's shifting self-perception and its relationship to the 'West' emerged from the writings of Ali Shariati. With reference to the anti-dependency theory of Al-e Ahmad and the Islamic-reformist writings of Mehdi Bazargan, Ayatollah Mottahari and others, Shariati developed a comparably critical position toward imperialism and cultural, political and socio-economic dependency on the 'West'. During his education at the Sorbonne in Paris, Shariati was in contact with figures of the French left, whose political outlook and intellectual paradigms influenced his later writings. These included Catholic Islamologist Louis Massignon to whom he was a research assistant between 1960 and 1962; the Jewish-Russian émigré George Gurvitch who was his professor in

---

[13] See further Mirsepassi, *Transnationalism in Iranian Political Thought*.
[14] Jalal Al-e Ahmad, *Plagued by the West (Gharbzadegi)*, New York: Caravan, 1982, pp. 10 ff.
[15] Jalal Al-e Ahmad, 'The outline of a disease', in Lloyd Ridgeon (ed.), *Religion and Politics in Modern Iran: A Reader*, London: I.B. Tauris, 2005, p. 168.

sociology; Islamologist Jacques Berque whose class on the 'Sociology
of Islam' Shariati audited in 1963–1964; Frantz Fanon whose seminal
The Wretched of the Earth he translated (in collaboration with others)
into Persian; and Jean-Paul Sartre whose attempt to reconcile existen-
tialism with Marxism and humanism had an important influence on
Shariati's own attempt to synthesise social scientific concepts with
Shia-Islamic political thought.[16]

Like many Iranians of his generation. Shariati was also heavily
influenced by the Cuban revolution and he introduced Ernesto Che
Guevara's *Guerrilla Warfare* into Persian. As with Al-e Ahmad, who
moved from communism to experimenting with Islamist ideas, the
milieu out of which Shariati emerged was distinctly cosmopolitan (if at
times naively utopian), imbued with revolutionary ideas from the international Left, and from third-world movements that were galvanised by
global processes of decolonisation. As a recent book about his enduring
legacy in Iran and the world demonstrates, Shariati 'immersed himself in
various revolutionary debates and radical anticolonial and anti-
imperialist activities taking place at the time'.[17]

In one of his main publications, titled *Bazgasht be khish* (Return to
oneself), which appeared as serialised articles in the Iranian daily
Kayhan between 22 April and 22 June 1976, Shariati juxtaposed what
he considered as the perfectly true and authentic identity of Iran as a
nation, whose inner structure is expressed in the epic of Imam Hussein's
shahadat (martyrdom), with the inauthentic status of the fallen present
under the Pahlavi shahs, whose inner structure made Iran susceptible to
the corrupting influences of 'Western' culture. For Shariati, the former is
rectitude and totality, the latter disintegration and inadequacy.[18]

As lay religious intellectuals whose ideas appealed to the disillu-
sioned middle-class urban youth in 1970s Iran, Shariati and Al-e
Ahmad introduced revolutionary ideas to a wide audience outside the

---

[16] See Ali Rahnema, *An Islamic Utopian: A Political Biography of Ali Shariati*,
London: I.B. Tauris, 2000, pp. 119–128.

[17] Siavash Saffari, *Beyond Shariati: Modernity, Cosmopolitanism and Islam in
Iranian Political Thought*, Cambridge: Cambridge University Press, 2019, p. 7.
A fascinating map compiled by Maryam Rabiee and Ali Rahnema traces the
footprint that Ali Shariati left in Paris, charting the favourite places that he
visited. It is available at www.makanism.com/shariati-the-preoccupied-flaneur-
in-paris, accessed 12 August 2019.

[18] Ali Shariati, 'Civilisation and modernisation', in Ridgeon (ed.), *Religion and
Politics in Modern Iran*, pp. 192–193.

religious seminaries. This interaction gave impetus to the emergence of a systematic, Muslim liberation theology which gave impetus to a culture of revolt. Translated by the organised political movements into revolutionary action, the force of this systemic movement transcended the powers of both its makers and its agents – it engendered its own dynamism, its own 'utopian reality' rendered transcendent by its intoxicating claims. Introjected with such a powerful, authoritative discourse, Iranians were driven by the belief that the revolution *was* a revolt against the *mostakbaran* (oppressors), that the shah *was* the incarnation of Yazid, that Iran *was* the battlefield where the party of God (*hezb'allah*) was struggling against the Greater and Lesser Satan, that Khomeini *was* the messianic chaperone guiding the slave revolt in its mission to smash the idols (*bot*) of the imperial masters. This revolutionary reality penetrated Iranian thinking to its core; and not only the mindset of Iranians. Even Michel Foucault, and others in the 'West' such as Oriana Fallaci, Peter Scholl-Latour and the *Independent*'s foreign affairs correspondent Robert Fisk, could not escape its awesome force as evidenced in their initially positive take on the events in Iran. 'When I first saw Yassir Arafat – admittedly he was no Khomeini – I was mesmerized by his eyes,' wrote the flamboyant, hyper-feminist and self-professed Islamophobe journalist Oriana Fallaci after she interviewed Khomeini:

What big eyes you have, I wanted to say. When I first met Hafez al-Assad of Syria, I was captivated by the absolute flatness of the back of his head, so straight I could have set a ruler against it without a crack showing. I spent an evening at dinner with King Hussein, perpetually astonished at how small he was, irritated that I couldn't get him to stop playing with the box of cigarettes that lay on the table between us. And now here was one of the titans of the twentieth century, whose name would be in every history book for a thousand years, the scourge of America, the Savonarola of Tehran, the 'twelfth' Imam, an apostle of Islam. And I searched his face and noted the two small spots on his cheek and the vast fluffy eyebrows, the bags under his eyes, the neat white beard, his right hand lying on his knee, his left arm buried in his robe . . . We were the foreign consuls arriving at the oriental court, waiting to hear the word of the oracle.[19]

---

[19] Robert Fisk, *The Great War for Civilisation: The Conquest of the Middle East*, London: Harpers Perennial, 2006, p. 151.

So even Fallaci, well known for her antipathy to Islam in general and Islamic politics in particular, could not escape the gnomic appeal of revolutionary Iran in that winter of 1978–1979. Fallaci found Khomeini intelligent, and 'the most handsome old man I had ever met in my life. He resembled the "Moses" sculpted by Michelangelo.' Khomeini was

not a puppet like Arafat or Qaddafi or the many other dictators I met in the Islamic world. He was a sort of Pope, a sort of king – a real leader. And it did not take long to realise that in spite of his quiet appearance he represented the Robespierre or the Lenin of something which would go very far and would poison the world. People loved him too much. They saw in him another Prophet. Worse: a God.[20]

Despite her brash attitude, Fallaci was perceptive when it came to judging character. Khomeini *was* a charismatic revolutionary who had the ruthlessness to demand and pursue total change.[21] At the right time for his gigantic enterprise he said no – no to the shah, no to the interim government of Shapour Bakhtiar, no to Israel and no to the United States. But Khomeini was also a Machiavellian politician: when necessary he compromised in truly pragmatic fashion to fulfil his revolutionary vision, for instance during the Iran–Iraq War and the so-called Iran-Contra affair when he accepted US weapons via Israeli intermediaries in order to resupply the Iranian military with their much-needed arsenal. With the ruthlessness that revolutionaries are wont to display – certainly Lenin and Mao – he uprooted the monarchy and replaced it with an Islamic Republic that he envisaged as a clerical, even godly, enterprise in the service of his definition of Islam. In this massive political explosion, it was not only Iran's revolutionary generation that was caught up in the powerful reality of late 1970s Iran: the revolutionary momentum engendered trans-cultural reactions. Thus, it should not have come as a surprise that after toppling the shah, the Islamic Republic institutionalised the revolutionary utopias as central ideological precepts of the state. Ultimately, it was this process that established Iran as a revisionist power in international affairs and that reintroduced religion as an expression of revolution into the study of political events worldwide.

[20] Quoted by Margaret Talbot, 'The Agitator: Oriana Fallaci directs her fury toward Islam', *New Yorker*, 5 June 2006.
[21] See further Arshin Adib-Moghaddam (ed.), *A Critical Introduction to Khomeini*, Cambridge; Cambridge University Press, 2014.

The song of Rooygari makes it clear that religious passion was a central force in this revolution. The revolutionary reality transmuted the paradigms of *Gharbzadegi* and *Bazgasht beh khish* into a radical counterculture that succeeded in destroying one of the most powerful states in the Persian Gulf. Glorifying the symbols of Iranian and Shia romanticism – the aesthetics of *shahadat* (martyrdom), the sufferings of their Imam Hussein, the just age of the Imam Mahdi (twelfth imam of the Shia who is said to have gone into occultation until judgement day) – this generation of Iranians extracted, channelled and dispersed their emotional energy to the receptive revolutionary masses.[22] Once internalised, this emergent culture appeared as an objectified reality to its agents. This aestheticised political reality had its own structure, meaning, symbols and imagery. Hence, the *Shuhada* (martyrs) were not merely freedom fighters giving their lives for the revolutionary cause. The revolutionary reality represented them as the 'candles of society [who] burn themselves out and illuminate society'.[23] Martyrdom was not a loss, it was a choice 'whereby the warrior sacrifices himself on the threshold of the temple of freedom and the altar of love and is victorious'.[24] Likewise, Imam Hussein – the exalted, almost eponymous hero of the revolutionary play – was not merely a religious-political personality among others. 'He was that individual who negated himself with absolute sincerity, with the utmost magnificence within human power.'[25] This 'ideal man', Shariati contended,

holds the sword of Caesar in his hand and he has the heart of Jesus in his breast. He thinks with the brain of Socrates and loves God with the heart of Hallaj ... Like the Buddha, he is delivered from the dungeon of pleasure-seeking and egoism; [l]ike Lao Tse, he reflects on the profundity of his primordial nature; ... [l]ike Spartacus, he is a rebel against slave owners ... and like Moses, he is the messenger of jihad and deliverance.[26]

---

[22] One of the main tenets of Iran's *Ja'afari* or Twelver Shi'i school is that the Twelfth Imam went into hiding (*gheiba*) and will return to establish the just rule of God on earth (together with Jesus).

[23] Mortada [Morteza] Mutahhari [Mottahari], 'Shahid', in M. Abedi and G. Leggenhausen (eds.), *Jihad and Shahadat: Struggle and Martyrdom in Islam*, Houston, TX: Institute for Research and Islamic Studies, 1986, p. 126.

[24] Ali Shariati, 'Arise and bear witness', available at htttp://www.shariati.com, accessed 24 March 2003.

[25] Ibid., 'A discussion of Shahid', in Abedi and Leggenhausen (eds.), *Jihad*, p. 233.

[26] Ali Shariati, *On the Sociology of Islam: Lectures by Ali Shari'ati*, trans. Hamid Algar, Berkeley: Mizan Press, 1979, p. 122.

These grandiose interpretations set the cornerstones of the Islamic polity that emerged, even if Shariati and al-e Ahmad were against the orthodox clerics. They toyed with too many inventions to which they gave a new 'Islamic' colouring to expect a secular-pluralistic order that would ensure the liberties of Iranian citizens without religious restrictions. In the end and involuntarily, they have to be seen as co-conspirators in a revolutionary play that they never really directed.

Making an Islamic Republic: A 'Godly' Sovereignty

It has been my proposition that the events of 1979 can be explained in terms of inventions of political identity and culture. The factors that I have highlighted favour this ideational analysis over other interdependent factors such as the socio-economic situation in 1970s Iran. Undoubtedly, the emergence of an urban underclass, the rampant hyper-modernisation policies of the shah and the class differences of 1970s Iran gave impetus to the revolutionary process. But despite inflationary pressures and the socio-economic gulf between the cronies of the shah and the Iranian underclass who lived in the 'favelas' surrounding the urban centres, the country was largely an economic success story in the 1970s. The revolution took place in a society far more socio-economically developed than was Russia in 1917, Cuba in 1959 or China in 1949. Half of the Iranian population lived in cosmopolitan urban areas, per capita income was about $2,000 per annum, Iran was one of the biggest recipients of US foreign aid, and Iranians were materially better off than a decade before due to a sustained period of economic growth, that was only matched by Japan.

The discourse of Khomeini, his supporters and the counterculture of 1970s Iran heavily influenced by the themes of Shariati's 'return to the self', and al-e Ahmad's 'westtoxification' favour an analysis of the revolution based on ideas. Khomeini knew very well the intoxicating effect that religion can have when he famously declared that people do not become revolutionaries for the price of watermelons. The images and symbols that he espoused were certainly not based on economic calculations; he was not content with selling a business enterprise to the Iranians. Rather, this was an identity revolution steeped in themes of self-redefinition, cultural renewal, anti-imperialism, third-world emancipation and other emotive rallying calls that tied the events in Iran to global history and the dialectics between state and society that the combative '68 generation provoked all over the world, certainly in terms of the powerful Iranian intelligentsia and the students. In this battle for a new invention of the meaning of Iran and the state, the Khomeinists emerged as the most forceful, uncompromising and ideologically radical of all the competing factions. In their radicalism, they turned the revolution from an anarcho-libertarian event that was meant to create a democratically accountable state in Iran, into a polymorphic yet centralised polity that employed Islamised inventions for the purpose of power.

Hence, immediately after the revolution in 1979, the Khomeinists began to implement their vision of the new state with full force. Alternative ideas of a rather more libertarian and democratic Islamic Republic, put forward by the old guard of religious nationalists such as the first prime minister of the Islamic Republic Mehdi Bazargan or his foreign minister Ibrahim Yazdi, were marginalised. Khomeini and his followers remained stoic, uncompromising, immoveable. As Barzagan himself admitted at the height of the revolutionary excesses in Iran:

Look, Khomeini is a rough and primitive man, but he's also a genius. I've never known anyone who has his capacity to interpret the mood and will of the masses, to communicate with them by a simple look or a few words spoken at a distance. Moreover, he hasn't been chosen only by the masses. Many intellectuals, too, have followed him from the start like orphans in search of a teacher, a father. So it's natural that he feels like something more than a religious leader – like the custodian of the revolution, its supervisor, its guardian ...

If we in the Freedom Movement [Bazargan's political party] – namely, we who believe in God and Islam but not in the clergy – had been more alert; if, instead of being distracted, we had behaved like a party – then this mess wouldn't have occurred. Yes, we could have prevented it. The fact is that we were so overwhelmed by the country's problems, by the urgency of getting it back in shape, by the need to prevent excesses, that we didn't realize we were missing the boat.[27]

Only a few months after the return of Khomeini to Iran on 1 February 1979, the 'students following the line of the Imam [Khomeini]' stormed the US embassy in Tehran (hostage crisis 4 November 1979 to 20

---

[27] 'Everybody wants to be boss', *New York Times*, 28 October 1979, p. 5, available at www.nytimes.com/1979/10/28/archives/everybody-wants-to-be-boss-an-interview-with-mehdi-bazargan-prime.html, accessed 2 June 2018.

January 1981), a huge compound that was at the heart of the efforts to keep the shah in power, as a powerful pro-US ally. The students were certainly motivated by the real fear that the Carter administration would repeat a scenario such as the 1953 MI6/CIA-led *coup d'état* which deposed Iran's first democratically elected prime minister, Mohammad Mossadegh, and reinstated the dictatorship of the shah, a pivotal event in world history that has been comprehensively re-examined by Ervand Abrahamian and succinctly narrated by Malcolm Byrne and Mark Gasiorowski around the uniquely useful primary material compiled in the National Security Archive at George Washington University.[28] After all, the occupation happened two weeks after the shah was finally admitted to the United States for medical treatment as he was dying of cancer. There was, then, a very immediate political rationale triggering the occupation: it was meant to demonstrate that this Iranian generation would not accept another 'Operation Boot/Ajax', another CIA/MI6-engineered coup that would reinstall the shah. Mousavi Khoeiniha, who acted as the spiritual guide of the *khatt-e imam* student movement, would write in retrospect that the

historical memory of the Iranian nation, and in particular the revolutionaries, of the United States-inspired coup of August 1953, that resulted in the overthrow of the government of Dr. Mohammad Mossadegh, needs an honest appraisal. That event resulted in the return of Shah Mohammad-Reza Pahlavi to Iran and the continuation of his dictatorial regime. When all the implications of this tragic episode in our history are taken into consideration, an unbiased arbiter would surely judge the students' action as having been the only real avenue for seeking justice from the American government.[29]

---

[28] See Ervand Abrahamian, *The Coup: 1953, The CIA, and the Roots of Modern US–Iranian Relations*, New York: The New Press, 2013. Mark J. Gasiorowski and Malcolm Byrne (eds.), *Mohammad Mosaddeq and the 1953 Coup in Iran*, London: Syracuse University Press, 2004. See further the National Security Archives webpages, in particular newly declassified documents about the clerical involvement in the *coup d'état* against Mossadegh which exonerated the main Iranian source of emulation Grand Ayatollah Boroujerdi, whilst implicating others such as Ayatollah Kashani and Ayatollah Behbehani, available at https://nsarchive.gwu.edu/briefing-book/iran/2018-03-07/new-findings-clerical-involvement-1953-coup-iran, accessed 18 November 2019.

[29] Preface to Massoumeh Ebtekar, *Takeover in Tehran: The Inside Story of the 1979 US Embassy Capture*, Vancouver: Talon Books, 2000, p. 26.

A letter by the Iranian Ministry of Foreign Affairs to their counterparts in Panama (21 December 1979), which had acquiesced to demands by the US government to admit the shah, is equally instructive about Iranian perceptions of world politics during that period:

In demanding the extradition of Mohammad Reza Pahlavi, the Iranian people do not seek to quench a thirst for vengeance, but legitimately desire that the deposed Shah answer to his crimes and unmask all the plots which enabled him, during 25 years, to establish a veritable organised terror and to smother the voice of the people in the sombre prisons of Savak.

In demanding this extradition, the Iranian people wish to demonstrate that oppressed nations of the world will no longer allow imperialist powers to play with their destiny, scorn their national pride, forge coups d'état at the whim of their interests or impose upon helpless people tyrants servilely devoted to foreign orders.

In this anti-imperialist struggle, all oppressed peoples should be united, and we hope that the people and the government of Panama will understand the true direction of this fight and will refuse to submit to the diktats of the United States of America.[30]

Bruce Laingen, then US ambassador to Iran, understood that prevalent mood in the infant Islamic Republic. In July 1979, that is three months before the shah was admitted to the United States for medical treatment and four months before the US embassy was occupied, he advised then US Secretary of State Cyrus Vance that giving

refuge to the Shah would almost certainly trigger massive demonstrations against our embassy. With luck, they may stop at that, without a physical assault of the kind we experienced last February. But there could be no assurance of that, since Iran's regular military and police force remain largely demoralised and cannot yet be relied on to apply force that might be needed to prevent violence against us.[31]

There was compelling evidence for direct US interference. Even before the revolution succeeded, the Carter administration sent a highly decorated US general by the name of Robert Huyser to Iran in order to

---

[30] 'Ministry of Foreign Affairs of the Islamic Republic. Extradition Request for Shah in Panama (Tehran, 21 December 1979)', available through the Carter Library.

[31] US Department of State, Incoming Telegram, US Ambassador to Iran Bruce L. Laingen to US Secretary of State, 'Shah's Desire to Reside in the US', Tehran, July 1979, available through the Carter Library.

stabilise the last government of the shah, led by Prime Minister Shapour Bakhtiar. Recently declassified documents reconfirm that Huyser was meant to organise things in favour of a civilian government and to keep the generals in check who were toying with the idea of an interim military government to support the monarchy.[32] After the departure of the shah on 1 February 1979, the Carter administration continued to meddle in Iranian affairs. Parallel to efforts to reach out to the liberal segments of the newly established Islamic Republic such as its first president Abol-Hassan Bani Sadr (who was subsequently forced into exile), and even Khomeini himself,[33] Carter pursued military options to try to rescue the diplomatic personnel held in the US embassy in Tehran. 'Operation Eagle Claw' proved to be a huge and tragic embarrassment for the US armed forces and its newly established 'elite' Delta One task force. Eight helicopters were sent to accomplish the mission, but only six arrived at the landing zone in Iran (the imaginatively named 'Desert One'). The technical failures included hydraulic problems and a cracked rotor blade. As an additional helicopter was deemed unfit for purpose, the mission was aborted. When the US forces prepared to leave the Iranian desert of Tabas, one of the helicopters crashed into a transport aircraft staffed by servicemen which was full of jet fuel. The resulting explosion destroyed both aircraft, killing eight. On the one side, the debacle was the main reason why President Carter lost the election against Ronald Reagan in November 1980. On the other, it buttressed Iranian suspicions about US government policies, adding to the memory of US interventions in Iranian affairs.[34]

As indicated, the Iranian students involved in the hostage-taking at the US embassy, which in the end lasted 444 days, wanted to radicalise the situation in Iran further in support of Khomeini's revolutionary agenda. The botched US military intervention gave impetus to this trend. Khomeini himself used the occasion to link the opposition to

---

[32] 'Declassified diplomacy: Washington's hesitant plans for a military coup in pre-revolution Iran', *The Guardian*, 11 February 2015. www.theguardian.com/world/iran-blog/2015/feb/11/us-general-huysers-secret-iran-mission-declassified, accessed 12 August 2016.

[33] Ibid.

[34] See further Laura Lambert, 'Operation Eagle Claw', *Encyclopaedia Britannica*, 20 January 2015, available at www.britannica.com/event/Operation-Eagle-Claw, accessed 12 July 2016.

US designs for the region, in a first major step to create a clear dichotomy between the 'righteous revolutionaries', who were positioned under the protection of God, and the 'deviant and perverted' counter-revolutionaries who were reprimanded as stooges of the 'Great Satan':

I would like to remark that the perverse and deviated groups in Kurdistan, which are anti-Islam, committed the troubles. In the colleges, the leftist groups, pro-America, did all that turbulence and tumult in the sacred places. The disturbances and clashes that the illegitimate government of Iraq is doing at the borders; it appears that all these are linked with tangible proof to the assault of Carter and his military intervention.[35]

For Khomeini and many of his followers, it was of primary importance to monopolise the revolution around the godly ordained sovereignty of the clerical philosopher-king, the *valiy-e faqih* or Supreme Jurisprudent. Khomeini lived through the turmoil of twentieth-century Iran, the Constitutional Revolt of 1906, the rule of Reza Shah Pahlavi (1921–1941), his deposition by the British, the Mossadegh interlude between 1951 and 1953 and the return of Mohammad Reza Shah thereafter. He wanted to create a stable, deified Leviathan in Iran, spearheaded by a clerical *Übermensch*, the perfect Muslim *zoon politikon*. This is why I have called Khomeini a 'clerical revolutionary' elsewhere.[36] His bias towards the clerical strata of Iranian society was apparent right from the outset:

These days, through the agents of the Shah and his lackeys, attacks have increased on the true clergy, who in fact, both at the time of the Shah and at the time of his father, were among the most distinguished strata of the nation, who through their numerous uprisings against the corruption of the regime engaged in struggle and divulged the crimes of the regime. Throughout the rightful struggles of the noble nation against the Shah and America, the clergy led the struggles that led to victory. Exactly at the time when the clergy started its irrepressible struggle against the traitorous Shah in the years 1962 and 1963, the Shah called the committed and responsible clergy black reactionaries, because the only serious threat to him and to his rule came from the struggling clergy, who had roots in the depth of the souls

---

[35] Ruhollah Khomeini, 'The failure of the US Army in Tabas', 25 April 1980, available at en.imam-khomeini.ir/en/NewsPrint.aspx?ID=7819, accessed 12 April 2012.

[36] See further Adib-Moghaddam, *A Critical Introduction to Khomeini*, 2014.

of the people and stood up against him and against his oppression. Now, the agents of the Shah have again put the word reaction into the mouths of my children who are unaware of the depth of the issues, in order to crush the clergy, who are the foundation of independence and freedom of this country. My beloved and revolutionary children: Today the insulting and the weakening of the role of the clergy is a blow against independence, freedom and Islam. Today, it is treason to follow the path of the traitorous Shah and use the word treason concerning this respected class, who are among the most distinguished strata, not accepting either the yoke of the East or that of the West.[37]

The other institutions of the newly established Islamic Republic reflected this ambition to place the clerical class of Iranian society at the heart of the political system. Institutions that had never existed in human history before, such as the Assembly of Experts (*Majles-e khobregan-e rahbari*) whose members are elected from and approved by the Guardian Council which is composed of eight clerics appointed either directly or indirectly by the Supreme Leader. In turn, the Assembly of Experts consists of eighty mujtahids or Islamic legal experts, who are elected, after approval by the Supreme Leader, from lists of vetted candidates by direct public vote for an eight-year term. The Assembly of Experts is tasked with the nomination and subsequent supervision of the Supreme Jurisprudent's performance. The Council of Guardians, probably the most powerful institution of the Iranian state, is staffed by six senior Islamic theologians appointed by the Supreme Leader and six jurists nominated by the judiciary and approved by parliament. Members are elected for six years on a phased basis, in order for half of the membership to change every three years. The Council has invasive powers: it approves all bills passed by the parliament and has the power to veto them if they are deemed inconsistent with Islamic law. In its constitutional task to vet candidates for the democratic institutions of the Iranian system – the presidency, the parliament and the municipal councils – the Council of Guardians has barred many candidates from standing in the elections.[38]

Before Khomeini passed away in November 1989, he reconfirmed the deistic sovereignty of the Iranian Leviathan in a now legendary

---

[37] Ruhollah Khomeini 'We shall confront the world with our ideology', *Middle East Report*, June 1980, p. 25.

[38] See further Asghar Schirazi, *The Constitution of Iran: Politics and the State in the Islamic Republic*, trans. John O' Kane, London: I.B. Tauris, 1998.

statement. In direct contradiction to thirteen centuries of Islamic *fiqh* (jurisprudence), Khomeini argued that the Islamic state (by implication Iran) can even go as far as to abrogate the five pillars of Islam, which had been considered sacrosanct even by the prophet Muhammad himself. In an explosive and highly controversial statement, Khomeini said:

I must reiterate that our government is a branch of Mohammed's vice-regency and is one of the first precepts of Islam. It takes precedence over all religious practices such as prayers, fasting or the Hajj pilgrimage ... I openly say that the government can stop any religious law if it feels that it is correct to do so ... The ruler can close or destroy the mosques whenever he sees fit ... The government can prohibit anything having to do with worship if these things would be against the interests of the country ... The Islamic government can unilaterally abrogate its contracts with and obligations towards the public whenever such contracts are against the interests of the country and Islam ... The government can prevent its citizens from performing the Hajj pilgrimage which is one of the divine duties ... Government is an institution ordained by the Almighty and founded with absolute power entrusted to the prophet Mohammed and as an entity it supplants as secondary statutes of the canonical law of Islam.[39]

The historical context is important here. The nascent revolutionary state was ideologically and economically exhausted after eight years of war with Saddam Hussein's Iraq. The Islamic Republic faced internal turmoil, not least from the so-called Mujahedin-e Khalgh (MKO), which had metamorphosed into an obscure sect-like movement with terrorist pedigrees under the bizarre leadership of Maryam Rajavi and which had launched several military campaigns against Iranian forces in collusion with Saddam Hussein.

Khomeini responded with institutional force and religiously sanctioned violence precisely because of the ongoing challenges from the outside and because, in his dying days, he wanted to secure the longevity of his interpretation of the Islamic Republic against competing forces. Apart from fortifying the power of the state, as theologically highly provocative directives such as the one above exemplify, Khomeini disowned his successor designate Ayatollah Montazeri,

---

[39] 'Asserting his authority, Khomeini rewrites Koran', *Los Angeles Times*, 31 January 1988, available at http://articles.latimes.com/1988-01-31/opinion/op-39482_1_islamic-government, accessed 10 January 2010.

seemingly for being too liberal in favouring the current Supreme Jurisprudent of the Islamic Republic, Ali Khamenei, due to his 'political competence' rather than theological status.[40]

In typical Machiavellian style, Khomeini then moved on to eliminate the MKO opposition and 'leftist' members of other movements, which led to the mass execution of thousands of inmates in Iranian prisons, a tragedy that continues to divide opinion in the Islamic Republic and that was flagged up by Ayatollah Montazeri as a historical crime, both at the time and in his memoirs.[41] Comparable to the decree above, Khomeini used distinctly divisive religious tropes to legitimate his policies, blaming the MKO for being *mohareb* and *mortad*, which in his radical interpretation of the terms meant 'enemies of god' and 'apostates', who deserve capital punishment as they are waging a war against 'god'. Here as well, then, Khomeini equipped his Leviathan with a godly sovereignty, a prophylaxis that he buttressed with theological reinterpretations that hadn't much to do with established traditions in Islamic jurisprudence, as Ayatollah Montazeri pointed out at the time, but much more with his totalitarian interpretation of the mandate of the Islamic Republic at that historical juncture.

This uncompromising stance and zero-sum approach also explains why Khomeini sought further confrontation with the 'West' by issuing the infamous fatwa for the death of Salman Rushdie. All of these extreme measures were meant to rally the revolutionary forces behind the state and to demonstrate to the world that Iran continued to be strong, and that it could react with systematic violence, if necessary. Khomeini, like other revolutionary leaders before him, did not shy away from instituting a Robespierrian *régime de la terreur* to that end. This 'easy' recourse to violence, recurrently arbitrary exactly because it lacks due process or legal legitimacy, continues to be tolerated at the heart of the 'deep state' in Iran, certainly among the extreme right wing. The precedent was set by Khomeini, which explains why the Iranian state continues to lash out (e.g. in November 2019) when it feels 'cornered', in terms of both domestic challenges and an adverse international context. This internal–external dialectic of violence is

---

[40] See further the recent book by Sussan Siavoshi, *Montazeri: The Life and Thought of Iran's Revolutionary Ayatollah*, Cambridge: Cambridge University Press, 2017.

[41] Ayatollah Hosseinali Montazeri, *Khaterat*, Los Angeles: Ketab Corporation, 2001.

what 1988, the massive retaliation against the 'Green Movement' in 2009, and the lethal force in subduing the protests in November 2019 have in common.[42]

The constitutional changes of 1989, implemented by a twenty-man assembly appointed by Khomeini, were meant to strengthen the state in order to prepare for the transition after his death. The post of prime minister was abolished and his powers were transferred to the presidency, which emerged as a rather more powerful institution in the new constitutional set-up. In addition, a new Supreme National Security Council, headed by the president and composed of representatives from the military and security services as well as the diplomats of the Foreign Ministry, was instituted in order to stabilise Iran's internal and external security. Furthermore, the new constitution downgraded the required qualifications of the Supreme Jurisprudent. In the original constitution the *faqih* had to be both a *marja-e taghlid* (source of emulation, highest Shia rank) and possess outstanding political competency. In consequence, the designated successor of Khomeini, that is, the current Supreme Leader Ali Khamenei, was a mid-ranking cleric (or *hojatol-eslam*); the requirement of *marjaiyyat* (highest Shia clerical rank) was abolished in favour of the ability to lead the Islamic Republic effectively in the political realm. Finally, yet another institution was formed: the so-called Expediency Council was introduced into this complex constitutional set-up as an advisory body to the Supreme Leader, vested with the powers to adjudicate in disputes over legislation between the parliament and the Guardian Council. The members of the Expediency Council, who are prominent religious, social and political figures, are appointed by the Supreme Leader (in October 2005, Ali Khamenei gave the Expediency Council 'supervisory' powers over all branches of government – delegating some of his own authority as is permitted in the constitution). In July 1989, about a month after the death of Ayatollah Khomeini, these immense constitutional changes were approved in a national referendum, much in the same way as Iranians voted in favour of the Islamic Republic at the beginning of the revolution. The departure from the revolutionary decade between 1979 and 1989 into a 'period of reconstruction' gave decisive

---

[42] On the 'Green Movement' and Khatami see most recently Pouya Alimagham, *Contesting the Iranian Revolution: The Green Uprisings*, Cambridge: Cambridge University Press, 2020; and Paola Rivetti, *Political Participation in Iran: From Khatami to the Green Movement*, London: Palgrave, 2020.

impetus to what I have called a 'pluralistic momentum' in Iranian politics, which continues in many ways to this day.[43]

The Pluralistic Momentum Revisited

Some of the descriptive paragraphs that I included in order to summarise the political landscape in Iran can be conveniently, and probably better, chartered online, even in some of the think-tank manuals about Iran. But what I have tried to intimate at the same time is that the Islamic Republic is not a monolith. This is the conceptual element that scholarship has to add in order to depart from description and journalistic representations. A critical approach is tasked to summarise what happened, but more importantly to ask 'why?'. To that end, each chapter in this book has been framed with a musical piece and conceptual, theoretical signposts which may be useful to demonstrate to the reader how to analyse Iran.

The musical piece for this chapter was chosen because it evokes the emotional vigour and romanticism underlying the utopian yearnings of the revolutionary generation, which could only be disappointed precisely because they were dreamed of in a moment of delirium during that exhilarating suspension of history that any grand revolution of human history simulates for a very short period of time, a feeling of intense hope that will never be recaptured and relived thereafter. Compared to this liberating impulse that Iranians felt in 1979, the period from 1989, so appropriately dubbed the 'period of reconstruction' under the aegis of the new supreme leader Ali Khamenei and the pragmatic President Ali Rafsanjani seems bland and technocratic. But from 1989 onwards no institution in Iran could escape further differentiation in the face of the socially driven pluralistic momentum to reform state and society. The revolutionary decade was truly over and Iranians began to detoxify from the psycho-political paraphernalia introjected by the political culture that delivered the Islamic Republic in 1979.

The central characteristic of this pluralistic momentum in Iran is that the clerical establishment can no longer take for granted the allegiance

---

[43] Arshin Adib-Moghaddam, 'The pluralistic momentum in Iran and the future of the reform movement', *Third World Quarterly*, Vol. 27, No. 4 (2006), pp. 665–674.

of their client social strata. Pluralism engenders competition, and state policies have to be 'sold' to an audience that is no longer obliged to 'buy' from one source.[44] This is one of the reasons why nowadays the clergy has a notably diminished role in the parliament of Iran. In the first parliamentary election in 1980, 61 per cent of the majlis was won by clerics. At the time of writing, they only occupy 6 per cent of the parliamentary seats. In fact, there are more female members of parliament (seventeen) than the number of clerics.[45]

In this 'market situation', then, the monopoly on political power is increasingly dissected. As a result, institutions and elites operating within the domain of the state have to organise themselves in such a way as to mobilise their respective constituencies – appeals to ideology are not sufficient. They enter into a competitive situation with other groups who follow the same political rationale. Comparing electoral campaigns in urban and provincial centres all over Iran for the past fifteen years, my primary research and fieldwork has shown that the presidential candidates, including so-called conservatives such as Mahmoud Ahmadinejad in 2005 or reformist clerics such as Mohammad Khatami in 1997, scarcely employed Islamic imagery or referenced the political will of Ayatollah Khomeini to further their agenda. The campaign of the current president Hassan Rouhani (2013–) was very similar – geared to specific issues rather than abstract slogans. In short, Iranian leaders understand that it is public opinion that matters and not utopian-romantic sloganeering.[46]

Secondly, all institutions attached to the state are under pressure to produce results, especially in the economic sphere. In turn, the pressure to produce results in a competitive situation engenders the rationalisation of policies. This explains why both reformers and conservatives advocate economic growth and public participation in the political and cultural process. In a pluralistic situation where political parties become marketing agencies of the state, reform ceases to be a monopoly of self-declared reformist parties. In other words, the reform

---

[44] Ibid.

[45] See further 'Revolution at 40: politics by the numbers', *The Iran Primer*, US Institute for Peace, 5 February 2019, available at https://iranprimer.usip.org/blog/2019/feb/05/revolution-40-politics-numbers, accessed 8 June 2019.

[46] See further Dara Conduit and Shahram Akbarzadeh, 'The Iranian reform movement since 2009', in Dara Conduit and Shahram Akbarzadeh (eds.), *New Opposition in the Middle East*, London: Palgrave, 2018, pp. 119–149.

agenda is necessarily intrinsic to the political process comprising all state institutions. This differentiation of the state comes out very well in a study by Eva Rakel; similarly Melody Mohebi and Eskandar Sadeghi-Boroujerdi focus on this dialectic between reformism and political thought.[47]

Studies like these transcend the monocausal conservative–reformist divide because they show that the functioning of the whole state apparatus depends on formal and informal public participation. Public relations with the client social strata, lobbying, fundraising, involvement with the secular economy – the Islamic Republic is dependent on the country's civil society in all these aspects of affairs of state, even if it doesn't want to be. In such an interactive situation it is impossible (for conservatives and reformists alike) to sell policies to a population of consumers without taking their wishes concerning the content of those policies into account. As such, the current president Rouhani is a surface effect of these dynamics, and his reconciliatory foreign policies, especially towards the United States under the Obama administration, reflect the preferences of the mainstream of Iranian society, as a young professor at the Islamic Azad University in Ahwaz rightly argues.[48] The ability of Iranian civil society to provoke decisive concessions from the state are exactly due to this pluralistic momentum. The most recent empirical examples in terms of women's rights are indicative of this ongoing trend: In October 2019, the Iranian authorities lifted the moralistic and ultra-conservative ban on women watching male team sports in the country's stadiums, and in the same month the Guardian Council ratified a bill that allows children born to Iranian women and foreign men to obtain Iranian citizenship. Both concessions were made after a long campaign by women's rights activists – in the case of access to the stadiums accelerated by the tragic

---

[47] See Eva Patricia Rakel, *Power, Islam and Political Elite in Iran: A Study on the Iranian Political Elite from Khomeini to Ahmadinejad*, Leiden: Brill, 2008; Melody Mohebi, *The Formation of Civil Society in Modern Iran: Public Intellectuals and the State*, London: Palgrave, 2014; Eskandar Sadeghi-Boroujerdi, *Revolution and its Discontents: Political Thought and Reform in Iran*, Cambridge: Cambridge University Press, 2019.

[48] See Hossein Karimi-fard, 'Siasat-e taneshsodai-ye Rouhani dar ghabal-e Amrika: Ahdaf va mavaneh', *Faslname-ye Siasat*, Faculty of Law and Political Science: University of Tehran, Vol. 49, No. 1 (1398) (2019), pp. 205–224, available at https://jpq.ut.ac.ir/article_70954.html, accessed 16 July 2019.

death of Sahar Khodayari who set herself on fire in protest at the stadium ban.

We are still concerned here with the 'why?' questions that conceptualise the contemporary domestic politics of Iran. The pluralistic momentum that I have offered is underpinned by a set of sociological factors that indicate the capacity of Iranian society to continuously provoke the state. In 1980, at the beginning of the revolution, there were just 175,000 students and 15,000 lecturers spread around twenty cities in Iran. In 2012, there were 4 million higher education students and over 110,000 lecturers in 120 cities. In 2017, Iran ranked higher than China, Peru and Turkey in the United Nations' Human Development index, which demonstrates a constant improvement across the indices since 1990.[49] According to Britain's Royal Society, the number of educational publications in Iran increased from 736 in 1996 to 13,238 in 2008, the fastest such growth in the world.[50] In addition, the number of internet users rose dramatically, a monumental 13,000 per cent.[51] In 2017, over 60 per cent of Iranians had access to the Internet, according to the World Bank.[52] This massive increase is reflected in the number of social media users, which explains why all major political personalities, media outlets and governmental institutions of the Islamic Republic have a prominent presence on Twitter, Facebook, Instagram, Telegram etc.[53]

According to the Canadian social media management platform Hootsuite and the UK-based marketing and advertising agency 'We Are Social', the number of Iranians using social media platforms is

---

[49] 'Human development reports', *United Nations Development Programme*, Available at http://hdr.undp.org/en/composite/HDI, accessed 12 August 2019.

[50] 'Iran and global scientific collaboration in the 21st century', *Association of Professors and Scholars of Iranian Heritage*, 3 September 2011, available at www.apsih.org/index.php/news/english-news/275-iran-and-global-scientific-collaboration-in-the-21st-century, accessed 18 June 2018; https://royalsociety .org/topics-policy/projects/knowledge-networks-nations/report/, accessed 8 November 2020. On the growth of science sectors, see also The Royal Society, 'Knowledge, networks and nations: global scientific collaboration in the 21st century', London, March 2011, available at http://royalsociety.org/ uploadedFiles/Royal_Society_Content/policy/publications/2011/4294976134 .pdf, accessed 12 July 2018.

[51] The Royal Society, 'Knowledge, networks and nations', p. 65.

[52] 'Individuals using the internet', *The World Bank*, 2019, available at https://data .worldbank.org/indicator/IT.NET.USER.ZS?locations=IR, accessed 19 May 2019.

[53] See further Babak Rahimi, *Social Media in Iran: Politics and Society after 2009*, New York: State University of New York Press, 2015.

increasing 135 per cent year by year. In their 2018 'Global Digital' report, the authors say that there are about 40 million active social media users in Iran, which amounts to almost half of the population. Approximately 23 million Iranians joined a social media network for the first time in 2017, which amounts to 63,000 new users every day and 43 for every minute in that year.[54] With over 40 million users, the social media app Telegram is the most prominent, and Iranian presidential candidates used it readily to spread their message, before the recent elections in 2017. Instagram, the photo-sharing spinoff of Facebook, is almost equally popular, its service used by approximately 24 million or 29 per cent of the population, making the country the seventh biggest market for this application. About 55 per cent of Instagram users are men and 45 per cent are women.[55]

There are equally impressive sociological indices across other sectors of Iranian civil society. For instance, in 2012, Iran announced the establishment of a nanotechnology centre and allocated 4 per cent of its GDP to research and development as a part of a comprehensive plan for science. This is one of the highest allocations for research in the world and has yielded an impressive research infrastructure and several scientific advances despite the harsh sanctions that have targeted Iranian scholars and scientists. Iranian researchers produce world-class research even in cutting-edge fields such as artificial intelligence and machine learning. According to the leading international journal for science, *Nature*, Iran was ranked eighth in the world in those fields, based on high-impact and high-citation articles – the only country from the region in the top ten.[56] Thus, the geography of knowledge in Iran is seriously expanded, which in turn has had an effect on the preference setting of Iranian civil society. Insofar, then, as the highly educated Iranian population has access to the instruments of global communication/social media, their preference setting is reflecting this. This is an important prerequisite for the emergence of a pluralistic society. The ability to choose and evaluate alternative worldviews

[54] 'Latest data on Iran: surge in social media use', *Financial Tribune*, 6 February 2018, available at https://financialtribune.com/articles/sci-tech/81536/latest-data-on-iran-surge-in-social-media-use, accessed 21 June 2018.
[55] Ibid.
[56] 'Iran ranks 8th for top papers in AI', *Tehran Times*, 2 September 2019, available at www.tehrantimes.com/news/439876/Iran-ranks-8th-for-top-papers-in-AI, accessed 5 September 2019.

requires the freedom to go beyond state-manufactured 'facts'. Such freedom depends on socio-economic conditions which provide access to alternative worldviews, not least through the means of education and mass communication.

Analytically it is crucial to push the point that the pluralistic momentum in Iran has created an interactive situation in which it is impossible for so-called reformers and conservatives to sell policies to a population of consumers without taking into account their wishes concerning the content of those policies. I am not claiming that the institutions within the domain of the state have conceded their formal powers – they have retained them, of course. But the pluralistic momentum has 'functionally differentiated' the *Machtkonsens* (power consensus) amongst the political elites in Iran. During the first decade of the Islamic Republic, it was Ayatollah Khomeini who authoritatively expressed that consensus. His legitimacy, albeit not total, was sufficiently massive and durable to maintain the political elites within the revolutionary framework (the Islamic Republican Party was the most influential manifestation of the power consensus dictating Iranian domestic politics in the first decade of the revolution). That framework expanded after his death in 1989 once and for all. Not that Iran emerged as a 'republican democracy' in the Habermasian sense.[57] But the differentiation of the revolutionary polity into competing factions has contracted the ability of the state to conduct politics in a unilaterally consensual mode.

The pluralistic momentum, emerging from below, negates the binary and total opposition between political 'masters' and 'slaves' at the root of state–society relations. Where there is pluralism there is critique, defiance and opposition exercised from innumerable points within society. This is the reason behind the recurrent demonstrations which are all geared to reform: the so-called Green Movement in 2009, the demonstrations in the provinces in late 2017 and November 2019 are very good examples.[58] The former was driven by the urban middle class in Iran, the latter by workers and the lower-income strata, whom the government of Rouhani failed. The pluralistic momentum is hence not something that can be channelled, redirected or hermetically

[57] See further Jürgen Habermas, 'Three normative models of democracy', in Ronald J. Terchek and Thomas C. Conte, eds., *Theories of Democracy: A Reader*, Oxford: Rowman & Littlefield, p. 238.
[58] See further Alimagham, *Contesting the Iranian Revolution*.

contained by a political faction or stratum of society. It goes beyond class lines and political preferences. There is no single locus, no unitary institution, no ideational agent, no sacrosanct HQ to be conquered. The pluralistic momentum in Iran is, by definition, an omnipresent yet polymorphous phenomenon. It is a propeller of demands for reform, and it is geared to the libertarian core principles of the revolutions and revolts of contemporary Iranian history, certainly the revolution of 1979, that are so powerfully expressed in the song of Rooygari that musicologically frames this chapter. At the heart of the lyrics of the song is this intense yearning for freedom and justice: 'Tomorrow when spring arrives, we will be free and we will rest, no injustice and no chain, we will be in the service of God.' It should be clear that in this liberation theology, God is a destination, a metaphor and analogy for liberty. No wonder, then, that the post-revolutionary generation are holding their parents to account for this failure to achieve a freer society and political system in Iran.

These demands articulated by activists, workers, students and intellectuals do not, by themselves, determine the substantive content or direction of political and socio-economic reforms. They simply generate the dynamic that change is possible. There is a common theme to the foregoing: Iran's oppositional civil society on the one side and the technological opportunities that are available to the highly educated population of the country on the other have provoked the demonopolisation of Iranian politics. The mass distribution of ideas through the Internet and satellite television have de-emphasised the importance of the state-controlled media and have, quite literally, penetrated the Iranian living room with a whole new set of ideas, values, norms and worldviews. In this struggle, the state has repeatedly yielded its function as the monopolist of political ideas and its ability to impose renunciations and restrictions upon society have atrophied under the pressures of a 'cumbersome' population which is no longer bound to accept a single ideology.

Such an analysis alerts us to another methodological factor crucial to our understanding of contemporary Iranian domestic politics. The pluralistic momentum in Iran is not a commodity that can be possessed by this or that group; there is no engine that can be localised here or there. It must be analysed as a 'gliding' phenomenon that is in constant motion. A trajectory of its infinitesimal movements requires analysis of the multifarious discourses, ideas, political cultures that constitute the

Iranian polity. Therefore, I have studied the pluralistic momentum in Iran in the way I have approached the mechanisms of state power all over the world. Such an approach avoids identifying some single locus of the pluralistic momentum, such as 'the state' or 'the ruling elites'. It does not analyse it in terms of the interests and motives of political parties and institutions in a top-down fashion – from the 'ruling classes' to the 'proletariat' as Marxists suggest. Instead, it focuses as much as possible on the vehicles of the pluralistic momentum in Iran: students, NGOs, women-rights activists, writers, workers, poets, intellectuals, film-makers etc. It pays attention to processes of differentiation, reification, deconstruction, theorisation and other ideational sources of reform emanating from Iranian civil society. It establishes, in short, a genealogy of reform emancipating 'the subject', i.e. Iranian society vis-à-vis 'the object', i.e. the state.

This pluralistic momentum is the main conceptual factor behind the ongoing differentiation of major institutional sites of the Islamic Republic, including the military and security organs which are at the heart of the 'monopoly over legitimate violence' claimed by any state in the world. It is these institutions that harass, incarcerate and, if necessary, kill, under the cover of the 'law'. Here, in one of his first decrees as the leader of the revolution, Khomeini proclaimed that it is of central importance to create an ideological army under the command of the Supreme Jurisprudent in order to uphold the tenets of the Islamic revolution. As a state-builder, Khomeini created parallel institutions in order to ensure a balance of power amongst them and to link the interest of various factions to the state apparatus, so that the Supreme Jurisprudent could position himself, as much as possible, beyond the day-to-day requirements of governance. The Islamic Revolution Guards Corps (IRGC) is one such institution created immediately after the revolution. It was baptised in blood during the devastating Iran–Iraq War between 1980 and 1988. Khomeini was adamant that the IRGC should keep out of politics, and this was largely the case until his death in 1989.

Yet the activities of the Guards in Iranian society, politics and economics increased exponentially thereafter, in particular because of the increased budget and ideological legitimacy that the IRGC enjoyed after the Iran–Iraq War. But as opposed to some of the hysterical analyses about this issue, the Guards have been affected by the pluralistic momentum as well. Indeed, the main reason why the Guards have been spearheading a powerful military-industrial complex that has become a major factor in the Iranian national economy can be considered a rather normal process of state-building. Similar trends can be discerned in other countries, most importantly the United States of course. The process of 'civilianisation' of the Guards turned war-experienced generals into accountants, which is one way of tying them ever closer to the system – an economic peerage mechanism of sorts that gives them access to the spoils of the Iranian economy in return for their allegiance. After all, ideological commitment is always also buttressed by economic incentives in order to keep the state secure. As Mohsen Rezai, the primary architect of the IRGC and its central commander for sixteen years, argued, assessing the domestic roles of Iran's Islamic Revolutionary Guards Corps:

> once someone had asked Imam [Khomeini] as to why he lends so much support to the IRGC. The Imam had answered 'why not?' and the interlocutor had warned him that it may result in staging a coup [if the IRGC became too strong]. The Imam had answered, 'It doesn't matter; it stays in the family [if they stage a coup]; as they are our own guys.'[59]

Here too, then, the IRGC has to be analysed as part of a differentiated state that is constantly under pressure by its civil society to deliver the lofty promises of the revolution. Contemporary Iranian politicians know that many Iranians are wary about the involvement of the military in politics and that there is a general sense that the IRGC is overbearingly powerful. The current Iranian president Hassan Rouhani has been aware of this perception, which is why he signified repeatedly that the 'IRGC is above and beyond political currents, not beside them or within them', which should be interpreted as an attempt to both remind them of their impartiality and to signal to Iranian society that the Guards have a special place in the Iranian system. 'The IRGC has a higher status,' Rouhani said, 'which is that of the whole nation.' My analytical point here is that even the military institutions of the Islamic Republic are under scrutiny, if they are perceived to be deviant and corrupt. Capital redistribution, social justice and equality, after all, were major planks of the revolution of 1979 itself.

---

[59] Mohsen Rezai quoted in Frederic Wehrey, Jerrold D. Green, Brian Nichiporuk, Alireza Nader, Lydia Hansell, Rasool Nafisi and S. R. Bohandy, *The Rise of the Pasdaran: Assessing the Domestic Roles of Iran's Islamic Revolutionary Guards Corps*, Santa Monica: RAND Corporation, 2009, p. 80.

Even the IRGC could not escape this fundamental dynamic, which is why it has to repeatedly legitimate itself via both a wide-ranging network of security institutions and media/educational outfits that are meant to calibrate public relations, as the important research of Narges Bajoghli clarifies.[60] Therefore, the Revolutionary Guards do not only have powerful representatives in all the major security institutions of the Iranian state, such as the Supreme National Security Council, the parliament (majlis), the Expediency Discernment Council and the Supreme Council of the Cultural Revolution. The Guards do not only encompass the Quds (Jerusalem) elite force, with its systematic influence in Iraq, Syria and Lebanon, and the Baseej voluntary force with its bases in every town in the country and their representatives in all the major public institutions of the Islamic Republic. The IRGC has evolved into a hybrid organisation with immense psychonationalist stamina, primarily through its cultural, 'smart' power manifesting itself in media conglomerates such as *Tasnim, Daneshju News, Nasim, Javan Newspaper* and *Fars News Agency*. This cultural power is galvanised by film-making entities such as Owj, and a set of social and cultural organisations under the wings of the Baseej such as the Imam Hossein University, and the Imam Hossein Military and Revolutionary Guards Academy, with its sophisticated counter-terrorism and cybersecurity programmes. This intricate web of IRGC institutions that spreads across the country and beyond, is aided and abetted by powerful business conglomerates such as Khatam al-Anbiya Constructions, a multinational engineering firm controlled by the IRGC and the largest contractor in Iran, and other entities such as the IRGC Cooperative Foundation (*Bonyad-e Taavon-e Sepah*).[61]

Therefore, the IRGC does not exercise its power by brute force alone. The organisation has turned from an ideological army that was at the heart of the Iranian defence against the invading forces of Saddam Hussein, into a socio-economic hydra conscious of public opinion and well versed in public relations. Undoubtedly, the Guards continue to have the militaristic power to proclaim and sustain a securitised state of exception in Iran, most recently evidenced by their

---

[60] Narges Bajoghli, *Iran Reframed: Anxieties of Power in the Islamic Republic*, Stanford: Stanford University Press, 2019.

[61] 'The Islamic Revolutionary Guards Corps: structure and missions', *IranWire*, 9 April 2019, available at https://iranwire.com/en/features/5735, accessed 28 May 2019.

response to the demonstrations in November 2019 against a sudden increase in fuel prices which triggered another violent chapter in the dialectic between state and society in Iran. It was symptomatic that the Guards threatened and partially implemented what they called a 'revolutionary response',[62] precisely because it is this quasi-monopoly over the sovereign use of violence that was inscribed into the organisation in the revolutionary process and more fundamentally during the Iran–Iraq War. But this sovereignty has metamorphised, under the pressures of new political dynamics, and the preference setting of Iranian society. The conceptual point being that the pluralistic momentum in Iran differentiated the IRGC, too, and that even this core institution of the Iranian revolution does not merely rely on its legitimacy from the Iran–Iraq War or even its brute power resources to subdue Iranian civil society – the IRGC as well needs to speak to the Iranian public, and as a result it has ceased to function in a one-dimensional mode.

Post-revolutionary Iran

It should be clear by now that our analysis departed from the deep sentiments embedded in Reza Rooygari's song. Revolutionary Iran was a utopian destination; today's Iran is a realistic assessment. In the first decade of the revolution and in particular during the Iran–Iraq War, the Revolutionary Guards were represented as those tulips that faded away in the blaze of one of the most devastating wars in human history. Today, the IRGC co-sponsor the flower beds that adorn almost every major infrastructural nodal point in Tehran and the other major cities in Iran. In short: Iran has turned into a post- and increasingly into a non-revolutionary country, that is dealing with the traumas of a particularly rapturous recent history. The hocus-pocus has faded away, and the state is being judged upon its performance – the magic tricks are simply not enough anymore to govern a highly educated society such as the Iranian one. As Amir Hassan Cheheltan, one of the doyens of contemporary Iranian literature, opined in the aftermath of the tragic accidental shoot-down of Ukraine International Airlines flight 752 in January 2020, which was only admitted by the

---

[62] 'Iran's Guards threaten petrol protesters with "revolutionary" response', *Rudaw*, 18 November 2019.

IRGC after three days of denials, and which was followed by a massive PR campaign to address the protests of the Iranian public: Iranians don't accept incompetence and lies anymore,[63] exactly because Iranian society has outgrown the capacity of the state. At the time, the students of Amir Kabir University declared in a similar spirit:

The only way out of our current crisis is a return to popular politics. A politics that neither clings to the coattails of (imperial) arrogance [*istikbar*] from fear of oppression, nor legitimizes tyranny in the name of anti-imperialism and resistance. Indeed, the only way out of our current predicament is the simultaneous rejection of both domestic despotism and imperial arrogance. We need a politics that doesn't merely claim security, freedom, and equality for a select group or class, but that understands these rights as inalienable and for all people. Today, the urgent need for social democracy has become clear to all. In such a democracy, the government will not be inattentive to the needs of the people, but will safeguard security, freedom, and equality for all.[64]

Even the Grand Bazaar in Tehran, which was so central to the infrastructure of revolt in the sprawling Iranian capital, turned from a hub for the opposition, whose power base was the traditional lower middle class, into a relic of a bygone era, in the shadows of the capital's glitzy malls and brand-driven boutiques which have been cultivated in typically neo-liberal economic fashion. In the build-up to the revolution, the bazaar played a major role in the day-to-day affairs of Tehran's population and it clearly benefited from the sustained economic growth that Iran experienced in the 1970s. The bazaar was a city within the city, home to a population brimming with political and socio-economic grievances against the shah. But these grievances were primarily about values, the cultural alienation that these traditionalists opposed. Thus, under the beautifully arched ceilings first erected in the seventeenth century, a civil society infrastructure emerged geared to the revolutionary momentum that delivered the Islamic Republic. In this labyrinthine matrix that makes the Grand Bazaar of Tehran such a fascinating urban space, the revolutionaries were able to keep up their

---

[63] Amir Hassan Cheheltan, 'Aus der Dunkelheit', *Frankfurter Allgemeine Zeitung*, 17 January 2020, p. 11 (my transcription).

[64] 'Statement by university students in Tehran protesting downing of flight 752', *Jadaliyya*, 13 January 2020, available at www.jadaliyya.com/Details/40488, accessed 21 January 2020.

organisational autonomy in the face of intrusions by the shah's security forces. At the height of the revolution, the *bazaaris* gave out free drinks and food to the demonstrators and helped them hide from the monarch's dreaded secret service, SAVAK. After the revolution, the Grand Bazaar became a major institutional focal point in the chain of 'Islamic' sites that galvanised the power of the newly formed Islamic Republic. Yet ironically, as Arang Keshavarzian rightly argued in his comprehensive book about the topic, this alliance with the state transformed the bazaar into an economic unit, with waning political centrality. Whereas in 1979 the bazaar was a hub for revolutionary agitation, today it is complementary to the state.[65] Comparable to the other institutions of contemporary Iran, then, the bazaar too has experienced rather dramatic changes. The pluralistic momentum is a useful analytical device to charter some of these transformations. It shows how domestic politics in Iran works and it provides a good transition to understanding the changes in the foreign policy of the country. This is the topic of the next chapters.

---

[65] See further Arang Keshavarzian, *Bazaar and State in Iran: Politics of the Tehran Marketplace*, Cambridge: Cambridge University Press, 2007.

3 | *Strategic Preferences – Transnational Interests*

Musical Piece:

'Vatan' (Homeland)
By: Alireza Assar (1970–) and Foad Hejazi (1970–)
Release Date: 2005

Adaptive, free translation of lyrics:
Oh Homeland, the mother of history making
Oh your soil (territory), is all I need to worship
Your desert is the paradise of my life
You, my eternal love, my Iran
Oh from you, my roots (origin) gain sustenance
There is nothing on my mind, apart from (serving) your goals (vision)
You have heroes like Arash (the archer),[1] ready to shoot an arrow
(And) the bare hands of Bahram to wrestle with lions[2]
(And) Kaveh the Blacksmith,[3] who kills Zahhak[4]
You yourself are an enemy slayer ending Zahhak (tyranny)
You unleash Rostam[5] who charges with (his mighty stallion) Rakhsh[6],

---

[1] Heroic archer figure in Persian mythology.
[2] A reference to the legendary story of the Sasanian king Bahram 'Gur' in the Book of Kings (*shahnameh*) of Ferdowsi, when Bahran is said to have killed a lion with his bare hands.
[3] Another mythological figure from the *shahnameh* where Kaveh leads a popular uprising against the tyranny of Zahhak.
[4] Symbol of evil and foreign tyranny in Persian mythology, including in the Book of Kings (*shahnameh*) of Ferdowsi. In Zoroastrianism, Zahhak is an opponent of Ahura Mazda, the highest deity in Zoroastrianism.
[5] The most legendary hero of the *shahnameh*; a symbol of power and justice.
[6] Rakhsh is the loyal and powerful stallion of Rostam according to the *shahnameh*. It is first noticed by Rostam amongst the herds of horses brought over from Zabulistan and Kabul. According to this legend, no one but Rostam ever rides Rakhsh, and Rakhsh recognized no one but Rostam as its master.

For the awareness (and presence) of them, your enemies will never find
you asleep (unprepared)
Your border guards are courageous (and ready to sacrifice their life)
Your victorious soldiers (Guards) stand in dense lines (in formation)
They have given their heart and soul for your streams and prairies
They returned Khorramshahr
Oh, Homeland, Oh you mother of my Iran
Mother of my ancestors and children
My home, My Baneh[7], My Tous[8]
Every inch of your territory (soil) resembles my honour
Alas! If I witness your derelictions
If I witness your (rank) and files emptied of your champions (heroes)
Without your soil, my life and existence is void
Without the existence of you (your soil), my life shall cease (is
meaningless)

Homeland signifies all the water and territory (soil) there is
Homeland means complete love and purity
It resembles a cradle, when you are an infant
It becomes a remedy for your pains, at old age
Homeland means father, mother, and ancestry
It signifies pledging your blood for the sake of the country and its soil
(territory)
Homeland means identity, origin, and roots
An opening, an ending and an eternity
Homeland signifies cliffs, rocks, seas (and the lake of) Hamun[9]
Aras, Zayanderud,[10] Arvand,[11] and Karun[12]
Homeland signifies the close (concordant) existence connecting Turks and
Persians
Homeland means the Gulf, which stays forever Persian
Homeland signifies the complete sacrifice (of life if necessary)
To reach the level (of resistance) at Tangestan and Dashtestan[13]

---

[7] A town in western Iran.   [8] A town in eastern Iran.
[9] Refers to the lake and wetlands along the Afghan–Iran border in Sistan province.
[10] Largest river of the Iranian plateau that runs through Isfahan. In Persian
Zayanderud means 'life-giver'.
[11] Refers to the Shat al-Arab river that runs between Iran and Iraq by the
confluence of the Euphrates and Tigris.
[12] Iran's most navigable river that runs through Khuzestan province, including
Ahvaz connecting to the Arvand and the Persian Gulf.
[13] Refers to the Tangestan and Dashtestan region in southern Iran known for its
resistance to the invasion by British forces in the late nineteenth century and the
beginning of the twentieth century, in particular under the leadership of Rais Ali

To purify the country from despotism and detestation
With the sacrifice of our warm blood filling the fountains of Fin Garden[14]
Homeland means calling for a prayer (tale) of love
Homeland means removing the clouds of dust from love
Homeland means intention (and) gallantry
Homeland means dignity and martyrdom
Homeland signifies the past, the present and tomorrow (the future)
The nation and its share of (status in) the world
Homeland, whether prosperous or in ruin
Homeland is exactly here
It means (that is)
Iran

Homeland means being liberated from fire and giving blood
(It means) Kaveh's roar[15] and Fereydoon's[16] anger (outcry)
Homeland indicates the demise of Simorgh[17]
The tradition of Zal's power[18] and the (wide) wings of Simurgh
The Army of Life marched to Khuzestan
(They) embraced martyrdom with open arms
They took a prayer of (drenched in) blood in Khooninshahr
They dislodged the invader from Khorramshahr
Homeland means calling for a prayer (tale) of love
Homeland means removing the clouds of dust from love
Homeland means intention (and) gallantry
Homeland means dignity and martyrdom
Homeland signifies the past, the present and tomorrow (the future)
The nation and its share of (status in) the world

Delvari, a committed Iranian independence fighter and anti-colonial activist. The group he headed was eventually referred to as 'Daliran Tangestan' – their story was turned into an Iranian TV series in the 1970s.

[14] Fin Garden, located in Kashan, Iran, is the oldest extant garden in Iran. It contains Kashan's Fin Bath, where Amir Kabir, the much-lauded chancellor during the Qajar dynasty, was murdered by an assassin sent by Nasereddin Shah in 1852.

[15] Kaveh is the most famous of Persian mythological characters symbolising resistance against despotic foreign rule in Iran, in favour of Iranian unity.

[16] Iranian mythical king symbolising victory, purity, justice and generosity. In the *shahnameh*, Fereydoon, together with Kaveh (see above), revolted against the tyrannical rule of Zahhak, and defeated and arrested him in the Alborz mountains. According to this myth, henceforth, Kaveh assumed the throne and ruled for 500 years.

[17] Simurgh is a gigantic, benevolent bird in Iranian mythology and literature, comparable to other mythological birds such as the phoenix.

[18] Father of Rostam. Recognized as one of the greatest warriors of the *shahnameh*.

Homeland, whether prosperous or in ruin
Homeland is exactly here
It means (that is)
Iran

Revolutions and the International System

The grand revolutions of the twentieth century, certainly in Russia, China, Cuba and Iran, were never confined to the place where they happened. These were revolutions that attempted to reveal themselves on a global canvas. Typically modern, they were based on utopian notions of total change, the possibility to re-engineer everything, indeed the very consciousness of individuals, their psychology, their lives, their thinking, even their bodies. The Iranian variant of this type of biopolitics, as it developed during the revolutionary period, bestowed upon the humble Iranian nation-state the mandate to spearhead a cosmic struggle of the 'oppressed' against the 'oppressors', in Khomeini's Manichaean *mostazafan–mostakbaran* dichotomy. Khomeini was quite explicit about this export of the revolution, much in the same way as Lenin, Castro and Mao, in Russia, Cuba and China before him.

It should be kept in mind here that Khomeini himself emerged out of a particular political current in Iranian and global history. He was the child of an intensely action-driven manifestation of political Islam, as it encompassed the region from the Arab world to the Indian subcontinent. Moreover, Khomeini was promiscuous in his discourse. Certainly, his emphasis on the anti-imperialist terminology of the Iranian left which was typical of the country's third-world populist and socialist zeitgeist during the 1970s, was meant to appeal to the intelligentsia and the students, to galvanise the revolution beyond the pious and the clerical establishment in Iran. To that end, Khomeini appropriated many ideas to appeal to a wider spectrum of Iranian society. Hence also his reference to a global battle, not only between the 'forces of arrogance' and the 'dispossessed', but also between justice and injustice.[19] According to that ideological dualism, the ongoing clash between the 'oppressed', who have been deprived of their political, cultural, natural and economic resources, and the 'oppressors', who have subjugated the 'disinherited'. was zero-sum in nature. In this vein,

---

[19] See further Ervand Abrahamian, *Khomeinism: Essays on the Islamic Republic*, London: I.B. Tauris, 1993.

Khomeini urged Muslim scholars 'to struggle against all attempts by the oppressors to establish a monopoly over the sources of wealth or to make illicit use of them. 'They must not allow the masses to remain hungry and deprived', he maintained, 'while plundering oppressors usurp the sources of wealth and live in opulence.' This mission was closely related to the Shia imamate, and here especially to the life of Imam Ali, cousin and son-in-law of the prophet Muhammad, who became the 'Commander of the Faithful' (*amir-ol momenin*) as the fourth caliph in Muslim history. In this process of historical reimagination, the role of Ali was reinterpreted as thoroughly revolutionary:

The Commander of the Faithful (upon whom be peace) says: 'I have accepted the task of government because God Exalted and Almighty, has exacted from the scholars of Islam a pledge not to sit silent and idle in the face of the gluttony and plundering of the oppressors, on the one hand, and the hunger and deprivation of the oppressed, on the other.'[20]

'Khomeinism' elevated the Iranian nation-state to the status of a vehicle of divine substance. Modern Iranian states have not been humble: the shah invoked Cyrus the Great, Khomeini referred to God.[21] Inevitably, the Islamic Republic felt destined to change what was perceived to be an overbearingly hierarchical world order. This was by no means merely an abstract self-perception. It was formalised, inscribed into the current constitution of Iran which declares that the revolution aims to bring about the triumph of the *mostazafan* against the *mostakbaran*, that it 'provides the necessary basis for ensuring the continuation of the Revolution at home and abroad'. Illustrated in accordance with the Quranic verse 'This your nation is a single nation, and I am your Lord, so worship Me (21:92)', it is further declared that the Constitution 'will strive, in concert with other Islamic and popular movements, to prepare the way for the formation of a single world community'.[22] At the same time, other sections of the Iranian

---

[20] Ayatollah Ruhollah Khomeini, 'The necessity for Islamic government', in Lloyd Ridgeon (ed.), *Religion and Politics in Modern Iran: A Reader*, London: I.B. Tauris, 2005, p. 209.

[21] See further Arshin Adib-Moghaddam, 'Global grandeur and the meaning of Iran: from the shah to the Islamic Republic', in Henner Fürtig (ed.), *Regional Powers in the Middle East: New Constellations after the Arab Revolts*, London: Palgrave, 2014, pp. 43–58.

[22] Hamid Algar, *Constitution of the Islamic Republic of Iran*, trans. Hamid Algar, Berkeley: Mizan Press, 1980, p. 19.

constitution accentuate abstention from 'aggressive intervention in the internal affairs of other nations' (see, for example, Article 154). In fact, and in many ways to this day, the Islamic Republic has adopted an overall anti-militaristic, if rhetorically confrontational, posture in international affairs. But Khomeini also explicitly endorsed the export of the revolutionary idea, whilst cautioning against applying force. On the one side he proclaimed that

we have set as our goal the world-wide spread of the influence of Islam and the suppression of the rule of the world conquerors ... We wish to cause the corrupt roots of Zionism, capitalism and Communism to wither throughout the world. We wish, as does God almighty, to destroy the systems which are based on these three foundations, and to promote the Islamic order of the Prophet ... in the world of arrogance.[23]

On the other side, he also cautioned that this 'does not mean that we intend to export it by the bayonet. We want to call [*dawat*] everyone to Islam [and to] send our calling everywhere.'[24] Although covert support to 'liberation movements' in Afghanistan, Iraq, Lebanon, Latin America, Africa and Palestine was openly justified, exporting the *idea* of the Islamic Republic without military confrontations was rather more central. Reliance on *dawat* (calling) and *tabligh* (propagation, advertisement, dissemination) substituted for the militaristic coercion periodically characteristic of the shah's foreign policy. In accordance with that disposition, the Islamic Republic cancelled the shah's multi-billion-dollar defence contracts with the United States and western Europe, left the Central Treaty Organisation (CENTO) which was meant to function as an extension of NATO, and abandoned Iranian military installations in Oman.

Revolutionary Iran felt very self-conscious about the potential appeal of the movement to the Muslim world in particular and the 'non-Western' world in general. Such attitudes can be discerned from the dozens of wills and testaments that exemplify the distinctly romantic feelings that some of the revolutionaries truly felt. Some of these

---

[23] *Bayan*, No. 4, 1990, p. 8. Quoted in Ali Rahnema, *The Constitution of Iran: Politics and the State in the Islamic Republic*, trans. John O' Keane, London: I.B. Tauris, 1997, p. 69.

[24] Ayatollah Ruhollah Khomeini, *Sahifey-e nur*, vol. 18, Tehran: Vezarat-e Ershad, 1364 (1985), p. 129.

emotional texts read like odes of love, tragic narratives often written at the nexus between life and death. Caught in the momentum of revolutionary intoxication, these revolutionaries relied on their ideological power transmitted by the charisma of Ayatollah Khomeini and transplanted by sympathising movements in the region and beyond, rather than military aggrandisement. The idea came first; the institutions that I have discussed in Chapter 2 were built upon them and the international affairs of the country were radically altered accordingly.

In this highly charged atmosphere, and the anarchy that the revolution brought about, the storming of the US embassy in November 1979 should not have come as a surprise. The students involved in occupying the embassy were clearly motivated to prevent another *coup d'état* as in 1953. A banner set up at the US embassy compound said it all: 'CIA, Pentagon, Uncle Sam: Vietnam wounded you, Iran will bury you'. Khomeini stoked up the flames of revolution in order to demonstrate to the world that the past was gone, once and for all. It was this confidence about the 'justness' of the revolutionary cause and the spiritual superiority of religious values that became central to the self-perception of the Islamic Republic. Iran was to be the citadel of a new world order. The US embassy takeover was the first event to signal this goal to the world.

So confident was Khomeini in his project that in January 1989 he wrote a letter to Soviet leader Mikhail Gorbachev attempting to persuade him to consider spiritual values in general and Islam in particular as an alternative to the materialism of capitalist societies. You have got to be very self-righteous to believe that an atheist empire steeped in Orthodox Christian traditions would take seriously an offer to embrace Islam. But Khomeini repeatedly claimed such authority. He argued in a similar vein in his response to a letter from Pope John Paul II (in the midst of the hostage crisis) in May 1980. All of these examples are meant to demonstrate the confidence that the Iranian revolutionaries felt – a sense of grandeur that is also reflected in the foreign policy of the country, in many ways to this day:

I ask His Honor to warn the US government of the consequences of its oppressions, cruelties and plunders, and advise Mr. Carter, who is doomed to defeat, to treat nations desiring absolute independence of global powers on the basis of humanitarian principles. He should be advised to observe the guidelines of Jesus Christ and not to expose himself and the US Administration to defamation.[25]

If these hubristic goals to change the world in total were characteristic of the revolutionary momentum, they were decisively challenged when Saddam Hussein started the devastating eight-year war in 1980. At the same time, the war buttressed the politics of Khomeini. Judging from his character and his stoic political persuasions it was to be foreseen that Iran was reluctant to retreat from its ideological positions after it had been invaded by Saddam Hussein's Iraq in 1980. The official discourse of the newly established Islamic Republic represented the war as a re-enactment of the eternal battle between absolute evil, represented by Saddam Hussein, and absolute justness, represented by Ayatollah Khomeini who was only too willing to exploit those sentiments for his revolutionary project. In my (off-the-record) conversations with members of the military establishment in Iran, the strategic calculus to continue the war after 1982, when Saddam Hussein offered a ceasefire, is intimately related to this confidence: Iran was in the ascendancy on the battlefield, the demand that Saddam Hussein step down was not met, and there was a general feeling that Saddam Hussein was buying time in order to rearm his troops and that he would launch another invasion with greater force. Hence, Iran marched on.

The fact that after Iranian advances in 1982, the Iraqi leader received overwhelming global support, including all the equipment he needed from Western companies to be able to use chemical weapons against Iranians and his own population, gives credence to the scepticism towards the 'international community' shown by Iranian decision-makers at that time.[26] Even United Nations Security Council Resolution 598 which ended the war in 1988 was biased towards Iraq, as it did not name that country as the invading party. Neither did the UN condemn the Iraqi chemical weapons attacks which I have comprehensively documented elsewhere.[27] In fact, the forces of Saddam

---

[25] 'Letter from Ayatollah Ruhollah Khomeini to Pope John-Paul II', in Massoumeh Ebtekar, *Takeover in Tehran: The Inside Story of the 1979 US Embassy Capture*, Vancouver: Talonbooks, 2000, p. 246.

[26] See further Arshin Adib-Moghaddam, 'Inventions of the Iran–Iraq War', in Nargues Bajoghli and Amir Moosavi (eds.), *Debating the Iran–Iraq War in Contemporary Iran*, London: Routledge, 2018.

[27] See further Arshin Adib-Moghaddam, 'The whole range of Saddam Hussein's war crimes', *Middle East Report*, No. 236 (2006), pp. 30–35.

Hussein tried to reinvade Iran even after UNSCR 598. The Iraqi forces were repelled, and Iran recaptured 600 square kilometres of Iraqi territory, but eventually withdrew to the recognised borders. Undoubtedly, without the massive support to Saddam Hussein's war effort before – and rather more overtly after – 1982, Iran would have won the war. The primary material available supports this assessment:

The Reagan Administration secretly decided to provide highly classified intelligence to Iraq in the spring of 1982 – more than two years earlier than previously disclosed – while also permitting the sale of American-made arms to Baghdad in a successful effort to help President Saddam Hussein avert imminent defeat in the war with Iran, former intelligence and State Department officials say. The American decision to lend crucial help to Baghdad so early in the 1980–88 Iran-Iraq war came after American intelligence agencies warned that Iraq was on the verge of being overrun by Iran, whose army was bolstered the year before by covert shipments of American-made weapons ... In the end, officials acknowledged, American arms, technology and intelligence helped Iraq avert defeat and eventually grow, with much help from the Soviet Union later, into the regional power that invaded Kuwait in August 1990, sparking the Persian Gulf war last year.[28]

When the Iraqi army entered Iran in 1980, it accentuated the interaction between the manufactured identity of the Islamic Republic and that of the totalitarian and secular Ba'athist state in Iraq. This antagonistic interaction engendered the notion among Iranian soldiers that they were fighting in order to defend 'justice', not only in Iran, but globally. Shia Islam's holy places, Karbala and Najaf, were to be liberated from the 'Pharaoh of the age', even if it meant that a whole generation of Iranians would perish in the war trenches. For them the conflict had nothing to do with 'revenge'. Rather, it was perceived to be a war for 'Islam, country and honour'.[29]

The metaphysics, symbolism and imagery that engendered the 'pseudo-reality' that Iranians were fighting for a transcendental cause was consciously engineered by Khomeini and the newly established Islamic state, as Kusha Sefat, a supremely gifted Cambridge-educated

[28] Seymour M. Hersh, 'US secretly gave aid to Iraq early in its war against Iran', *New York Times*, 26 January 1992, p. 1, available at www.nytimes.com/1992/01/26/world/us-secretly-gave-aid-to-iraq-early-in-its-war-against-iran.html, accessed 14 June 2017.

[29] Husein Golchin, *Namazi dar atash va khun* [A prayer in the midst of fire and blood], Tehran: Cultural Centre for Islamic Propaganda, 1372 (1993), p. 9.

scholar currently at Shahid Beheshti University in Iran, innovatively argued in his research.[30]

In turn, for many of their addressees among the receptive revolutionary generation, this pseudo-reality was synonymous with an 'age whose every moment is light and illumination, wisdom and perfection'. The aforementioned wills and testaments are clear about such sentiments: 'Yes my brothers,' reads one of them written by an Iranian soldier who died in the war, 'we have witnessed Islam, its Prophet and his valuable traditions, and the innocent Imams; in a short span of time we have felt, with all our existence, the rich history of Islam which [previously] we had only read or heard about'.[31] Now that Iranians were entrenched in this (pseudo-)reality it seemed that the legendary story of Imam Hussein was repeating itself, 'in the matter of guardianship and leadership, in the [presence of] sincere disciples and companions of falsity, in belief, sacrifice and martyrdom, in blasphemy, belligerence and dissension, in the expansion of Islam and the multiplicity of enemies'.[32] In this dichotomic order, Khomeini was perceived to represent 'the spirit of God. [W]e have made a compact with you, heard your words and endeavoured to implement them', it is proclaimed in another will.

[W]e have written your message onto the face of history with our blood saying: In our time, we were with our Imam, and if we were not in Karbala to assist Hossein, we have added his child and this way our duty. Oh Imam! I have understood your command when you stated: The present war is a conflict between truth and falsehood and since truth is the victor, we are victorious. Since I wished to join the ranks of the combatants of truth, I entered the scene and this was my message ...[33]

---

[30] Kusha Sefat, 'Things and terms: relations between materiality, language, and politics in post-revolutionary Iran', *International Political Sociology*, Vol. 14, No. 2(2020), pp. 175–95, available at https://doi.org/10.1093/ips/olz031, accessed 14 December 2019.

[31] 'Martyr Ahmad Sanezadeh', in Majid Zamanpour (ed.), *Jelveha-ye Nur* (The Faces of Light), Tehran: Cultural Centre of the Revolutionary Guards, Spring 1373 (1995), translated and quoted by Nader Nazemi, 'Sacrifice and authorship: a compendium of the will of Iranian war martyrs', *Iranian Studies*, Vol. 30, Nos. 3–4 (1997), p. 265.

[32] Ibid.

[33] 'Martyr Bijan Muhammadian', in Zamanpour (ed.), *Jelveha*, pp. 131–132. Translated and quoted by Nader Nazemi, 'Sacrifice and authorship', p. 266. For translated poems on the death of Ayatollah Khomeini in 1989 see Naser

There is a lot more primary material that demonstrates the immense morale that inspired the Iranian military to repel Saddam Hussein's forces and take the war onto Iraqi territory. Some of these themes are closely analysed in the recent research of Soudeh Ghaffari.[34] The melancholic memories are the primary reasons why the war created a bond between its protagonists, that became central to the core ideological cohesion of the post-revolutionary generation – a brotherhood baptised in a common trauma drenched in blood, that shared the terror of the chemical weapons attacks by Saddam Hussein and the immense support that he received from the most powerful actors in the world to that end. This is the reason why the war continues to be central, even to the rhetoric of contemporary Iranian leaders. It reinvigorated the age-old Iranian suspicion towards 'imperial' powers and their designs for the country. As the current foreign minister Javad Zarif replied in 2018 to the Trump administration's reimposition of sanctions against Iran:

Iran has 7,000 years of history. We've lived through more difficult times. For eight years [the Iran–Iraq War], we lived through a war that was imposed on Iran and everybody supported the aggressor, Saddam Hussein. The United States supported it, the Soviet Union supported him, the Europeans supported him. The Soviets gave him MIG [jet] fighters, the French gave him Mirage [jet] fighters, the Brits gave him Chieftain tanks, the American gave him AWACS reconnaissance, the Germans gave him chemical weapons, the Saudis gave him $70 billion worth of assistance.[35]

Over three decades after the Iran–Iraq War, then, this generation of Iranian decision-makers continues to perceive world politics through the lens of a history of real and exaggerated foreign conspiracies against the country. Therefore, securing the independence of Iran

Shakuri, Alireza Emami, Mohammad Ali Bahmani, Fatemeh Rake'i, Parviz Abbasi-Dakani and Reza Esma'ili, 'Elegies for a lost leader: six poems on the death of Khomeini', trans. Paul E. Losensky, *Iranian Studies*, Vol. 30, Nos. 3–4, (1997), pp. 277–289.

[34] See Soudeh Ghaffari, 'From religious performances to martial themes: discourse of Shia musical eulogies, war and politics in Iran', *Journal of Language and Politics*, Vol. 18, No. 4, pp. 617–633, available at https://benjamins.com/catalog/jlp.18059.gha, accessed 24 July 2019.

[35] 'Transcript: Iran foreign minister interview', *USA Today*, 5 November 2018, available at https://eu.usatoday.com/story/news/world/2018/11/05/iran-foreign-minister-interview-us-nuclear-deal-mohammad-javad-zarif-trump-administration/1892350002/, accessed 10 January 2019.

against all odds continues to be a major motivational factor behind the country's foreign policies

Rivers of Blood

This historicisation of Iran's spirit to 'resist injustice', a derivative of the Hussein paradigm so crucial to Shia eschatology, is central to the song of Alireza Assar and Foad Hejazi that frames this chapter.[36] In 'Vatan' (Homeland), Assar invokes the spirit of the war veterans who 'liberated' Khorramshahr, the south-western Iranian town that was recaptured by Iran two years after the invasion by Saddam Hussein's forces in 1980. Immediately after the occupation, Khomeini referred to the town as *Khooninshahr* or town of blood. Assar uses this allegory in his lyrics when he refers to the Iranian troops who died in the battle to recapture the town. For many Iranians, the realist, and therefore explicit, photography of Bahman Jalili (1944–2010), captured the horrors of this battle, and installed its memory in popular Iranian culture, certainly in the 1980s. Moreover, the famous poem of Simin Behbahani (1927–2014) called *benevis, benevis, benevis* (record, record, record), written in September 1980 when Khorramshahr was occupied, gave the battle a tragic, yet romantic colouring.

> *Record, record an epic of resilience . . .*
> *The Lionhearted, the Hero.*
> *Exalt, exalt the death*
> *Those guardians of the Land.*
> *Record those who uttered:*
> *'Either death or glory',*
> *Who bravely pressed on till Death.*
> *Record, yes, Record.*[37]

The liberation of Khorramshahr is celebrated on 24 May with great fanfare to this day, as it became a metaphor for the sacrifices of the Iranian war veterans in this 'holy defence' or *defaye-moqadas* as the Iran–Iraq War is still referred to in the official discourse of the Islamic Republic. As part of 'Operation Jerusalem', the recapture of

---

[36] Alireza Assar and Foad Hejazi, 'Vatan', 2005.
[37] 'Remember Khooninshahr', *The Iranian*, 29 October 2007.

Khorramshahr gave impetus to the reconquest of Iranian territory and the eventual push of Iranian forces into southern Iraq thereafter.

Behbahani's poem connects to the tropes and metaphors that can be discerned from the musical piece that frames this chapter. With dramatic lyrics and with his unmistakably penetrative voice, the song of Assar (and Hejazi) sounds like an ode of patriotic love and loyalty for Iran that combines mythological themes and embeds them in a poetic, yet psycho-nationalistic romanticism, characteristic of this genre of Iranian 'pop' music promoted by the state.[38] Assar celebrates the war veterans as the 'army of life' who accepted death for their homeland and liberated Khorramshahr from Saddam's forces. In typical prose for this kind of popular music in Iran, the nation is represented as a source of identity, love, roots, endeavour, and the status of a people in the world. With repeated reference to the great heroes of Iranian mythology taken from the *shahnameh* of Ferdowsi, and Zoroastrian mythologies, Assar's song is a story of love for Iran that signifies the country as the centre of a global struggle against injustice.

The militaristic drumbeats and trumpets and the anthropomorphic, emotive lyrics make 'Vatan' quite comparable to the song of Rooygari that I used for the previous chapter, with the difference that Assar sounds far more Irano-centric than Rooygari, whose lyrics were rather more dominated by religious, Shia-Islamic tropes. In 'Vatan', the ancient figures of Iranian mythology such as 'Bahram Lionheart' and 'Arash the Archer' are positioned next to famous events depicting the tragic fate of national heroes such as the famed Qajar chancellor Amir Kabir who was assassinated in 1852, and the anti-colonial fighter Rais Ali Delvari, killed in 1915. Delvari fought the British in the Tangestan and Dashtestan area of southern Iran, at the time when the first Iranian oil fields were commercially exploited by foreign companies.

In an epic tour de force, Assar turns these figures into contemporary heroes of Iranian resistance and power. Assar is a member of the postwar generation, that was less affected by the Islamic utopia than their parents envisaged, yet equally confident that Iranians could change history. The role of Iran in the world, the tenor of these songs reveals, was perceived to be special, even unique. Iran emerges as a vehicle of

---

[38] This aspect is highlighted in Nahid Siamdoust, *Soundtrack of the Revolution: The Politics of Music in Iran*, Stanford: Stanford University Press, 2017, especially ch. 5.

divine substance, the object of injustice, the divine agent of resistance to tyranny and the nodal point of history, indeed the universe. This kind of Iranocentric thinking has a long pedigree, and it is central to a proper understanding of the foreign policy of the country.

The song of Rooygari was emblematic for the romantic sentiments of many revolutionaries, whereas Assar's 'Vatan' is a rather more chauvinistic musical piece that is imbued with psycho-nationalist fervour. The song of Assar also displays in quite a vivid manner the confidence of this Islamic Republic and its adherents, as I started to argue above. Assar conceptualises Iran as an epic, the place where the eternal battle between the forces of darkness and the forces of light is decided in favour of Iranians. Psycho-nationalism always also entails these tales of bravery, love for the nation, blood and honour, which speak to a national egotism that reveals a narcissistic self-perception and an inflated sense of 'mission'.

Caught up in a gendered language, the nation becomes a feminised subject, protected by the heroism of its male guardians. In terms of policy, one immediate result of this kind of internalisation of patriarchally structured 'Iranian grandeur' can be seen in the persistent attempts to challenge the international status quo. It may also explain the vicious and inhumane treatment of homosexuality by the Iranian state, as queer politics challenge the retroactive claim of 'male guardianship' of the feminised nation. In this regard, Iranian national chauvinism is comparable to any other form of psycho-nationalism.

The Iranian revolutionaries, like the Russians, Chinese and Cubans before them, have been dangerously righteous and partially delusional about the ability of their country to bring about a global revolution. Thus, far from recognising the overbearing 'injustice' of the present, Iran's revolution was meant to strive for the transcendence of all the tensions between utopia and reality which those dichotomies opened up. Utopia by force, so to say – a hegemonic conception of the future which has caused many disasters in human history, especially during the twentieth century with its 'modern' pretensions. Iran was merely yet another example of this violent dialectic in global history. The lyrics of Assar's song partially reveal why, even when they depart from the religious tropes characteristic of the Khomeini decade.

No wonder, then, that the more international society turned against Iran, the more this reaction confirmed the self-perception of the Iranian state as the vanguard of 'global justice', facing the overwhelming force of the 'arrogant' powers. When Khomeini was still alive, the revolutionary state closely related this imagery to the 'Hussein paradigm', i.e. the killing of the Shia imam Hussein, grandson of the prophet Muhammad, during the battle of Karbala against the Umayyad monarch Yazid in 680 AD. Yet, it is crucial to underline in this analysis that the Shia notion of victimhood was turned by the Iranians into a psycho-national source of an immensely radiant, yet largely utilitarian, doctrine of power, sovereignty, legitimacy and governance: Hussein was not to be oppressed again. This Islamic Republic would not be victimised. There would be no need for concealment (*taqiyya*) anymore, no *suggestio falsi* that the Shia had to practise due to their prosecution as a minority sect within Islam. The disinherited would rule:

Imam Husayn was not to be killed again. Thus, he defeated Yazid [i.e. the shah] in Iran last year. Imam Husayn, who is now leading a battle against a greater Yazid [i.e. imperialism], will also triumph, God willing. The revolutionary Imam Husayn in Iran, who is fighting imperialism, is not alone now. In addition to some 35,000,000 Iranians who bravely and devotedly rally around him, there are billions of Muslims and non-Muslims everywhere in Syria, Libya, Algeria, Lebanon, Palestine, Pakistan, Africa, the Omani liberation front, Eritrea, the Chilean resistance, the Chadian liberation movement, the Canary Islands' liberation movement, the Futami liberation movement, Spain, Korea and many other places as well as the entire Islamic world, and the oppressed all over the world, who all support Iran, the revolution and Imam Husayn, represented in leader Imam Ayatollah Khomeini.[39]

This is a particularly confident form of psycho-nationalism that was distilled out of the anti-imperialist norm advocated by Al-e Ahmad and Shariati, which was translated into institutions by Iran's revolutionary generation and which became constitutive of the Islamic state. Iran was placed at the centre of a global struggle for empowerment; the Iranian nation became the carrier of a divine mission. The 'oppressed' became a pseudonym that translated resistance into power, not at all determined by a class theory that would emancipate the socio-economically deprived strata of Iranian society, but by a theory of power that would place the Islamic Republic firmly within a vanguard for a new world order.

[39] BBC *Survey of World Broadcasts*, Part IV (A), The Middle East, 24 November 1979, ME/6280/A/8.

Accordingly, the country's foreign policy culture, Iran's perception of international affairs and its role in world politics, were being transformed. This driving agency, which commanded its own reality, soon broke the boundaries between political idiom and political action. These conceptual links that are central to an understanding of Iranian foreign affairs come out succinctly in the work of Homeira Moshirzadeh, a professor in the Department of International Relations and the Centre for Women's Studies, at the University of Tehran.[40] In addition, some of the best theoretical scholarship with a similar approach is published by Prof. Mehdi Zakerian and his team in the Iranian *International Studies Journal*.[41]

The Islamic Republic, as many Iranians saw it during the revolutionary period, positioned itself into a severed, schismatic condition: on the one side of the Atlantic the 'great Satan', the governments of the United States, on the other the atheist giant, the Soviet Union (and in between other, 'lesser' enemies such as Apartheid South Africa, Israel and Saddam Hussein). Having completed their diagnosis of Iranian and Muslim civilisation, and their prognosis that revolutionary action will bring about the renewal of both, Iran's revolutionary generation was introjected with the idea that radical independence from both superpowers would ensure a process at the end of which the existing world order would be transformed. Hence the emergence of the *na sharghi na gharbi, jomhur-e eslami* norm (neither eastern nor western, only the Islamic Republic). Hence the country's decision to end its membership of Cold War institutions such as CENTO. Hence the prolonged war with Iraq which was perceived to be a part of an international conspiracy to subdue the revolution (which in many ways it was, of course). Hence the Islamic Republic's immediate support for the Palestine Liberation Organization (PLO) (Yassir Arafat was the first major foreign political leader to visit Iran, where he received the keys to what ceased to be the Israeli embassy in Tehran) and sympathising leftist movements all over the world, especially in Latin America. Hence, the Islamic Republic's decision to sever ties with Apartheid South Africa and thus also Iran's enduring antagonism toward the policies of successive US governments. The costs of these changes to the country's

---

[40] See for instance Homeira Moshirzadeh, 'Identity and Security in the Middle East', *Iranian Review of Foreign Affairs*, Vol. 4, No. 2 (2013), pp. 5–32.

[41] Most articles are now available as free PDFs. See www.isjq.ir/?lang=en.

international affairs were accepted, even if that meant that it would be isolated, and labelled as a 'rogue' or 'outlaw' state by prominent members of the international community. For ordinary Iranians, seeking international justice was a genuine sentiment, and for the Khomeinists erecting the core of the theocratic elements of the Iranian state, it was a ready-made ideological instrument to subdue competing forces and entrench their political ideology and their vision of a 'just' state.

National Interests, International Challenges

I have started to argue that Iran's contemporary foreign policy culture and strategic preferences are rooted in the revolutionary paradigms formulated in the 1970s and that this cultural system informs the country's grand strategic preferences. Institutionalised as central narratives of the state, the Islamic Republic followed the revolutionary utopias not only at the level of behaviour, but also of interest. In other words, the radical wing that took over the Iranian state did not see a contradiction between the revolutionary ideals and 'the' national interest of the country. On the contrary, from their perspective, realising those ideals *was* in the national interest of the Islamic Republic and – by implication – other nations with similar ambitions to create a new world order.

Iranian foreign police elites were aware that the appeal of the revolution in the Muslim world and beyond would be enhanced greatly if the counter-hegemonic rhetoric were to be backed up by action. If the US state was the 'imperial oppressor', conquering the moral high ground in world politics required confrontation. If the Islamic Republic wanted to propagate its revolutionary claim, it needed to confront real and perceived imperialism both at home and abroad. If the revolution was to act as a model for other third-world countries, it had to assert its legitimacy, if necessary, through violent action. In the Iranian case, then, as elsewhere, utopia offered both 'a vantage point from which to perceive the given, the already constituted' and, more importantly, 'new possibilities above and beyond the given'.[42]

The composition of Iran's current foreign policy culture shows both residual elements of the revolutionary utopias and signs of a strong 'counterculture' that signals loyalty to the country's commitment to

---

[42] 'Editor's introduction', in Paul Ricoeur, *Lectures on Ideology and Utopia*, ed. George H. Taylor, New York: Columbia University Press, 1986, pp. xxviii–xxix.

project its ideological power, yet less raucous methods to achieve that goal.[43] In the Iranian context, as elsewhere, culture does not appear as a monolithic system resistant to changes from below. 'The reality of any hegemony', the Welsh Cambridge professor Raymond Williams famously noted, 'is that, while by definition it is always dominant, it is never either total or exclusive. At any time, forms of alternative or directly oppositional politics and culture exist as significant elements in the society.'[44] Culture, Williams was right to note, changes in accordance with historical realities.

One needs only to consider the speeches of women activists and intellectual paradigms developed by a range of oppositional figures to conclude that Iran's post-revolutionary cultural order has undergone rapid transformations, as I have already argued in the previous chapter. Undeniably, this emergent counterculture – which has manifested itself in a multidimensional movement for a pluralistic democracy – has had an impact on the country's foreign policies. It would be reductionist, however, to attribute these policies to power struggles between pragmatic 'reformers' and hard-line 'conservatives' supported by the office of the current Supreme Leader Ayatollah Ali Khamenei.

This dichotomous notion, too often presented in monocausal terms (i.e. reformism equals pragmatism and pro-Western policies while conservatism equals pan-Islamism and anti-Western agitation), is inadequate to address why Iranian foreign policy elites have remained committed to certain core strategic principles of the state, and why even Ayatollah Khamenei repeatedly softened his stance towards the United States. The discourses shift within specific historical contexts, but the Islamic Republic continues to represent itself as a 'moral superpower', as a force for change in international affairs, as an agent of a just world order: It continues to challenge US foreign policies, in the Persian Gulf, in Iraq, in Syria, in Central Asia and in Latin America; it continues to support the Palestinian cause, with conferences, ideological propaganda, organised diplomatic initiatives, military equipment and money; its alliance patterns are incredibly pathdependent, exemplified by the close relationship with the Lebanese Hezbollah, whether under presidents Khatami, Ahmadinejad or the

---

[43] For the difference between 'residual', 'dominant', and 'emergent' culture see Raymond Williams, *Marxism and Literature*, Oxford: Oxford University Press, 1977, especially pp. 121–127.

[44] Ibid., p. 113.

current president Rouhani; the country remains committed to the slogan of independence which is why the nuclear issue became a matter of national pride and a marker of Iranian sovereignty, despite sanctions and recurrent threats of war by the United States and Israel; the country continues to intervene directly and indirectly in Yemen, Iraq and Syria etc., despite stringent threats by Saudi Arabia and others. Like any other state, then, decision-makers in Iran adhere to certain grand strategic preferences that transcend the fault-lines of day-to-day politics and unite the core political strata of the country around a set of 'state interests'.

Moreover, from the perspective of contemporary Iranian decision-makers there appears to be no contradiction between the utopian-romantic leitmotif of the revolution and multilateral engagement and détente – two themes that were central to the 'dialogue among civilisations' initiative put forward by the Khatami administration (1997–2005) and which have also been emblematic of the so-called 'pragmatic diplomacy' of the current Rouhani presidency. Although the Islamic Republic has distanced itself from some of the confrontationist policies characteristic of the first decade of the revolution, *tabligh* and *dawat* continue to provide the strategic means to realise the grand strategic preferences of the state as these tactics have transmuted into a *ghodrat-e narm* (soft power) doctrine that accentuates cultural diplomacy, for instance in the form of the burgeoning Islamic Azad University network that spans from almost every town and city in Iran to Syria, Iraq, sub-Saharan Africa and beyond (and/or cultural centres all over the region).[45] As Mohammad Khatami proclaimed in typical parlance for Iran's contemporary decision-makers:

Fulfilling the utopian vision of the revolution's devotees inside and outside of Iran is a pressing necessity to ensure our survival. To assert our identity it is necessary to be present in all world forums and to defend Islam and Iran effectively in all international tribunals and conventions. But we cannot ultimately flourish and make our weight felt in the international

---

[45] For an Iranian view by a young scholar from the University of Lorestan see Mahdi Zolfaghari, 'Iran's soft power in foreign policy', *International Journal of Management and Applied Science*, Vol. 4, No. 1 (2018), pp. 66–69. For a rather more analytical piece see Nargues Bajoghli, 'The hidden sources of Iranian strength', *Foreignpolicy.com*, 15 May 2015, available at https://foreignpolicy.com/2019/05/15/the-hidden-sources-of-iranian-strength, accessed 12 August 2019.

scene – whose rules are set by our opponents – unless we maintain our unique idealism.[46]

Despite his repeatedly problematic rhetoric and a generally confrontational demeanour, even the former president Mahmoud Ahmadinejad (2005–2013) pursued a comparable political rationale when he called for

> serious reform in the structure and working methods of the [UN] Security Council ... Justice and Democracy dictate that the role of the General Assembly, as the highest organ of the United Nations, must be respected. The General Assembly can then, through appropriate mechanisms, take on the task of reforming the Organisation and particularly rescue the Security Council from its current state. In the interim, the Non-Aligned-Movement, the Organisation of the Islamic Conference and the African continent should each have a representative as a permanent member of the Security Council, with veto privilege. The resulting balance would hopefully prevent further trampling of the rights of nations.[47]

The current President Rouhani (2013–) argued in a similar vein:

> In today's tumultuous world, the only way to overcome difficulties is through concerted international efforts based on mutual interests, and not the short-sighted demands of one or a few states. Unilateralism is fatal; while multilateralism is the only appropriate, inexpensive and effective course of action.[48]

To open a parenthesis here, I am not claiming that there is a consensus among the different factions of Iranian politics on every foreign policy decision. That would oversimplify the differences between the spectrum of political parties and institutions in Iran. After all, there are at least eight institutions involved in Iran's foreign policy process: the

---

[46] Mohammad Khatami, *Islam, Dialogue and Civil Society*, Canberra: Centre for Arab and Islamic Studies, 2000, p. 62. See also Javad Zarif, 'Indispensable power: hegemonic tendencies in a globalized world', *Harvard International Review* Vol. 24, No. 4, Winter 2003, pp. 72–75.

[47] 'Address by His Excellency Dr Mahmoud Ahmadi-Nejad President of the Islamic Republic of Iran before the 61st Session of the General Assembly', New York, 19 September 2006.

[48] Hassan Rouhani, 'Europe should work with Iran to counter US unilateralism', *Financial Times*, 1 November 2018, available at www.ft.com/content/3ecaed5e-dcfc-11e8-b173-ebef6ab1374a, accessed 1 September 2019.

office of the leader; the Foreign Ministry; the office of the president; the head of the Expediency Council; the Supreme National Security Council; the parliament (primarily through its national security and foreign policy commissions); the Strategic Council for Foreign Relations which was established in June 2006 to oversee the performance of the presidency; and the Revolutionary Guards with their huge underbelly which encompasses the Baseej voluntary forces that are present in each Iranian town and village. There is no doubt that sometimes these institutions follow different agendas. But there is a politically constituted consensus about the country's role in international affairs that is strong enough to transcend the factions of – and fractions in – Iranian politics.

This foreign policy culture refers to a higher level of abstraction than the day-to-day affairs of the state. It functions as the guardian of state identity, represents a web of shared ideals, images, norms, institutions, and provides for the foreign policy elites a coherent, if systematically abstract, overall orientation in the conduct of international affairs with a particular sensitivity towards safeguarding the legitimacy and sovereignty of the state. In this vein, foreign policy has become an important tool to recreate the self-image of the Islamic Republic of Iran as a major power in an increasingly multipolar international system.

It is not at all obvious, then, that Iran's current strategic preferences represent a break from some of the core ideas of the revolution. Nor is it clear, that they result from 'socialisation' in international structures, although – viewed from the perspective of Iran's current foreign minister Javad Zarif – the war against Saddam Hussein's Iraq played its part in confronting Iran with the brute realities of international life, with the immediate experience of 'war and destruction . . . in the battlefields . . . cities, neighbourhoods and homes', and the 'global indifference' regarding Saddam's war crimes.[49] Today, Iran has undoubtedly changed, in particular with regard to the country's international affairs and attitudes towards reconciliation with the United States. But these nuanced changes are tempered by the enduring strategic preferences of the state which will continue to guide the international affairs of the

---

[49] Mohammad Javad Zarif and Mohammad Reza Alborzi, 'Weapons of mass destruction in Iran's security paradigm: the case of chemical weapons', *Iranian Journal of International Affairs*, Vol. 11, No. 4, Winter 1999–2000, p. 513.

Islamic Republic for the foreseeable future. When Iran is confronted, it will react in accordance with the level of that confrontation.

At the same time, Iranian utopianism is alive and well within society because it is still in the process of realising its dual aim: democratisation at home and positioning Iran as a central international player abroad. The Khatami interlude, and of course the current presidency of Hassan Rouhani, effected an eclectic reinterpretation of these goals and did/do not represent a revolt against the system.[50] Khatami and Rouhani are surface effects of the demand for change, that is directed against the 'chiliastic' moment of Iran's revolution. The Iranian utopia of *imminent change* has transmuted into the utopia of *generic growth*. This appears to be the philosophical faultline of Iran's contemporary political culture: it manifests itself in the fight between an intellectual and scientific (enlightened) worldview and a theocratic or clerical (retroactive) worldview or a battle between progressive politics and right-wing conservativism which goes beyond the Iranian context.[51] Despite his problematic over-reliance on metaphysical imagery and idioms, the influential ideas of the contemporary Iranian philosopher Abdolkarim Soroush continue to be emblematic of the former:

If science develops, it would modernize and develop our politics, it would give meaning to justice and freedom ... and [it] would determine the rights of people. We should not forget that in the New World politics is scientific politics and management is scientific management. The new science modernizes even philosophy. Islamic philosophy is dear, but ... [w]e should not think that the answer to all questions could be found in this philosophy. Even on the scene of philosophy we should seek progress and renewal.[52]

The paradigmatic turn advocated by Soroush and others has engendered the critical deconstruction of Iran's pre-revolutionary identity discourse. According to the 'Kian school of Iranian philosophy', neither the 'return to the self' nor the idea of 'westtoxification' have

[50] See also Fariba Adelkhah, *Being Modern in Iran*, trans. Jonathan Derrick, London: Hurst & Company, 1999.
[51] See Arshin Adib-Moghaddam, 'Global intifadah? September 11th and the struggle within Islam', *Cambridge Review of International Affairs*, Vol. 15, No. 2 (2002), pp. 203–216.
[52] Abdolkarim Soroush, 'Scientific development, political development', *Kian Monthly Review* 10, No. 54, Oct.–Nov. 2000, available at www.drsoroush.com/English/By_DrSoroush/E-CMB-19990500-Seminar_on_Tradition_and_Modernism_held_in_Beheshti_University.html, accessed 8 November 2020.

sufficiently addressed Iran's conflict with itself. Instead of essentialising Iran's Islamic heritage and castigating the 'West', Soroush argues, Iranian thinkers need to evaluate critically the country's national (Persian), religious-Islamic (Shia) *and* Western heritage. This is something of a departure from the way the Khomeinists conceptualised the meaning of Iran and it is a good analytical signpost to understand why Iran could forge closer relations with the European Union (EU) and even with the United States in the build up to the JCPOA. The Western heritage of Iran makes this orientation entirely viable and culturally sustainable, once it was repackaged as 'authentic.'

The contemporary strategic preferences of the Iranian state oscillate between this emerging, liberal-humanitarian utopia articulated by an increasingly vocal civil society and the chiliastic meta-structure woven into the institutional and intellectual fabric of the country during the revolutionary process. A critical, discursive, reconfiguring continuation rather than a break with the ideals of the revolution, this emergent culture has guided the Rafsanjani, Khatami, Ahmadinejad and Rouhani administrations toward advocating reform at home, while prioritising an essentially conservative purpose: the preservation of the post-revolutionary, Islamic character of the Iranian system and the projection of Iranian power both regionally and globally.

Iran's seemingly 'eclectic' pragmatism during times of crisis – arms deals with the United States via Israel during the Iran–Iraq War (Iran-Contra affair), the diplomatic backing of the US invasion of Taliban Afghanistan in 2001, relative silence about Russian war crimes in Muslim Chechnya and Chinese suppression of Muslims primarily in the western provinces of the country, mute support of the war against Saddam Hussein in 2003, efforts to engage with the United States diplomatically, the nuclear agreement etc. – should be seen within that context. They exemplify instances when diplomacy and the anarchic spaces of world politics are/were exploited in support of Iran's strategic preferences.

The foreign policy elites of Iran do not think of the international system in an ad hoc fashion, then, they do not merely decide from crisis to crisis, their decisions are not singularly eclectic, they are not merely reactive, as even someone such as Soroush alleges.[53] Rather, they think

---

[53] Abdolkarim Soroush, *Reason, Freedom & Democracy in Islam: Essential Writings of 'Abdolkarim Soroush*, trans. and ed. Mahmoud Sadri and Ahmad Sadri, Oxford: Oxford University Press, 2000, p. 23.

of world politics in terms that have been bequeathed to them by preceding experience. As a result, a whole cultural ground exists upon which Iran's foreign policies figure as a surface effect. The nuclear issue is a case in point. The refusal of Iran to compromise mastering the full nuclear fuel cycle and the country's rights under the NPT until the JCPOA was signed in July 2015 can hardly be detached from cultural attitudes exemplified by the notion of 'mastering the machine' that was central to Al-e Ahmad's writings in the 1960s. When analysts say that the nuclear issue has become a matter of national prestige for Iranians, they are right. But they abstract from those cultural attitudes permeating Iranian society, which run deep and which are constitutive of some of the international behaviour of Iran.

This view of technology as a vehicle for change and, ultimately, prestige resonates with the utopian ideas of Iranian intellectuals from the 1960s until now. 'It's obvious that as long as we only use machines and don't make them,' warned Al-e Ahmad, 'we're Weststruck.'[54] Indeed, a critical analysis of Iran's nuclear strategy can be written only on the basis of what has been contemporaneous with it, that is in terms of the intellectual and theoretical a prioris established in the archives of Iran's contemporary history. It is in this sense that a cultural genealogy can give an account of the nuclear strategy, and thus opens a complex, emotionally charged area in which the history of Iran's resistance to foreign dominance can be explained. It is through such an understanding that the national consensus in defence of the nuclear programme can be linked to the 'tobacco revolts' of 1890 against the concession of exclusive tobacco rights in favour of Major G. Talbot (a British citizen); the nationalisation of the Anglo-Iranian Oil Company in early 1951 initiated by Prime Minister Mohammad Mossadegh; and the Islamic revolution of 1979 in the name of global empowerment.

These central struggles against imperial interference constantly frolic with the 'Iranian psyche', as the musical piece chosen for this chapter also demonstrates. The right of civilian nuclear self-determination reached a comparable emotional status. Ultimately, it engendered a political momentum uniting Iranians against what was perceived to be yet another imperial intrusion into the country's sovereignty. Once the rights of Iran were acknowledged, diplomatic contacts with the Obama

---

[54] Jalal Al-e Ahmad, 'The outline of a disease', in Ridgeon, *Religion and Politics in Modern Iran*, p. 170.

administration became possible. The ability of the Rouhani administration to change the perception of some rather more sceptical elements
of the Iranian state shouldn't be underestimated here. This is why for
some Iranian commentators, the current foreign minister of Iran, Javad
Zarif, the chief architect of the negotiations with the Obama administration, could be compared to such illustrious figures of recent Iranian
history as Mirza Hossein Khan Sepahsalar (1828–1881), Mohammad-
Ali Foroughi (1877–1942), Ahmad Qavam (1876–1955) and the iconic
Mohammad Mossadeq (1882–1967).[55]

The Foreign Policy Culture of Iran Revisited

We began the analysis with the assertion that utopian-romantic
ideals constituted the preference setting and goal orientation of the
revolutionary Iranian state. What had emerged as a counter-hegemonic
political culture during the 1960s and 1970s, it was argued, was
codified as a revolutionary narrative and appeared as a transcendent,
de facto reality, reacting on its agents. The introjection of the utopia of
the just state, mantled in the romantic imagery of the millenarian Shia
struggle for emancipation, constituted the pool of shared knowledge
that determined the foreign policy culture of the Iranian state after the
Islamic revolution in 1979. Once this aestheticised political reality was
internalised cognitively and legitimated institutionally, the self-
identification of the Iranian state as a 'just power' guided the country
toward challenging the international status quo that was perceived as
inherently unjust and overbearingly hierarchical. This is the conceptual
core that this chapter worked out, so far.

For the sake of foreign policy analysis, it can be demonstrated that
the morphology of Iran's foreign policy culture may be attributed to a
four-dimensional cultural genealogy: (1) The elite-driven invention of
utopian-romantic ideas in the 1960s and 1970s engendered a total
redefinition of Iran's relationship with the world, based on a new,
anti-imperialist, Muslim-revolutionary identity for the Iranian state;
(2) through the process of mass internalisation of the revolutionary

---

[55] See further Mohammad Mehdi Raji (ed.), *Āqā-ye Safir: Goftogu bā
Mohammad-Javād Zarif, Safir-e Pishin-e Irān dar Sāzemān-e Mellal-e Mottahed*
[Mr Ambassador: A Dialogue with Mohammad Javād Zarif, the Former
Ambassador of Iran to the United Nations], Tehran: Nashr-e Ney, 1392 (2013),
pp. 368ff.

ideals and institutionalisation in the post-revolutionary period, the utopias generated a powerful dynamism of their own (they attained systemic qualities); (3) socialised in this omnipresent, ideological system, Iranian foreign policy elites were habituated to accept Iran's new role as legitimate and a reflection of the revolutionary ideals as formulated by Ayatollah Khomeini and others; (4) that process of institutionalisation and habituation constituted Iran's contemporary role identity par excellence – it introjected foreign policy elites with the idea that Iran's self-attributed moral high ground legitimates the country's special place in international affairs, which, by necessity, motivated (and motivates) them to challenge the prevailing status quo.

A radical deviation from this institutionalised consensus about the way the Iranian state pursues its national interests abroad would require an equally radical shift in the way the Iranian state is constituted. It is this understanding that explains why successive US governments have tried to pursue 'regime change' in Iran, as the next chapter shows. They know that the strategic preferences of the Islamic Republic are not subsumable to US designs. The state would need to be changed in order to make it rather more amenable to US national interests. This is the rationale behind 'regime change' strategies in Iran, Venezuela, Cuba and elsewhere.

We can take this analysis one step further now: Since the revolution of 1979, the foreign policy culture of Iran has oscillated around five strategic preferences which set the general contours of the country's international relations. The current strategy of the Rouhani administration repackages these preferences but does not radically depart from them. The Iranian state, like any other state in the international system, has its national interests that it pursues. It has been an analytical mistake to assume that these are merely tactical and short-term, that Iran after the revolution acts ad hoc. Undoubtedly, there have been serious shifts in the way Iran positions itself in international affairs, Rouhani is not Ahmadinejad (in the same way as Barack Obama is not Donald Trump).

But the strategic preferences of any state do not suddenly and completely change with a change of government. Strategic preferences are systemic, cultural, institutionalised. They have depth and longitude that go beyond the politics of the day. Rouhani is the surface effect of gradual changes in Iran's domestic politics after the revolution, a product of a post-revolutionary generation yearning for reforms, but he is still operating within the general contours of the strategic preferences of the Islamic Republic as they emerged after the revolution in 1979.

The first strategic preference that has guided the ruling classes in Iran is geared to the idea of maximising economic independence.[56] This preference was inscribed into the Iranian constitution by the Sorbonne-educated liberals surrounding Ayatollah Khomeini at the beginning of the revolution, in particular the first prime minister Mehdi Bazargan and the first president Abol-Hassan Bani Sadr, differences notwithstanding.[57] At the heart of it is the conviction – similar to Islamic economic theories authored by Ayatollah Motahhari in Iran and Ayatollah Baqir al-Sadr in Iraq – that a 'just' welfare state should be at the centre of the economic system. While Iran has attempted to liberalise the economy in recent years and while it has tried to accede to the World Trade Organization in the past, the country continues to keep a relative distance from radical neo-liberal reforms. The ruling classes continue to pursue a form of economic nationalism which manifests itself, among the policies mentioned above, also in the emphasis on mastering the full nuclear fuel cycle on Iranian territory as indicated. This emphasis on nuclear sovereignty has fuelled Iranian psycho-nationalism in recent years. With the self-perception of a great power in human history, Iranians deem it their natural right to take advantage of nuclear energy without impingement by the United States. Hence, Rouhani is trying to present Iran more vigorously in international economic forums. There is certainly a technocratic emphasis in his policies which are carried out by a cadre of economic experts that he dotted around key ministries. But it is highly unlikely that the Iranian state and its underbelly, in particular the powerful conglomerates affiliated to the Revolutionary Guards, will liberalise the economy to the degree that they lose their privileged position. There will not be a neo-liberal *infitah* policy comparable to what happened in Egypt under Sadat or Tunisia under Ben-Ali. The Iranian economy will continue to be mixed and the state will ensure that it does not concede too much ground to the private sector and even less so to foreign investors.

[56] See further Maaike Warnaar, *Iranian Foreign Policy during Ahmadinejad: Ideology and Actions*, London: Palgrave Macmillan, 2013.
[57] Mehdi Bazargan resigned amidst the US hostage crisis. Abol-Hassan Bani Sadr fled the country into exile in Paris where he still lives today.

Second, since the revolution, Iran has allocated immense ideological and material resources to the Palestinian issue, with mixed results both for the Palestinians and Iran's national interest. Yassir Arafat was the first major political leader to visit Iran after the establishment of the Islamic Republic in 1979. The revolutionaries greeted him with great fanfare and handed him the keys of the Israeli compound in Tehran, which had served as a major centre for Israeli operations during the reign of the shah. Moreover, in an effort to institutionalise the pro-Palestinian sentiments of his followers, Ayatollah Khomeini designated the last Friday of Ramadan to the liberation of Jerusalem (so-called *Quds* day). 'The road to Jerusalem goes through Baghdad' was a prominent slogan of the millions of volunteers of the newly established Islamic Revolution Guards Corps, the elite 'Quds corps' (*Sepah-e Quds*) created for foreign operations, and their Baseej militia during the devastating Iran–Iraq War which drained the material and human resources of both countries for decades to come, exactly because the war was charged with immense ideological venom.[58]

Palestine has been appropriated by the Iranian state not least in order to claim regional leadership and a central role as the defender of Muslim rights. For instance, religious leaders in the country consider holy sites such as the Al-Aqsa mosque as Islamic *waqf* whose sovereignty should be shared by all Muslims and not only by the Palestinians. There is also genuine support to the Palestinian cause within Iranian civil society. Several NGOs are involved in fundraising efforts, and several Iranian hospitals provided free medical help to Palestinians wounded in the successive intifadas in the occupied territories. Rouhani has not broken from these policies, as Ali Alavi shows in an important recent study.[59] Iran recurrently hosts a high-ranking delegation of Islamic Jihad, there are recurrent efforts to engage the PLO and the country continues to have close relations with Hamas despite the fallout over Syria. At the same time there are nuanced shifts:

[58] For an excellent discussion of this period with a particular emphasis on the spectre of 'charisma' in the IRGC see Maryam Alemzadeh, 'The Islamic Revolutionary Guards Corps in the Iran–Iraq War: an unconventional military's survival', *British Journal of Middle Eastern Studies*, Vol. 46, No. 4 (2019), pp. 622–639.

[59] Seyed Ali Alavi, *Iran and Palestine: Past, Present, Future*, London: Routledge, 2019.

Iranian officials, quite comparable to the period of the reformist President Mohammad Khatami (1997–2005), have refrained from using the term 'Zionist regime' to denote Israel and Rouhani has not targeted the country in the way his predecessor Ahmadinejad did. In another parallel to the Khatami years, the current foreign minister Zarif repeatedly indicated that the Iranian government would accept any final settlement that the Palestinians would agree to. Asked if Iran would recognise the state of Israel if the Palestinian question would be resolved, Zarif replied:

> You see, that's a sovereign decision that Iran would make but it will have no consequence on the situation on the ground in the Middle-East. If the Palestinians are happy with the solution then nobody, nobody outside Palestine could prevent that from taking place. The problem for the past 60 years is that the Palestinians have not been happy. The Palestinians have not been satisfied and they have every right not to be satisfied because their most basic rights continue to be violated and people are not ready to address those rights.[60]

Third, the revolution has buttressed a sense of grandeur in the historical consciousness of Iran which was equally apparent in the thinking of the shah.[61] But whereas the shah's dependence on the West did not allow him to act upon his imperial mentality, the revolution turned Iran into an antagonist to US (and Israeli) hegemony in West Asia and North Africa (WANA) and the wider international system, in a grand effort to position the country as a major actor in world politics. As such, Iran sees itself as a central competitor to US influence in WANA and beyond, which is exemplified by the country's stringent opposition to NATO forces and US military bases in the Persian Gulf, Central Asia and elsewhere in Iran's immediate geostrategic neighbourhood. But in this regard as well, Iran has initiated a gradual shift in its foreign policies. For Rouhani and his administration, competition with the United States does not preclude establishing full diplomatic ties between the two countries.

---

[60] 'Zionist media fabricate Iranian FM's remarks on Tehran's recognition of Israel', *Fars News Agency*, 5 February 2014, available at http://english.farsnews .com/newstext.aspx?nn=13921116001667, accessed 12 February 2014.

[61] See further the work of Roham Alvandi, *Nixon, Kissinger and the Shah: The United States and Iran in the Cold War*, Oxford: Oxford University Press, 2014.

In my conversations with Iranians close to the decision-making process, the model of China is repeatedly invoked. China and the United States have serious differences in eastern Asia, not least over the contentious issue of Taiwan. But the two countries have close economic ties and they have managed to liaise diplomatically as well. Many Iranian decision-makers agree that the future of Iranian–American ties could be similar. On issues of agreement, the territorial integrity of Iraq, opposition to the Taliban in Afghanistan and al-Qaeda groups throughout the Muslim world, Iran and the United States have a lot of reason to foster enduring diplomatic links. On issues of disagreement, Palestine/Israel, Syria and Hezbollah, the two countries are likely to tiptoe around each other and try to pursue their national interests without a zero-sum mentality that would antagonise the other side. Such a mitigated 'cold peace' could be a major factor in stabilising the region. I will expand on this topic in Chapter 4. Suffice it to say at this stage that this 'cold peace' was entirely possible when both Rouhani and President Obama campaigned on the basis that they would talk to the other side. The outcome was the Joint Comprehensive Plan of Action (JCPOA), which resolved the stand-off over Iran's nuclear energy programme until the agreement was breached by the Trump administration. The erratic approach to the region that has characterised Trump's foreign policy triggered an adverse reaction from Iran. As Rouhani explained in an opinion piece:

Over the past two years, US foreign policy has emerged as a new and complicated problem, as America creates new challenges on a variety of fronts in international relations. We see US complicity in the daily atrocities in Yemen and in the humiliation and gradual perishing of the great nation of Palestine, which has daily inflamed the emotions of one-and-a-half billion Muslims. We believe the American government has explicitly supported criminal groups like ISIS, who value no human principles, exacerbating the problems of our region ... In brief, the US administration's policies of unilateralism, racial discrimination, Islamophobia, and the undermining of important international treaties, including the Paris Climate Accord, are fundamentally incompatible with multilateralism and other socio-political norms valued by Europe ... The nuclear deal demonstrated that Iran is committed to reason and dialogue. We have initiated political consultations with Europe on key issues of mutual interest, especially on regional crises, with the aim of finding appropriate solutions ... Iran believes in multilateralism and is prepared to join other peace-loving nations in this path. Cooperation between Iran and Europe will secure the long-term interests of both parties, and ensure international peace and stability.[62]

Fourth, since the revolution of 1979 Iranian foreign policy elites have called for the empowerment of the 'third world'. To that end the Islamic Republic immediately ceased its membership of CENTO and became a strong advocate of the Non-Aligned-Movement. This policy has transmuted into a discourse accentuating the need for a multipolar world order that is not dominated by one superpower alone. Naturally, Iran perceives itself as one of the poles in such an international system, together with Brazil, India, China, Russia, the EU and the United States. The non-aligned policy encapsulated in slogans such as *na sharghi, na gharbi, jomhur-ye eslami* (neither eastern nor western, only the Islamic Republic) has manifested itself in Iran's close relations with like-minded governments in Latin America, in particular the 'Bolivarian' vanguard in Venezuela, Bolivia, Cuba, Ecuador and Nicaragua. Iran has fostered close political and economic relations with these countries in the past decades. The former president of Brazil, Lula, even took the audacious step, together with Turkey's Prime Minister Erdogan, of proposing a solution to the nuclear impasse during the Ahmadinejad presidency, which was rejected by the White House. While it is a priority of the Rouhani administration to manage ties with the United States, Rouhani has continued to deepen the existing relations of Iran with Latin America.[63] The support to President Maduro in the challenge to his rule in Venezuela throughout 2019 is the latest indicator of Iran's investment in South American affairs.

And finally, since the Islamic revolution of 1979 the discourse of Iran's ruling elites has focused on the ideal of Islamic communitarianism which the Iranian state pursues primarily through the Organisation of Islamic Cooperation (OIC) and the network of *bonyad*s (foundations) that operate in the country's clerical 'Vatican', Qom. While the symbols and imagery of the revolution were steeped in

---

[62] Hassan Rouhani, 'Europe should work with Iran to counter US unilateralism', *Financial Times*, 1 November 2018, available at www.ft.com/content/3ecaed5e-dcfc-11e8-b173-ebef6ab1374a, accessed 1 September 2019.

[63] 'Iran firm to boost ties with Latin America: President Rouhani', *IRIB World Service*, 10 February 2014. http://english.irib.ir/news/iran1/item/178359-iran-firm-to-boost-ties-with-latin-america-president-rouhani, accessed 12 February 2014.

Iranian psycho-nationalist traditions, Khomeini was adamant in portraying the revolution as pan-Islamic, indeed as a global revolt for justice, in order to extend the claim for leadership beyond the confines of the Shia minority within Islam. To that end, the revolutionaries instituted 'unity week', a culturally driven policy to institutionalise ecumenical unity between Sunni and Shia. At the same time, Iran has never really sacrificed the country's national interest to the pan-Islamic utopia. The ruling classes of the country have been very careful not to criticise Russia and China for their brutal policies against their Muslim minorities in Chechnya and Xinjiang province respectively, in order not to jeopardise the cordial relations of Iran with the two countries. Similarly, Iran tends to support Christian-Orthodox Armenia in its territorial dispute with Shia-majority Azerbaijan. There is no automatic pan-Islamic solidarity that the Iranian state can afford to pursue on every occasion. While closer cooperation between Muslim-majority countries is pursued through various institutions, the pan-Islamic ambitions of the revolution have been circumscribed by the the Iranian nation-state outfit which demands *raison d'état*, a state-centric rationality.

As indicated, these five strategic preferences of the Iranian state continue to be salient during the Rouhani presidency and they will remain central to Iranian foreign policies after him. The bargaining position of the Iranian president has been particularly strong because he has repeatedly received the backing of the Supreme Leader Ayatollah Ali Khamenei who made it unmistakably clear that the president has a green light to pursue his policies of constructive engagement. Of course, his re-election in 2017, which was foreseeable, strengthened the hand of President Rouhani even further. Hence, and in many ways for the first time in Iran's post-revolutionary history, the two most powerful institutions of the Iranian state emphasised détente and diplomacy in international affairs as a means to maximise the national interest of Iran, even if the Islamic Republic continues to extend its strategic depth from Afghanistan, Yemen and Iraq to Lebanon and Syria.

This emphasis on smart, diplomatic power is exemplified in the cultural imagery of the Islamic Republic. In the current discourse, and discernible from one of the central policy speeches of the Supreme Leader Khamenei accentuating 'heroic flexibility' in Iran's dealings with international adversaries, the Islamic Republic accentuates the pragmatism of Imam Hassan, the grandson of the prophet Muhammad and the third imam of the Shia. Addressing senior veterans of the Revolutionary Guards, Khamenei maintained that a 'technical wrestler also shows flexibility for technical reasons sometimes, but he would never forget who his rival is and what his main goal is'.[64] Hence, whereas the revolutionaries of yesterday emphasised the romantic 'heroism' and sacrifice of Hassan's younger brother, Hussein, who together with his family was killed by the armies of Yazid in the seventh century CE, today the ruling classes in Iran repeatedly refer to his older brother Imam Hassan who is known for his pragmatism, level-headedness and accommodating strategies. Hence, whereas the Hussein paradigm emphasises revolutionary change à la Che Guevara manifesting itself in Hussein's self-sacrifice during the battle of Karbala, the 'Hassan paradigm' symbolises pragmatism, exemplified in the peace treaty that Hassan signed with Muawiya when he voluntarily handed over to him the leadership of the *umma* in the seventh century CE. The song of Assar that I have used to frame this chapter speaks exactly to this distinctly post-revolutionary context of contemporary Iran.

Moreover, there are also concrete institutional changes in the foreign policy decision-making process of the Islamic Republic in recent years: for instance the nuclear dossier has been firmly in the hands of the foreign ministry, with no tangible interference by the conservative National Security Council. The foreign ministry itself was staffed with the best and the brightest of Iran's post-revolutionary diplomatic cadres. And in another sign of the consensual policies between Rouhani and the Supreme Leader, Ayatollah Ali Khamenei has repeatedly signalled to the Revolutionary Guards that they should not interfere in matters of diplomacy.

Yet, the lack of attention to the demands of Iranians within the country and outside continues to be one of the major shortcomings of successive Iranian governments, and the Rouhani administration is complicit in this failure. National security, after all, is always also dependent upon civil society and its capability to defend itself against security threats. A potent Iranian society, where human security is safeguarded by the state, is the most reliable source of independence, as the revolutionaries knew in 1979 when they likened the Islamic Republic to *esteghlal* (independence) and *azadi* (freedom) in their

---

[64] 'Supreme Leader underlines belief in insightful "heroic flexibility"', 17 September 2014, *Iranian Diplomacy*, www.irdiplomacy.ir/en/page/1921549/Supreme+Leader +Underlines+Belief+in+Insightful+quot%3BHeroic+Flexibilityquot%3B.html, accessed 12 February 2014.

famous chant *esteghlal, azadi, jomhur-ye eslami* (independence, freedom, Islamic Republic). No contemporary Iranian government has understood these connections between human security and national security. Hence the ongoing clashes with the society that the Iranian state has been mandated to represent.

Here, it is analytically central to reiterate that President Rouhani (and all the presidents before him for that matter) are products and not drivers of those changes which are determined by the preference settings of Iranian society. I have theorised this in Chapter 2 as a 'pluralistic momentum', that continuously impinges on the realm of the state through a bottom-up process, from Iranian society to the ruling classes. The central characteristic of this bottom-up process in Iran is that the foreign policy culture as well is modified in accordance with the preference setting of Iranian civil society.

These are the analytical reasons, then, why Iran has changed, in particular with regard to the country's international affairs and attitudes towards reconciliation with the United States. But these nuanced changes are tempered by the enduring strategic preferences of the state, which will continue to guide the international affairs of the Islamic Republic. These preferences of the Iranian state do not preclude closer relations with the United States and even a tacit accommodation of the issue of Israel. But they make it impossible that Iran emerges as a subservient pawn. Ultimately, for the world, the Iran of the future will not be the Iran of the shah. Every Iranian president after the revolution of 1979 has been voted into office to deliver Iran's national interest and to move the state towards more democracy and accountability. In my previous research, I have shown that these preference settings of Iranian civil society have been boosted by the Arab revolts which have demonstrated that the new yardstick of politics in the region is not ideology anymore, but democracy, respect for human rights and social equality. President Rouhani is merely the latest manifestation of these demands of contemporary Iranian society and its diaspora, whose demands for reforms have been repeatedly frustrated. Ultimately, then, Assar's 'homeland' is scattered along the cosmopolitan plane that carries the meaning of Iran beyond its national locus.

4 | *The United States, Israel and the Global Right Wing*

Musical Piece:

'YE MOSHT SARBAZ'
(A Bunch of Soldiers)
By: Soroush Lashkary aka HICHKAS (No one) (1984–)
Release Date: 2008

Adaptive, free translation of lyrics

No one is alone
We are a bunch of soldiers
A bunch of soldiers
Who put our lives on the line
The Angel of Death [Gabriel] is down with us

I want you to throw your hands up high, Higher!
Throw 0,2,1 up forever!
I am with a bunch of 'cool' soldiers
And each of them has their (own) story

Like 'Tripee Maa' I begin this verse in the name of God
God is with us because
We are ever thankful to him
In good times, yet also when we feel like cursing the world
We are a bunch of soldiers, with our lives on the line
The Angel of Death [Gabriel] is down with us
We help each other even though we are all in poverty
Take a taste of my Raps, they are bitter aren't they?
We have taken it to the limit and reached the point
We have monopolised everyone into listening to our Rap instead of the
'other side'
We are prepared to give our precious lives for 4 things
God, Homeland, our family and our friends

We have stayed in the streets for 4 reasons
First, because we have no other choice or place to go, the next reason is a
sense of honour-bound duty
The next reason is not appropriate to be mentioned here
The 4th reason is a bit romantic
The leaves of autumn

I want you to throw your hands up high, Higher!
Throw 0,2,1 up forever!
I am with a bunch of 'cool' soldiers
And each of them has their (own) story
I want you to throw your hands up high, Higher!
Throw 0,2,1 up forever!
I am with a bunch of 'cool' soldiers
And each of them has their (own) story

I don't feel the peace of mind I feel here anywhere else
All the young ones are learning from us
Learning that a true soldier doesn't just think of himself
They think of the future and tomorrow
We are a bunch of soldiers
With Masters degrees from the biggest university in Iran
I mean the streets, not formal education
I chose the pavement over the school chair
Remember to try and be different to us in this respect
We also made mistakes, however in any situation we find ourselves in we
build and make progress
Many tears and a lot of blood will be shed on our journey
But in the face of hopelessness and loss of faith
We are the trees that will not be swayed
We stand firm
We do not even fear to be axed
Not even a bit
Let them know that we are prepared for war if they force us

I want you to throw your hands up high, Higher!
Throw 0,2,1 up forever!
I am with a bunch of 'cool' soldiers
And each of them has their (own) story
I want you to throw your hands up high, Higher!
Throw 0,2,1 up forever!
I am with a bunch of 'cool' soldiers
And each of them has their (own) story

The flag is at full mast, never doubt that, never doubt that
Don't even worry my friend, no reason to fear
We are bunch of soldiers, there used to be more of us
Take my words seriously, I am not one to joke around
Many of our friends are no longer with us
This new year our thoughts will be with you
I want the martyrs to know that if we are keeping it real
It is due to their blood which was spilt on the grounds for us
All the people keeping it real, know that our flag is flying high
If you are a real man then we are with you too
I pray for the world to be secure and peaceful
Amen
We have felt (endured) enough fire
I hope the day (when) we are all safe and secure comes soon
So that we all may be happy together

Don't stand still because I want you to throw your hands up high,
Higher!
Throw 0,2,1 up forever!
I am with a bunch of 'cool' soldiers
And each of them has their (own) story
I want you to throw your hands up high, Higher!
Throw 0,2,1 up forever!
I am with a bunch of 'cool' soldiers
And each of them has their (own) story

I want you to throw your hands up high, Higher!
Throw 0,2,1 up forever!
I am with a bunch of 'cool' soldiers
And each of them has their (own) story
The flag is up, The flag is up, The flag is up

Iran Demonised

One serious ambition of critical Iranian studies has been to correct the false image that Iran is eternally in the grip of enigmatic, irrational revolutionaries led by intransigent, retrograde mullahs. This effort has been partially successful: in the past decade I have had the pleasure of supervising over two dozen PhDs and hundreds of masters dissertations at SOAS, University of London, and several other universities around the world. In this way, this team has managed to create a global knowledge network that tries to contribute to a better

understanding of the country and the region in conversation with all
strata of society, including the political class.

Of course, one wishes that in Iran itself there would be more space
for dissent in order to allow for a freer academic culture. As I have
repeatedly said in interviews for the *Tehran Times*, whose editorial
board has been successful in preventing censorship of my sugges-
tions, part of the problem is the Iranian state itself, with its self-
defeating psycho-nationalism and lack of self-reflection about the
revolution and its casualties. But this is an internal dialogue between
Iranians that history will deliver sooner or later. I am in no doubt
about that.

In order for this national dialogue to come to peaceful fruition, sober
scholarship which is devoid of ideological allegiances to any of the
toxic items on this historical menu is needed.[1] It is well and good to let
me express some of my criticisms from outside of the country. But
dissent in Iran itself continues to come at too heavy a price for many
activists and colleagues in academia. This betrayal of the liberation
theology underlying the revolution of 1979 itself, continues to be a
morally and politically unacceptable reality for many of us in the
global scholarly community. As I mentioned in an interview with the
Tehran Times which was republished in Persian by Mehr News
Agency: 'The people of the region yearn for democracy, human rights,
and social equality.'[2] Critical Iranian studies appreciates the adverse
context that exists in Iran for scholarship about the country and it
addresses its impact on a truer understanding of this particular
subject matter.

Moreover, it is a familiar story for everyone focusing on Iran from a
scholarly perspective that we are 'orphaned'. The Islamic Republic and
its diplomatic missions are largely dysfunctional when it comes to a
cultural diplomacy that would embrace the scholarly community.

---

[1] The interviews were primarily conducted by Javad Heirania and Payman
Yazdani. They are archived here: www.tehrantimes.com/tag/Arshin+Adib-
Moghaddam, accessed 12 August 2019. At the time of writing there were
thirty-one interviews listed. For interviews in Persian see www.mehrnews.com/
tag/مقدم+ادیب+آرشین.

[2] 'People of region yearn for democracy, human rights, social equality', *Mehr News
Agency*, 12 April 2019, available at https://en.mehrnews.com/news/143871/
People-of-region-yearn-for-democracy-human-rights-social-equality, accessed
3 June 2019.

A cultural attaché in a typical Iranian embassy doesn't do what his Chinese, Peruvian or Qatari counterpart does: reach out to academics, organise conferences, attract student exchanges etc. Scholars focusing on Iran made their career against all odds. Critical Iranian studies has also been about pooling our resources in the absence of this kind of platform, that is fairly normal for any other scholarly community. Iranian studies is hard hit because we are left alone to fend for ourselves. This situation has had real consequences for young scholars coming through, and has seriously contributed to the proliferation of 'fake news' about Iran, that the Islamic Republic itself purports to challenge.

Many scholars of Iran from the country itself fought discrimination and social prejudice when they were forced out of their homeland. This first generation of Iranian scholars made their career equipped only with the truth and their scholarly integrity. They didn't 'sell out' to make it. Despite the immensely debilitating odds, they carried the torch of knowledge into the darkness of the Orientalist catacombs that had kept the truth out for decades. When one of the contemporary doyens of Iranian studies self-reflects, in another book in the Cambridge Global Middle East series, that he is a 'traveller' who had to make a home in the United States, opting for the psychology of a nomad who is in-between cultures, and uses this position to zoom into the connective tissue and sinews that hold the world together at the rhizome of our intertwined history, he is defining this new breed of intellectuals who stand for a common humanity.[3] But this position came with a lot of struggle, and to maintain it without any of the structural support that 'organic intellectuals' and most of our 'privileged' colleagues take for granted proves to be even more arduous.

The other problem that emerges is the depiction of Iran from the perspective of the global right wing including many supporters of the Trump administration in the United States. The Islamic Republic has occupied a prominent place in the imagination of these influential figures. The less raucous and more presentable face of this loose network has recurrently had direct links to the decision-making process in the United States and immense resources to influence the public discourse in the country. These days they are competing with other

---

[3] Hamid Dabashi, *Reversing the Colonial Gaze: Persian Travellers Abroad*, Cambridge: Cambridge University Press, 2020, pp. 8–9.

image entrepreneurs in an increasingly diversified global media land-scape. However, given the devastating military capability of the US state, which can annihilate the rest of the planet, this ability to create false images of foreign countries needs particular attention. Together with their allies in the Likud party in Israel (some of whom are now members of Kadima) and, to a lesser extent, right-wing agitators in Europe, that nefarious coterie has manufactured an image of Iran through which they try to make the country's 'aggressive nature' an established fact amongst influential strata of international society.

The missing link in that cause–effect relationship is the role of a specific context (in our case right-wing politics) in the production of reality (in our case the image of Iran as an 'international aggressor' governed by irrational religious zealots). It would be a mistake to underestimate that dialectic, especially with regard to Iran's nuclear file and the confrontations that President Trump initiated over the JCPOA. For this ideological representation of Iran is governed by a strategy to expel from competing realities the notion of a country that attempts to exercise its right to national development, and suppress the view that Iranians are as rational as the Japanese, Germans or other 'normal' nations who have developed a peaceful nuclear energy programme. The point being that the right wing does not want a factual analysis of the Iranian nuclear dossier, but one that turns it into a legitimation for war. After all, the first baby steps towards an Iranian nuclear energy infrastructure were taken by the shah before the revolution, and they were aided and abetted by successive US governments.

In this chapter, I am not so much interested in quantifying the proliferation of anti-Iranian discourses in right-wing circles. It is rather more central to account for the way Iran is spoken about, to analyse who does the speaking, to explore the institutions which codify people to speak about the country, and to understand the political culture that signifies and legitimates the things that are said. This is the 'false consciousness' apparatus that needs to be recorded in history to be studied by future generations. What is at issue in this chapter, in short, is the overall discursive representation of Iran by right-wing ideology, the way in which Iran is misrepresented to us by a cumbersome, largely uneducated coterie of activists and decision-makers with an overtly hegemonic agenda that has repeatedly tried to bully foreign countries into complete submission.

For this chapter, I have chosen the musical piece 'A Bunch of Soldiers' (*Ye Mosht Sarbaz*) by the Iranian rap artist Hichkas (No one), for two reasons:[4] First, the lyrics of the song indicate a continuity of theo-nationalist tropes in contemporary popular music in Iran. In his unmistakable hip-hop style, in vogue among the post-revolutionary urban middle class in the country's bustling metropoles – in particular the capital Tehran – Hichkas alludes to the nation, God and the martyrs 'whose memory is always alive. God, the nation, family and friends,' the rap song continues, 'We help each other … We are a bunch of soldiers with masters degrees from the biggest university in Iran. I mean the streets not formal education. I chose the pavement over the school chair.' The rebellious tenor that is so characteristic of this genre of music is apparent here. Hichkas raps in the good old tradition of urban hip-hoppers who used their art to rebel against social injustice and/or other forms of discrimination. Most recently Hichkas sampled a rap song in memory of the victims of the crack-down on the protests in November 2019 entitled '*Dastasho mosht kardeh*' decrying the corruption in Iran and the lack of accountability and attention by the authorities: 'They don't want citizens,' say the lyrics of this song released in December 2019, 'they want slaves.'

Apart from those socio-economic themes, the lyrics of Hichkas are intertwined with mixed samples from the ancient classical music trad-ition in Persia, quite comparable to the jazz snippets used by US hip-hop artists such as Public Enemy in order to speak to different musical genres and listeners. This brings me to the second reason why I chose 'A Bunch of Soldiers' as a part of my loosely defined discursive musicology: With an eye on the overarching goal of all my work so far, that is to present points of communication and peaceful interaction between peoples from different parts of the world, I chose this rap song to demonstrate the circularity of art and ideas on the global canvas of human activity. Hip-hop and rap music developed as a musical genre out of the political and social grievances of inner-city African Americans in the 1970s. In terms of style, this sampled music accom-panied by rhythmic and rhyming chanting called rap, became the language of protest for generations of disadvantaged African Americans in the United States. Hichkas and other rappers in Iran have a similar background and ambition. From this perspective, we

---

[4] Hich-Kas, 'Ye Mosht Sarbaz', 2008.

can draw a clear line from the beautifully emancipative rap music of the New York–based (Long Island) group Public Enemy to the Tehran-centric musings of Hichkas. Both are urban, both are dotted with themes of emancipation and socio-economic grievances about inequality and political marginalisation and both are radical in their own way as they target the injustices of the state. For Public Enemy, of course, the issue of race was paramount, whereas Hichkas takes the economic inequalities of post-revolutionary Iran as his primary subject.

As I have argued in more depth elsewhere:[5] certainly since the Iranian revolution in 1979 there have been immense efforts on both sides to convince us that Iran and the United States are essentially different entities, that there is an inherent epistemological difference between these two national constructs. The anti-Americanism permeating the revolution was a post-colonial reaction to the history of imperial interference in Iranian affairs – that much has been established. But upon closer inspection the hyphen in 'Iranian-American' reveals itself as a conjunction, a grammatical particle, a *via media* that indicates that in the word formation 'Iranian-American' nothing is detachable, autonomous, at liberty. We are confronted with a particular form of disjunctive synthesis which binds Iran and the United States together in a mesmerising paradox.

The purpose of this chapter is to demonstrate why it is that Iran and the United States repeatedly have had antagonistic interstate relations. But the wider ambition of this analysis is to show that it is not in the interest of both countries to listen to the preachers of hate, but to build upon a common narrative much in the same way as happened in the build-up to the JCPOA. The circularity of the hip-hop tradition from the United States to Iran and back again via the Iranian-American community is a good example to hold up against the irrationality of narratives of hate perpetuated by the global right wing. The following paragraphs will disassemble these political constellations in order to suggest alternative, rather more rational and loving, forms of interaction.

War Engineering

No manufacturing of consent, no engineering of facts, no ideological effort to produce 'reality', no campaign to transform a specific political consciousness can function if, through a pattern of institutions, functionaries, media outlets or social media 'bots', it does not constitute an

---

[5] Adib-Moghaddam, *On the Arab Revolts and the Iranian Revolution.*

overall strategy. And, inversely, no such strategy can achieve lasting effects if it is not based on a consensus serving, not as a headquarter, conspiracy or predetermined, static outcome, but as the smallest common denominator among its adherents. With regard to Iran, that consensus is constituted by influential, idea-producing conglomerates established by right-wing functionaries and activists with close links to influential lobbying organisations and like-minded parties in Israel and, to a lesser extent – in recent years – in Saudi Arabia and the United Arab Emirates (UAE) too. These all adhere to a common interest: to subvert the Iranian state and, by extension, to recode Iranian behaviour in accordance with right-wing interests in West Asia and beyond, which always also implies being mute about the rights of Palestinians, as the research of two of my former PhD students demonstrates.[6]

It is no secret that there are strong ideological and institutional links between the right-wing coterie surrounding the White House and various parties in Israel. 'No lobby has managed to divert US foreign policy as far from what the American national interest would other-wise suggest,' wrote Mearsheimer and Walt audaciously in a seminal book on the subject, 'while simultaneously convincing Americans that US and Israeli interests are essentially the same.'[7] More recently, Ilhan Omar, the first naturalised citizen from Africa to enter the US Congress, came under attack when she criticised the influence of The American Israel Public Affairs Committee (AIPAC), probably the most influential lobbying group in the United States.[8] Criticising most, if not all, Israel-related policies almost immediately provokes a systematic response organised by an institutionalised movement that is profes-sionally networked. It is such political constellations that prevent the truth from entering mainstream public discourse, especially in a strictly chaperoned political culture that is so central to the way the United

---

[6] Alavi, *Iran and Palestine*; Jonathan Gerwin Leslie, 'Fear and Insecurity: Competing Narratives of the Iran–Israel Relationship', PhD dissertation, SOAS, University of London, 2019.

[7] The authors accurately observe that the lobby includes prominent Christian evangelicals and non-Jewish neo-conservatives such as former CIA director Woolsey and former education secretary William Bennett. See further John Mearsheimer and Stephen Walt, 'The Israel lobby', *London Review of Books*, Vol. 28, No. 6, 23 March 2006, available at www.lrb.co.uk/v28/n06/mear01_.html, accessed 23 May 2006.

[8] 'Ilhan Omar's victory for political sanity', *New Republic*, 7 March 2019, available at https://newrepublic.com/article/153229/ilhan-omars-victory-political-sanity, accessed 18 June 2019.

States is governed today. Any presidency, including the Biden administration of course, works within the context of this political culture,
which continuously produces destructive sentiments of war, aggression
and/or sanctions.

Let me put forward a general definition here. Right-wing thinking in
all its manifestations – certainly also in its anti-Semitic or Islamophobic
variant – does not refuse aggression. On the contrary, it habituates us
to accept war as rational, it puts into operation an entire machinery for
producing false images in order to legitimate militaristic policies. Not
only does the right wing speak of aggression and urge everyone to do
so; they also present an 'aestheticised' version of war. Via right-wing
strategy, justice, patriotism, morality, even love, find an opportunity to
deploy themselves in the discourse of war.

Here, serious scholars have connected slogans such as 'Make
America great again' and 'America First', which are central to the
language of Donald Trump, to the terms and idioms used by Nazi
sympathisers in the United States before the start of the Second World
War. 'It is small comfort that in foreign policy Trump does not emulate
the Hitlerian goals of wars of conquest and genocide, because the
prospects for peace and stability are nevertheless seriously threatened,'
the Holocaust historian Christopher Browning wrote in the *New York
Review of Books*. 'Escalating trade wars could easily tip the world
economy into decline, and the Trump administration has set thresholds
for peaceful settlements with Iran and North Korea that seem well
beyond reach.'[9] Browning is not even known for particularly progressive opinions, yet he rightly indicates that the Trump administration
espoused a political language that promotes war, in particular with
Iran, which has repeatedly served as a convenient 'villain' in the politics
of demonisation that is so predominant in the contemporary United
States. As Trump declared in his speech of May 2018, that announced
the withdrawal of the United States from the JCPOA:

As we exit the Iran deal, we will be working with our allies to find a real,
comprehensive, and lasting solution to the Iranian nuclear threat. This will
include efforts to eliminate the threat of Iran's ballistic missile program; to
stop its terrorist activities worldwide; and to block its menacing activity

[9] Christopher R. Browning, 'The suffocation of democracy', *New York Review of
Books*, 25 October 2018, available at www.nybooks.com/articles/2018/10/25/
suffocation-of-democracy/, accessed 1 September 2019.

across the Middle East. In the meantime, powerful sanctions will go into full effect. If the regime continues its nuclear aspirations, it will have bigger problems than it has ever had before.[10]

This was the reincarnation of the 'axis of evil' analogy that was used by George W. Bush in 2002 to refer to Iran (together with Iraq and North Korea) as the enemies of the United States. Iran has repeatedly functioned as a convenient target for this type of right-wing rhetoric, whether in its neo-conservative variant dominant in the George W. Bush administration, or in the language of the presidency of Donald Trump.[11] The latter's erstwhile national security advisor, John Bolton, may have tried to differentiate himself from neo-conservatives and liberal internationalists because of their '"theological" attachment to principles – the principle that treaties and alliances are good (in the case of internationalist liberals) or that democracy must be spread at the expense of all else (in the case of neoconservatives)'.[12] But the reality is, of course, that neo-conservatism shared an equally pronounced distaste for multilateral organisations, a similar belief in the supremacy of 'America' (based on a rather racialised 'white' designation of what it means to be 'American') and a disdain for independent countries such as Iran, Cuba or Venezuela. For John Bolton the 'greatest hope for freedom for mankind in history is the United States, and therefore protecting American national interest is the single best strategy for the world'.[13] This is quintessentially the imperial project that neo-conservatives subscribed to, as one former US army captain rightly indicated with reference to the Iran-war agenda that John Bolton has pursued for over a decade now, even as the US ambassador to the United Nations in the administration of George W. Bush.[14]

[10] 'Remarks by President Trump on the Joint Comprehensive Plan of Action', 8 May 2018, available at www.whitehouse.gov/briefings-statements/remarks-president-trump-joint-comprehensive-plan-action/, accessed 6 March 2019.

[11] I covered the Bush presidency here: Arshin Adib-Moghaddam, 'Manufacturing war: Iran in the neo-conservative imagination', *Third World Quarterly*, Vol. 28, No. 3 (2007), pp. 635–653.

[12] 'John Bolton: Trump's shrewd national security advisor', *The Atlantic*, 8 March 2019, available at www.theatlantic.com/magazine/archive/2019/04/john-bolton-trump-national-security-adviser/583246/, accessed 9 August 2019.

[13] Ibid.

[14] See Michael Morford, 'John Bolton is trying to steer Trump and the US into another Mideast war. Don't let him', *USA Today*, 7 March 2019, available at

Therefore, this illiberal moment for democracy in the United States could only deliver someone like Donald Trump, exactly because right-wing ideology has been professionally institutionalised as a dominant part of the country's political culture for decades now, as the research of David Ryan at University College Cork in Ireland beautifully captures.[15] In *US Foreign Policy and the Other*, he and Michael Patrick Cullinane present several essays that explore how the very idea of 'America' has been invented and sustained through the creation of 'monsters' and the counter-identities imagined by US strategists in order to tell US citizens and the world fairy tales about those foreign enemies.[16] My distinguished colleague at SOAS, Stephen Chan, echoes such scholarship, when he argues that US foreign policies are premised on paranoia, a manufactured fear of 'evil'.[17] Iran has been a major object in this self-realisation of successive US governments. Hence, the Trump administration easily lodged into what neo-conservatives left behind after the presidency of George W. Bush, moving US politics further to the right. Demonising Iran is merely one of many continuities in this salient policy tradition.

We can take the process of manufacturing war one step further now: through institutionalisation, an ideology is transmuted into another sphere of synthesis, a coherent policy. In other words, by creating more and more interlinked foundations, think tanks and lobbying organisations, goals, causes, norms and ideas are brought together in artificial unity as a whole and complete political action. It is this synthesis that has repeatedly brought right-wing ideology close to the foreign policy process in the United States. Even when there are relatively cordial interludes, such as the presidency of Barack Obama, the institutional underbelly of the global right-wing movement routinely surfaces, and the foreign policies of the Trump administration were merely a very recent example for this recurrent trend.

eu.usatoday.com/story/opinion/2019/03/07/john-bolton-neoconservatives-steer-trump-america-war-iran-column/3061161002/, accessed 10 June 2019.

[15] See among other works David Ryan, *Frustrated Empire: US Foreign Policy from 9/11 to Iraq*, London: Pluto, 2007; and Michael Patrick Cullinane and David Ryan (eds.), *US Foreign Policy and the Other*, London: Berghahn Books, 2014.

[16] Ibid.

[17] Stephen Chan, *Out of Evil: New International Politics and Old Doctrines of War*, London: I.B. Tauris, 2004.

Influence on the levers of power in Washington is not only secured through lobbying efforts. There is also persuasive evidence for covert activity. In August 2004 it was revealed that classified documents including a draft National Security Presidential Directive devised in the office of then undersecretary of defence for policy, Douglas Feith, was shared with AIPAC and Israeli officials. The document set a rather more aggressive US policy toward Iran and was leaked by Lawrence Franklin, an 'expert' on Iran who was recruited to Feith's office from the Defense Intelligence Agency.[18] An FBI counterintelligence operation revealed that the same Franklin met repeatedly with Naor Gilon, the head of the political department at the Israeli embassy in Washington, and other officials and activists tied to the Israeli state and pro-Israeli lobbying organisations. Franklin was sentenced to twelve years and seven months in jail in January 2006 for disclosing classified information to Steven Rosen and Keith Weissman. Both were members of AIPAC.[19]

Feith, whose office invented the idea that Saddam Hussein had ties to al-Qaeda, which in turn was used to legitimate the invasion of Iraq in 2003, has long-standing loyalties to the Israeli right wing. His collusions became clear when the chairman of the Senate Armed Services Committee, Carl Levin, released the declassified 'Pentagon Inspector General Report on Intelligence Assessment Activities of the Office of Under Secretary of Defense Doug Feith' in April 2007. It was stated that Feith concluded incorrectly that 'intelligence indicates cooperation [between the regime of Saddam Hussein and al-Qaeda] in all categories' and that he asserted wrongly that an alleged meeting in April 2001 in Prague between an Iraqi intelligence officer and lead 9/11 hijacker Mohammed Atta was a 'known' contact.[20] Feith is also

---

[18] Brian Bennett, Elaine Shannon and Adam Zagorin, 'A web of intrigue: inside the Israel espionage investigation', *Time*, 5 September 2004.

[19] 'Pentagon man jailed over spying', *BBC*, 20 January 2006. The district court found Franklin guilty of count 1 'Conspiracy to communicate national defense information to persons not entitled to receive it', 18 U.S.C. §§ 793 (d), (e) and (g) counts 2–4 'Communication of national defense information to persons not entitled to receive it', 18 USC § 793 (d), and count 5 'Conspiracy to communicate classified information to agent of foreign government' 50 U.S.C. § 783, 18 U.S.C. § 371. Rosen was found guilty on counts 1–3 and Weissman on count 1. The full indictment is available at http://fl1.findlaw.com/news.findlaw .com/nytimes/docs/dod/usfrnklin80205ind.pdf, accessed 12 February 2007.

[20] The full declassified report is available at www.fas.org/irp/agency/dod/ ig020907-decl.pdf, accessed 14 April 2007.

co-founder of 'One Jerusalem', a Jerusalem-based organisation whose ultimate goal is securing 'a united Jerusalem as the undivided capital of Israel'.[21] In 2009, he became one of several Bush administration officials under consideration for investigation of possible war crimes in a Spanish court, headed by Baltasar Garzón under claims of universal jurisdiction.

A second co-founder of 'One Jerusalem' is David Steinmann who is chairman of JINSA (Jewish Institute for National Security of America). He is also a board member of the Center for Security Policy (CSP) and chairman of the executive committee of the Middle East Forum which publishes biased analysis about the region. Two other co-founders of One Jerusalem are directly tied to the Likud party: Dore Gold was a top advisor to former prime minister Ariel Sharon, and Natan Sharansky was Israel's minister of diaspora affairs from March 2003 until May 2005 (he resigned from the cabinet in April 2005 to protest plans to withdraw Israeli settlers from the Gaza Strip).

Currently, the Trump administration's Iran policy is being flanked by David Wurmser, yet another member of the neo-conservative guard that delivered the Iraq War of 2003. Wurmser was formerly at the American Enterprise Institute (AEI) and former special assistant to John Bolton at the State Department. He was a strong advocate against the 'land-for-peace' formula in the Israeli–Palestinian negotiations. In May and June 2019, Wurmser wrote several memos to then national security advisor John Bolton. In the documents, Wurmser argued that sudden disruptive actions – such as the killing of General Soleimani which eventually happened in January 2020 – would, in Wurmser's words, 'rattle the delicate internal balance of forces and the control over them upon which the [Iranian] regime depends for stability and survival'.[22]

The flamboyant annual meetings of yet another institution tied into this right-wing coterie, that is the Zionist Organisation of America (ZOA), have been repeatedly used as a platform to agitate against Iran. At their gala in 2018, the aforementioned Bolton justified the renewed sanctions against Iran and the withdrawal of the Trump administration from the JCPOA. At the same meeting, Alan

---

[21] See https://onej.org/, accessed 12 August 2012. The organisation is chaired by the aforementioned Natan Sharansky.

[22] 'Trump's latest plan for Iran: regime disruption', *Bloomberg*, 14 January 2020.

Dershowitz, who acts as the legal representative of President Donald Trump, spoke about how he talked to Qatari leaders about adopting rather more pro-Israeli policies (presumably without success).[23] Dershowitz is the author of the book *The Case against the Iran Deal* which was published in 2015, when the Obama administration adopted the JCPOA and fostered a diplomatic dialogue with the Islamic Republic. Dershowitz's book acted as a blueprint for the Trump administration's subsequent withdrawal from the deal. Like Bolton, Dershowitz has a long-standing anti-Iranian track record based on myths that serve the interests of the right wing in Israel. In 2004, for instance, he argued that '[b]y deliberately placing nuclear facilities in the midst of civilian population centres, the Iranian government has made the decision to expose its civilians to attacks ... [I]f all else fails,' he demanded, 'Israel, or the United States, must be allowed under international law to take out the Iranian nuclear threat before it is capable of the genocide for which it is being built.'[24] Dershowitz, therefore, serves as a tragic example of the effort to launch 'legal' wars.

Jewish Iran

We have already gathered several recurring themes in this anti-Iranian discourse. Quite comparably to the way Iraq was portrayed before the US invasion of 2003, likening Iran with absolute evil, in contemporary world politics always epitomised by Nazi Germany, is a central pillar of the right-wing campaign to demonise the country. For instance, the French philosopher Bernard-Henri Lévy, whose ideas must be considered among the most uneducated in modern continental philosophy and whose political attitudes are vile and full of anti-humanistic anger, made the following point in one of his books. The extraordinarily illiterate section deserves to be quoted in full:

On 21 March 1935, Persia decided to change its name to Iran under orders from Germany. Why? Why? Because Iran, in Persian, in Farsi, means 'the

[23] 'Bolton declares: "Iran will never get nukes" at star studded ZOA gala in NYC', *Jewish Voice*, 11 July 2018, available at http://thejewishvoice.com/2018/11/07/bolton-declares-iran-will-never-get-nukes-at-star-studded-zoa-gala-dinner-in-nyc/, accessed 10 July 2019.

[24] Alan Dershowitz, 'Amend international law to allow preemptive strike on Iran', *Forward*, 20 August 2004.

land of the Aryans'. And, as it was on the rise at the time, **Nazi Germany offered the Persians the 'deal of the century'.** **Nazi Germany told the Persians: 'We'll make you the Aryans from the East, we'll be the Aryans from the West, we'll have a great adventure together, we'll dominate the world.' And the Iranians accepted the deal, and we have this incredible 'semantic coup'!** Because Persia is not nothing. Persia is poetry, it is porcelain, it is extraordinary art, it is so many things, it is an immense civilization, it is Achaemenid civilization, it is a glorious past, and Persia decides that day to draw a line under that past to align itself with Nazi Germany ... It's when the Islamic revolution happens that it gets really interesting. Back then, the issue was raised once more. People said, alright, now in 1979 let's go back to Persia, go back to our greatness as an extraordinary civilization! And yet for several new reasons, **philosophical reasons** tied to the presence in the entourage of the ayatollahs of young philosophers, admirers of the Nazi philosopher Heiddeger, **who thought it perfect to be both islamist and Aryan,** thought it wonderful to forge an islamic Aryanism, or an Aryan islamism. Thus, the islamic revolution created the 'Islamic Republic of Iran'. And this story is interesting because it's quite uncommon for such a thing to occur, because it's extravagant ; but above all, because **it reveals the true undertones that we can feel about Iran, these dark undertones left unsaid, over which islamism, the brown wave, can spread!** The victims of this brown wave are Iranian women, forced to wear the veil, Iranian homosexuals who are jailed, adulterous women who are stoned or threatened to be stoned, like Sakineh Mohammadi Ashtiani and so many others. **And it also says a lot about radical islamism** and what we call jihadism. Because this is Shia islam, but such things are equally found in Sunni islam. This jihadism is rooted in two different origins. Of course, these people, jihadists, radical islamists, are Muslims. The fact that they claim to speak in the name of the Qu'ran is a very serious thing to consider. But they are also among the people who never stepped away from the dark, tragic, atrocious past of the twentieth century; the last people who still haven't gone through denazification.[25]

Of course, anyone with a shred of knowledge about Iran knows that the country had been called as such by Iranians since ancient times, that there is a direct link between the Achaemenid Empire's distinction between *aryan*, a designation reserved for Persians, and *anarayan*, denoting the 'other'. Two and a half thousand years before being

[25] '"The Nazi origin of Iran's name": another fake news from Bernard-Henri Lévy', *Les Crises*, 4 June 2018, available at www.les-crises.fr/the-nazi-origin-of-irans-name-another-fake-news-from-bernard-henri-levy-bhl/, accessed 26 January 2019. Emphasis in original.

'Aryan' became a tenet of European race theories and pseudo-sciences such as phrenology, the term Aryan was used by the Persian king Darius (522–486 BC). In an inscription at Naqsh-e Rustam, close to Iran's ancient capital Persepolis in Fars (Persian) province, this passage authored by Darius reads as follows:

I [am] Darius the great king, king of kings, king of countries possessing all kinds of people, king of this great earth far and wide, son of Hystaspes, an Achaemenid, a Persian, the son of a Persian, an Aryan, of Aryan lineage.[26]

Reza Shah simply gave credence to this ancient terminology – one of the first that expressed a civilisational superiority of the 'Iranians' vis-à-vis others. Although there existed racially charged themes in the discourse of the Pahlavis, these were primarily directed against Arabs and not Iranian Jews. In fact, it was during the reign of Reza Shah that Iranian Jews were fully emancipated by law and that they started to serve in the newly constituted Iranian national army and to enrol in the state schools that Reza Shah promoted.

At a time when Jews were being persecuted all over Europe including in France, they acquired the right to hold jobs in the Iranian government. Even though Nazi Germany declared non-Jewish Iranians to be immune from the Nuremberg Laws, Iranian Jews, who had been living in the country for millennia, were not persecuted or handed over to the Germans. Rather the contrary: despite occasional diatribes against the Semitic race by Iranian ethno-nationalists, the Iranian Jewish community was increasingly integrated into the new national narrative promoted by the Pahlavi monarchs.

Moreover, at a time when Nazi Germany was busy implementing the *Endlösung*, Iranian diplomats offered hundreds of Iranian passports to European Jews in order to facilitate their exodus, especially from Poland (there continues to be a small Polish-Jewish minority in Iran to this day). After the abdication of Reza Shah in favour of his son, which was forced upon him by the Allied forces in 1941, the Iranian monarchy continued with pro-Jewish policies. For instance, the 'Iranian Schindler', Abdol-Hassan Sardari, who was in charge of the Iranian consular office when Paris was under Nazi occupation in 1942, facilitated the transfer of many European Jews to Iran,

---

[26] 'Darius iii, Darius I, the Great', *Encyclopaedia Iranica*, available at www.iranicaonline.org/articles/darius-iii, accessed 11 May 2019.

an amazingly courageous act under dire circumstances in Nazi-dominated Europe.[27]

This support for European Jews was the topic of a series sponsored by Iranian state TV in 2007. It is based on the story of Sardari, and traces the life of an Iranian student, played by Shahab Hosseini who had also starred in the Oscar-winning movie *A Separation* directed by Asghar Farhadi. The student played by Hosseini travels to Nazi-occupied Paris where he falls in love with a French Jewish woman. In the Nazis' book this romance would have been categorised by law as *Rassenmischung* (racial mixing) which was likened to *Völkermord* (national annihilation), in accordance with the cod science of the Nazis. This is another example where contemporary Iran and Nazi Germany are worlds apart.

So the sheer lies of a charlatan such as Bernard-Henri Lévy, one of the advocates of the war against Libya in 2011, are part of a wider context – a global right wing as I have called it. A very similar message, i.e. Iran equals Nazi Germany, has been spread by many other protagonists of this narrative including John Bolton. In an article entitled 'Iran's plans for a second Holocaust must be stopped' published in the prominent neo-conservative outlet *Newsmax*, Bolton stated:

Iran's objectives in seeking nuclear weapons are clear.

First, Tehran prizes them as the ultimate trump card against Israel (the 'little Satan' in the words of Ayatollah Ruhollah Khomeini, leader of the 1979 Revolution) and the United States (the 'great Satan').[28]

The same link between an impending holocaust and an Iranian nuclear weapon has been made by Israeli Prime Minister Binyamin Netanyahu for over a decade now. In 2018, speaking at the Munich Security Conference, Netanyahu had the following to say:

Today we gather two-and-a-half years after another agreement was signed in another city in the heart of Europe. There too, noble men and women, high-minded leaders hoping to avoid war, signed an agreement that brutalizes its own people and terrorizes its neighbors. Let me be clear. Iran is not Nazi Germany. There are many differences between the two. Well, for one, one

---

[27] See further Lior Sternfeld, '"Poland is not lost while we still live": the making of Polish Iran, 1941–45', *Jewish Social Studies*, Vol. 23, No. 3 (2018), pp. 101–127.

[28] John R. Bolton, 'Iran's plan for a second Holocaust must be stopped', *Newsmax*, 26 March 2012, available at www.aei.org/publication/irans-plan-for-a-second-holocaust-must-be-stopped/, accessed 12 June 2015.

advocated a master race, the other advocates a master faith. Jews in Iran are not sent to the gas chambers, although religious and ethnic minorities are denied basic freedoms. And there are obviously many other differences. But there are also some striking similarities. Iran openly declares its intention to annihilate Israel with its six million Jews. It makes absolutely no bones about it. Iran seeks to dominate our region, the Middle East, and seeks to dominate the world through aggression and terror. It's developing ballistic missiles to reach deep into Europe and to the United States as well ... Through its proxies, Shiite militias in Iraq, the Houthies in Yemen, Hezbollah in Lebanon, Hamas in Gaza, Iran is devouring huge swaths of the Middle East. Now, there has been one positive consequence of Iran's growing aggression in the region. It's brought Arabs and Israelis closer together as never before. In a paradoxical way, this may pave the way for a broader peace and ultimately also for a Palestinian–Israeli peace. This could happen. But it will not happen if Iran's aggression continues to grow, and nowhere are Iran's belligerent ambitions clearer than in Syria. There Iran hopes to complete a contiguous empire, linking Tehran to Tartus, the Caspian to the Mediterranean.[29]

In order to accentuate this link between Iran's alleged acquisition of a nuclear bomb and the Holocaust, Netanyahu presented President Obama with the Book of Esther at a meeting in the White House in March 2012. The Book of Esther is a biblical story in which the Jews of Persia are threatened with mass slaughter by the Persian king Xerxes. What Netanyahu failed to add is that at the end of the story the Jews are not actually killed. In fact, the reverse is said to have happened: Esther was the Jewish wife of Xerxes and when she pleads with him that his vizier Haman plans to destroy the empire's Jews, Xerxes allows them to defend themselves, which leads to the killing of 75,000 Persians and the slaughter of Haman's ten sons. Thereafter, Esther institutes a festival of redemption, the holiday of Purim which is celebrated throughout the world to this day. The story was a major theme for many European artists in the seventeenth century, for instance in some of the most aesthetically pleasing paintings of Rembrandt (van Rijn), Artemisia Gentileschi and Peter Paul Rubens.

But in Netanyahu's distinctly ideological reading of this story it is during Purim when 'we will read how some 2,500 years ago, a Persian

[29] 'Full text: Netanyahu's speech on Iran in Munich', *Haaretz*, 18 February 2018, available at www.haaretz.com/middle-east-news/full-text-netanyahu-s-speech-on-iran-in-munich-1.5826934, accessed 2 August 2019.

anti-Semite tried to annihilate the Jewish people'.[30] This utter nonsense was repeated by US Secretary of State Michael Pompeo. In an interview with the fundamentalist Christian Broadcast Network during a trip to Israel in March 2019, he was asked if 'President Trump right now has been sort of raised for such a time as this, just like Queen Esther, to help save the Jewish people from an Iranian menace.' In response, Pompeo replied that 'As a Christian, I certainly believe that's possible ... I am confident that the Lord is at work here,' revealing a deeply primitive theocentric worldview.[31]

Of course, Netanyahu and Pompeo failed to add that it was the Persians who got killed in the ensuing battle, and not Persia's Jews, as indicated. Iran is certainly not known for its intolerance towards the Jews of the Persian Empire. The Persian king Cyrus is mentioned in the Torah as a 'saviour' and 'saint' of the Jewish people, and the Old Testament describes him as God's 'anointed' and 'chosen ruler' because he gave refuge to the Jews when they were persecuted by the Babylonian king Nebuchadnezzar in the sixth century BC. The tomb of Esther is in Hamedan (ancient Ecbatana), in the north-west of today's Islamic Republic of Iran. The tomb draws pilgrims from all over Iran especially during Purim. The walls of the building explain the origins of Esther in Hebrew and they are not desecrated by swastikas or neo-Nazi slogans as some of the Jewish cemeteries elsewhere continue to be.

Netanyahu's omissions about today's Iran are almost as preposterous as an article published in Canada's *National Post* in 2006. *The National Post* is part of the media empire that used to be controlled by Conrad Black. The newspaper published an entirely bogus piece, where it was alleged that a new law would require Iranian Jews to 'be marked out with a yellow strip of cloth sewn in front of their clothes while Christians will be assigned the colour red. Zoroastrians end up with Persian blue as the colour of their zonnar.' The article ran alongside a photograph of a Jewish businessman in Berlin in 1935 with a yellow, six-pointed star sewn on his overcoat. After the lie was exposed, the *National Post* had to retract the piece and apologise.

[30] 'Netanyahu's speech at AIPAC', *The Times of Israel*, 6 March 2012, available at www.timesofisrael.com/netanyahus-speech-at-aipac-full-text/, accessed 2 February 2019.

[31] 'Pompeo says God may have sent Trump to save Israel from Iran', *BBC News*, 22 March 2019, available at www.bbc.co.uk/news/world-us-canada-47670717, accessed 21 July 2019.

In actual fact, Stars of David are publicly displayed in Tehran, for instance on the walls and signs of the Beheshtieh Jewish cemetery where dozens of Holocaust victims are buried.[32] In Tehran today there are eighteen synagogues, several kosher butchers, Jewish schools and a Jewish hospital. Comparable conditions exist in other Iranian cities with a sizeable Jewish community. The situation for all minorities in Iran is far from perfect, but the Islamic Republic guarantees the political representation of the Jewish community in the Iranian parliament, a political right that is codified in the Iranian constitution. The Jewish communities of Tehran, Shiraz, Isfahan, Boroujerd and Yazd continue to be the largest in West Asia outside of Israel. In fact, the 30,000–60,000 Iranian Jews can party more freely than the country's majority Muslim population, given that they are exempt from prohibitions on alcohol and attending mixed gender parties.

What is overlooked by Netanyahu and his court historians is that anti-Semitism, scientific racism per se, is a particularly European phenomenon; that race theory developed out of the ideological laboratories of the European Enlightenment period. There is no Iranian or Islamic theory of anti-Semitism. There have been anti-Semitic sentiments of course, but these have never really morphed into a fascist ideology or a cod science such as phrenology that identified Jews as subhumans. Opposition to Israel is a political stance and has nothing to do with scientific racism which fed into Nazi ideology, especially in Germany. Being opposed to the policies of the state of Israel is not the same as being anti-Jewish, as another of our studies in The Global Middle East book series clarifies with abundant vigour. The important book by Yaacov Yadgar shows how the right wing in Israel misappropriates Jewishness and subdues it to the stealthy sovereignty of the state 'with its obsession for a total "pure" confluence between territory and identity'.[33] Such clashes about the meaning of Israel itself explain why even such a controversial figure as the former Iranian president Ahmadinejad received the support of self-admittedly anti-Zionist Jewish organisations such as Neturei Karta International. Furthermore, in an interview with Oriana Fallaci in 1979, Ayatollah Khomeini himself, who institutionalised *Quds* (Jerusalem) day as a

---

[32] See the webpages of the Beheshtieh cemetery at www.beheshtieh.com, accessed 12 January 2014.
[33] Yaacov Yadgar, *Israel's Jewish Identity Crisis: State and Politics in the Middle East*, Cambridge: Cambridge University Press, 2020, p. 183.

global celebration of Palestinian rights, and who was firmly anti-Zionist, used the example of a Jewish protagonist in Shia theology to respond to a question about democracy in Iran:

When Ali succeeded the Prophet, and became head of the Islamic state – and this consideration had all the power, and his reign extended from Saudi Arabia to Egypt, and included a large part of Asia and also of Europe, he happened to have a dispute with a Jew. And the Jew had him called by the judge, and Ali accepted the summons of the judge, and went to him. And when he entered the room, the judge stood up, but Ali said to him angrily, 'Why do you stand up when I enter the room but not when the Jew entered? Before a judge the two contending parties should be treated the same way.' Afterward, he accepted the sentence, which was unfavourable to him.[34]

These are not the words of an anti-Semite. Khomeini may have been an authoritarian, uncompromising, culturally retroactive, cleric with a rather stoic and stern vision for the revolution, but he did not emerge out of a context with fascist undertones, exactly because such a tradition simply does not exist in Iran's mainstream political culture, and certainly not in mainstream Shia and Sunni Islam. Systematic, institutionalised anti-Semitism was a particularly European phenomenon, and it turned into a catastrophe for humanity at one particular time in global history.

The misguided effort to conflate opposition to the policies of the Israeli state with fascism and/or Nazism is another similarity to the build-up of previous invasions in the region. It was apparent in 1990 when the US media played a key role in reproducing, and thereby disseminating, the 'Saddam Hussein equals Adolf Hitler' analogy which was constitutive of the 'New World Order' narrative that was meant to buttress US global hegemony after the end of the Cold War and the impending disintegration of the Soviet empire.

In a study about the number of stories citing Saddam Hussein and Adolf Hitler (and the New World Order) in the *Washington Post* before, during and after the Second Gulf War (1990–1991), Shaw and Martin found a direct correlation between the intensity of conflict and the employment of the phrases by the *Post*'s reporters. In the pre-war period between 30 June and 1 August 1990, Hussein and Hitler

---

[34] Oriana Fallaci, 'An interview with Khomeini', *New York Times*, 7 October 1979, p. 8, available at www.nytimes.com/1979/10/07/archives/an-interview-with-khomeini.html, accessed 13 June 2018.

were mentioned twice (an average of 0.06 news stories per day) and the New World Order phrase not at all (obviously because the phrase had not yet entered the jargon of US policy-makers and Iraq had not yet invaded Kuwait). In the build-up to the US offensive between 2 August 1990 and 15 January 1991, the Hussein–Hitler analogy was used 118 times (an average of 0.71 news stories per day) and the New World Order phrase 50 times (an average of 0.30 stories per day). During the air war from 16 January 1991 to 22 February 1991, the Hussein–Hitler comparison was referred to 39 times (an average of 1.03 times per day) and the New World Order phrase was mentioned 45 times (an average of 1.18 stories per day). During the US ground offensive, that is in a period of four days between 23 February and 27 February 1991, the Hussein–Hitler analogy was mentioned seven times (an average of 1.40 stories per day) and the New World Order norm five times (an average of 1 story per day). The employment of both phrases decreased in the post-war period between 28 February and 30 March 1991: the Hussein–Hitler comparison was made seven times (an average of 0.23 stories per day) and the New World Order phrase was used 21 times (an average of 0.68 news stories per day).[35]

So, the theme that Iran equates to Nazi Germany, which is one of the many right-wing (and formerly neo-conservative) narratives, has a precedent. Again, there is no suggestion here that all minorities in Iran prosper – Iranians of all hues have been suffering from discrimination by successive governments throughout the contemporary era, probably as far back as to the end of the rule of Karim Khan-e Zand (1751–1779) who has been depicted by historians as a relatively benevolent and tolerant emperor judged by the global standards of his age. But it is one thing to denounce the lack of civil rights and another to talk about racism. If anything, Iranian Jews must be considered an integral part of the national idea of Persia since antiquity. There is a range of historical examples that place the Jews of Iran at the centre of Iranian self-perceptions.

There is, then, far more common ground between Israel and Iran than decision-makers in both countries would admit. The reasons for the Israeli–Iranian animosity are geostrategic, and they are buttressed

[35] See Donald L. Shaw and Shannon E. Martin, 'The natural, and inevitable, phases of war reporting: historical shadows, new communication in the Persian Gulf', in Robert E. Denton Jr (ed.), *The Media and the Persian Gulf War*, Westport, CT: Praeger, 1993, p. 53.

by political agendas of the 'hardliners' on both sides, but also by the objectively very real oppression of the Palestinians. Israel and Iran are at odds, not due to any incommensurable historical issues, then. They have clashing national interests. This is particularly apparent with reference to Palestine of course, which played such an emotive role in the imagination of the Iranian revolutionaries. But the anger towards Israel was also because of the support of successive Israeli governments for the rule of Iran's despised dictator, including the torture manuals that the shah's dreaded secret service SAVAK adopted from the vile methods of the Mossad (and the CIA).

The EU has largely moved on from one-dimensional depictions of the Iranian state as inherently evil and irrational. But with the Trump administration some of the idioms I have outlined so far have returned. This is due to that institutionalised coterie that I have linked to an international right wing in admittedly abstract terms. How easy it was for them to change the discourse about Iran from the constructive engagement of the Obama–Biden years which yielded the JCPOA nuclear agreement, to the current venom that the Trump administration has re-injected into Iranian–US relations. In his UN speech in October 2017, in which he threatened to abrogate the nuclear deal, Trump used the very same terms that have been floating around right-wing circles for years now: 'The Iranian dictatorship's aggression continues to this day,' Trump declared in a characteristically mono-causal manner. 'The regime remains the world's leading state sponsor of terrorism, and provides assistance to al-Qaeda, the Taliban, Hezbollah, Hamas, and other terrorist networks.'[36] As indicated in the prologue, Trump even went as far as to label General Soleimani a 'terrorist' and 'monster' after ordering his assassination in January 2020, in total disregard of, perhaps even disbelief in, the fact that he was considered a war hero by many Iranians and others beyond, who saw him as a symbol of security because of his role in the Iran–Iraq War and in particular because of his successful campaigns against so-called Islamic State and al-Qaeda in Iraq and Syria. Old habits die hard, not least because there are institutions, social media 'bots' and angry individuals out there who reproduce them on a daily basis.

---

[36] 'Iran nuclear deal: Trump's full speech', *BBC*, 13 October 2017, available at www.bbc.co.uk/news/world-us-canada-41617488, accessed 12 December 2018.

Iran As an Object

Questioned at the theoretical level, right-wing ideology, including sub-movements such as neo-conservatism (notwithstanding differences), is not ordered in accordance with a unifying headquarter or conspiracy. The contemporary right wing should be represented rather as an ideological space open in three dimensions. In one of these we have already situated the right-wing or neo-conservative functionary, for whom writing the script, the speech, the terminology of a specific political narrative is central (e.g. 'Iran is a part of the axis of evil' by David Frum or 'Iran is a threat to global security' reiterated by Mark Dubowitz and his Foundation for Defense of Democracies).[37] In a second dimension we may situate the decision-maker, the right wing's public face who proceeds by relating diversified but consensual narratives in such a way that they are then able to claim causal validity and strategic value (e.g. Richard Perle, Dick Cheney, Donald Rumsfeld, Paul Wolfowitz in the George W. Bush administration, or John Bolton and Steve Bannon in the Trump administration before they were ousted). These two dimensions are largely practical in that they are part of the day-to-day affairs of politics in Washington DC and the 'think-tank belt' scattered around Dupont Circle.

The third dimension is that of strategic value, which develops as a long-term state interest out of the latter; it forms a salient grand strategy and is hence not easily discarded or altered. It is here that we meet the legitimation of war, its translation from the empirical realms of day-to-day politics into theorised reality; it is this realm where it attains the level of a regime of (un)truth. In this dimension, Iran is meant to lose its subjectivity, its agency, its ability to speak for itself. It is here, in political science terms, where US governments attempt to erode the sovereignty of the country as a prelude to subordinating it to US state interests.

As such, Iran was mentioned as a primary target for US military action and sanctions in several National Security Strategies, and several key policy speeches. A short discourse analysis of these reveals that they are littered with such emotionally charged terms as 'ally of terror'

---

[37] See Ray Takeyh and Mark Dubowitz, 'The United States finally has an aggressive plan to defang Iran', *Foreignpolicy.com,* 21 May 2018, available at https://foreignpolicy.com/2018/05/21/the-united-states-finally-has-an-aggressive-plan-to-defang-iran-trump-pompeo/, accessed 27 June 2019.

or 'fanatical'. As Donald Trump said, in a typically arbitrary manner: 'Iran is under the control of a fanatical regime that ... forced a proud people to submit to its extremist rule. This radical regime has raided the wealth of one of the world's oldest and vibrant nations, and spread death, destruction, and chaos all around the globe.'[38] The effort is clear here: to subvert the Iranian state, its legitimacy and sovereignty and to take away the agency of the Iranian people to establish their own destiny. As indicated, this is a rather worn-out ploy spelled out in several previous speeches and strategy papers. The Bush administration, for example, established an in-house Iran Desk, Iran watch units in Dubai as well as US embassies in the vicinity of Iran, and a US$75 million programme aimed at 'expanding broadcasting into the country, funding nongovernmental organisations and promoting cultural exchanges'.[39] In another parallel to the build-up to the Iraq War in 2003, US officials set up an Iran Syria Policy and Operations Group (ISOG) whose actions included

increasing the military capabilities of Arab allies such as Saudi Arabia, the United Arab Emirates, and Bahrain ... providing covert assistance to Iranian dissidents and building international outrage toward Iran by publicizing its alleged role in a 1994 terrorist attack in Argentina.[40]

In another continuation of this failed neo-conservative strategy, the Trump administration designated the Islamic Revolution Guard Corps a foreign sponsor of terrorism in April 2019, a rather symbolic gesture that was meant to signal the tough stance that the Trump administration has pursued against Iran. It was flanked by 'regime change' rhetoric and institutions targeting social media networks and the Internet, such as the so-called Global Engagement Center, led by Daniel Kimmage, that is aimed at countering the growing influence of rising powers. 'We have teams focused on Russia, Iran and China,' Kimmage said in December 2018. 'We have a very active science and technology team that does data analytics ... That's how we went on

---

[38] 'Remarks by President Trump on Iran strategy', 13 October 2017, available at www.whitehouse.gov/briefings-statements/remarks-president-trump-iran-strategy/, accessed 28 June 2018.

[39] Available at www.washingtonpost.com/wp-dyn/content/article/2006/03/12/AR2006031201016.html, accessed 4 July 2006.

[40] Farah Stockman, 'US unit works quietly to counter Iran's sway, backs dissidents, nearby nations', *Boston Globe*, 2 January 2007.

offense against the Soviets ... We're mapping the online disinforma-
tion networks and we are giving media organizations in key regions
tools so that they can identify these narratives and go out and counter
them.'[41] This policy has been violating the Algiers Accords of
19 January 1981 which set out that the United States 'pledges that it
is and from now on will be the policy of the United States not to
intervene, directly or indirectly, politically or militarily, in Iran's
internal affairs'. Yet despite these legal restrictions, US intervention
has been repeatedly enforced by a parallel process probing tensions
between Iran's ethnic minorities and the central government in Tehran.
A research project to that end was implemented by the Marine Corps
Intelligence in 2006 which focused on 'crises and predeployment support to expeditionary warfare'.[42]

More recently, senior US military and national security officials have
been backing the politically defunct MKO (Mujahideen-e Khalgh)
organisation which is despised by most Iranians for its support of
Saddam Hussein during the Iran–Iraq War, when Hussein granted
the organisation a military base in the country from which they
attacked Iranian troops.[43] The group has been responsible for numerous terror attacks all over the world including on US targets.[44] And
yet, in a statement widely published by the MKO's propaganda outlets,
thirty-three former senior officials of the US military and national
security establishments endorsed the MKO's leader 'Maryam Rajavi's
10-point plan for the future of Iran'. According to the statement,

[41] Guy Taylor, 'State Department Global Engagement Center targets Russian
propaganda, "deep fakes"', *Washington Times*, 12 December 2018, available at
www.apnews.com/9f7892a163582b5fd0297e2a81124c35, accessed 1
January 2019.

[42] Guy Dinmore, 'US marines probe tensions among Iran's minorities', *Financial
Times*, 23 February 2006.

[43] In the build-up to the revolution of 1979, the group was notorious for targeting
US targets in Iran and beyond. See further 'A terrorist cult and its Trumpian
friends', *Habilian: Iranian Perspectives and News on Terrorism*, 19 March
2019, available at www.habilian.ir/en/201903193807/articles/a-terrorist-cult-
and-its-trumpian-friends.html#_ednref4, accessed 18 April 2019. The MKO is
led by Maryam and Massoud Rajavi and has a political wing that operates
under the name 'National Council for Resistance in Iran'.

[44] See further 'Iran rebels hit missions in 10 nations', *New York Times*, 6 April
1992, section A, p. 3, available at www.nytimes.com/1992/04/06/world/iran-
rebels-hit-missions-in-10-nations.html, accessed 12 June 2018; and 'The cult of
Rajavi', *New York Times Magazine*, 13 July 2003, available at www.nytimes
.com/2003/07/13/magazine/the-cult-of-rajavi.html, accessed 28 February 2018.

members of the American delegation to the 2018 annual gala event for a 'Free Iran' were eager to attend the MKO's rally in Paris in June 2018. Among the listed signatories of the statement were Joe Lieberman, Fran Townsend, Newt Gingrich, Gen. James Jones, Bill Richardson, Ed Rendell, Tom Ridge, Patrick Kennedy – and Rudy Giuliani. The latter declared at the rally that 'next year I want this convention in Tehran'.[45] This strand of US policies vis-à-vis Iran, unsurprisingly, is endorsed by functionaries tied into the global right wing, from the Netanyahu administration in Israel, sympathisers in Saudi Arabia, Bahrain and the UAE to ideological think tanks and neo-fascist parties, even in Europe. The links are far reaching and some-times paradoxical: For instance, the extremist Spanish right-wing party VOX, which is chaperoned by the former Spanish prime minister Jose Maria Aznar, a staunch supporter of the invasion of Iraq in 2003, was partially funded by the MKO.[46]

US Policy Failures and the Recipes for Peace

There is a response to this strategy to target Iranians in the lyrics of Hichkas. In the musical piece framing this chapter, there is a constant reminder to resist injustice peacefully, which stems from the traumatic experience of the global support for Saddam Hussein during the Iran–Iraq War: 'I pray for the world to be secure and peaceful. Amen. We have felt enough fire. I hope for a day when we will all feel safe and secure. So that we all may be happy together. Don't stand still because I want you to throw your hands up higher and higher.' Iran as a target – successive generations after the revolution have felt the serious repercussions of this tragic objectivisation of the country as the ultim-ate villain. And yet, the Islamic Republic has ruled Iran for over four decades now, the longest period that any state has managed to govern the country since the demise of the Qajar dynasty at the beginning of the twentieth century.

---

[45] See further Simon Tisdall, 'Rudy Giuliani calls for Iran regime change at rally linked to extreme group', *The Guardian*, 30 June 2018, available at www .theguardian.com/us-news/2018/jun/30/rudy-giuliani-mek-iran-paris-rally, accessed 12 July 2018.
[46] See further Sohail Jannessari and Darren Loucaides, 'Spain's Vox Party hates Muslims – except the ones who fund it', *Foreignpolicy.com*, 27 April 2019, available at https://foreignpolicy.com/2019/04/27/spains-vox-party-hates-muslims-except-the-ones-who-fund-it-mek-ncri-maryam-rajavi-pmoi-vidal-quadras-abascal/, accessed 12 May 2019.

Despite all these destructive efforts of the global right wing, the diplomacy surrounding the JCPOA stands out as a fine example of détente between Iran and the United States. In his first sit-down interview, which he symbolically gave to the Arabic satellite network Al-Arabiya after his election in November 2018, President Barack Obama addressed the leadership of Iran directly, asking them to 'unclench their fist' and to open up a new chapter in Iran's relations with the United States. On the occasion of the Iranian *Nowrouz* (new year) celebrations in March 2009, he reiterated his willingness to talk to Iranian leaders setting a markedly different tone than his predecessor George W. Bush. Biden too has adopted a rather less confrontational language in addressing Iran, certainly in comparison to Donald Trump and George W. Bush.

On the other side, then-president Mahmoud Ahmadinejad became the first Iranian leader in three decades to officially congratulate a US president-elect, a gesture acknowledged by Obama at a news conference in January 2009.[47] In parenthesis one should add that when the reformist President Mohammad Khatami had talked about dialogue and détente with the United States in the late 1990s, he was castigated by Iranian hardliners and blamed for sacrificing Iran's revolutionary ideals. There were no such complaints about Ahmadinejad's far more proactive overtures. There were two reasons for this: First Obama's cautious rhetoric set the stage for a new opening in relations between the two countries. And second, the Supreme Jurisprudent of Iran, Ali Khamenei, indicated before the elections in the United States that Iran would consider talking to any president other than George W. Bush.[48]

The diplomacy surrounding the nuclear agreement became possible because Iranian and US decision-makers stripped relations between the two countries of some of their historical baggage and discursive venom. This allowed rapprochement in accordance with congruent national interests and geostrategic considerations. There was accommodation despite some of the divergent goals of the two countries, for instance the pro-Israeli policies of the United States versus Iran's subversion of Israeli power within the region and beyond; US efforts to contain populist Islamic movements such as Hamas and Hezbollah versus Iran's support for them; and the United States' opposition to

---

[47] See further Ali-Reza Eshraghi, 'Our friend in Tehran', *New York Times*, 22 February 2009.

[48] 'Iran Leader suggests US ties possible in future', *Reuters*, 3 January 2008.

independence-driven socialist movements, especially in Latin America, which clashes with Iran's close cooperation with them.

So, on the one side we have Iran with its self-perception as a regional superpower. On the other side, the political elites governing the United States firmly believe in the Americo-centric configuration of world politics. These self-perceptions are in many ways mutually exclusive, but that did not mean that the United States and Iran remained perennial enemies. In the build-up to the JCPOA, Presidents Rouhani and Obama managed to establish what I called a 'Cold Peace' in the *Daily Star* published in Beirut, within three interrelated contexts and along three mutual interests:[49] In Iraq both the United States and Iran had an interest in the stability of the central government and the unity of the Iraqi nation-state, which yielded some low-level diplomatic engagement throughout 2007. In Afghanistan, an equally important strategic theatre, both states had an interest to stem the resurgence of the Taliban and to support the central government politically and economically. There is no reason why such a formula couldn't work in the future, as well, but the there will certainly be a concerted effort against any movement towards a lasting peace between Iran and the United States by the global right wing, as I have argued.

Such close collaboration came out in a detailed book by the resourceful former foreign secretary of the UK, Jack Straw, which was very quickly translated into Persian and published in Iran.[50] Generally, on a global scale, both the United States and Iran are enemies of al-Qaeda/ISIS-type movements which are virulently anti-American and anti-Shia/anti-Iranian. And finally, both the Obama administration and the Iranian state saw the benefits of a managed nuclear programme that was rightly heralded as a major step towards a functioning nuclear non-proliferation regime. These factors became components for a positive-sum game between the two countries – both benefited from dialogue and acknowledgement of each other's interests within a context of mutual respect and engagement. To my mind, such engagement could have become the cornerstone of a viable security architecture in West Asia, which could have fed into a rather more stable international system. Its abandonment, as the director of the

---

[49] 'We may be near a "cold peace" between the US and Iran', *Daily Star* (Beirut), 15 August 2008; 'How to make peace with Iran', *Opendemocracy*, 14 May 2010.

[50] Jack Straw, *The English Job: Understanding Iran and Why It Distrusts Britain*, London: Biteback Publishing, 2019.

admirably principled and factual Stockholm International Peace Research Institute (SIPRI) rightly argued, has threatened the global anti-proliferation efforts:

The JCPOA limits Iran's uranium enrichment programme until 2030 and contains monitoring and transparency measures that will remain in place long after that date. Along with other international experts, SIPRI's assessment from the outset has been that the agreement is technically sound with robust verification procedures. The International Atomic Energy Agency ... has consistently found that Iran is fully living up to its undertakings ... However, Saudi Arabia, Israel and most US Republican politicians opposed the agreement ... This makes it clear that, rather than an evidence-based technical objection to the agreement or its implementation, the US decision to withdraw from the JCPOA was a political measure aimed against Iran ... US withdrawal from the JCPOA risks seriously weakening trust and confidence in international institutions and arrangements that are essential parts of the global security architecture. In particular, the US action undermines the global effort for nuclear non-proliferation by sabotaging an important and effective anti-proliferation agreement.[51]

In opposition to such facts and calls for diplomacy, the right-wing ideology espoused by the Trump administration has functioned as a mediation between war and the target enemy, Iran in particular. To be more precise, by way of establishing a presence in public discourse through the (social) media and institutions, in politics and in the foreign policy process of the United States, the right wing transformed disparate crisis situations in West Asia into the myth that there is a clear and immediate threat to the 'national security' of the country and Israel, and that Iran is the prime mover. As a consequence, the Trump administration managed in a relatively short period of time to do away with the rapprochement between the United States and Iran that was achieved by the Obama administration. Social media sites such as Twitter were instrumental in that swift policy change, because they facilitate propaganda through the proliferation of false news disseminated by thousands of fake 'bot' accounts. In many ways, Twitter is the real *Volksempfänger* of our contemporary period – a central platform for nefarious political agendas.

---

[51] Dan Smith, 'The US withdrawal from the Iran deal: one year on', *Stockholm International Peace Research Institute*, 7 May 2019, available at www.sipri.org/commentary/expert-comment/2019/us-withdrawal-iran-deal-one-year, accessed 13 June 2019.

Sometimes what I have so conveniently termed 'a global right wing' has strange bedfellows from seemingly opposite political leanings, as the example of the cooperation between the formerly Marxist-Leninist guerrilla movement MKO and right-wing parties such as VOX in Spain exemplifies (see p. 140). The former UK prime minister Tony Blair, too, is not a right-wing politician in terms of his domestic politics, as he is a member of the Labour Party. But in the aftermath of the terror attacks on the United States in September 2001, he pulled the foreign policy of Britain into a dangerous direction, despite the massive protests of British civil society against his alliance with George W. Bush which aided and abetted the ill-fated invasions of Afghanistan and Iraq in the aftermath of 9/11. Blair was a willing collaborator in an essentially neo-imperial agenda, and one of the culprits for the criminal, humanitarian disaster that ensued throughout the region after those poorly executed wars 'for freedom and democracy' which were always also deemed to be godly ordained in the typically primitive parlance of the right wing in the United States and elsewhere. Declassified memos sent by Blair to Bush in the run-up to the Iraq War of 2003 exemplify the strength of the relationship between the two leaders, when the British prime minister pledged to support the US invasions 'whatever' would happen.[52] The memos show how Blair suggested manipulating public opinion to support the wars: 'Public opinion is public opinion,' he wrote in one of the memos. 'And opinion in the US is quite simply on a different planet from opinion here, in Europe or in the Arab world.'[53]

The memos sent between 2001 and 2007 were released alongside Sir John Chilcot's highly commendable report of his inquiry into the Iraq War (to which I was invited but to which I declined to contribute). The Chilcot Report condemned Tony Blair's role in the conflicts. My analytical point is that right-wing thinking advocates war and confrontation and that this type of worldview is promiscuous in its search for allies. Of course, this is not the only type of ideology that is distinctly antagonistic – leftist and Islamist extremism are equally destructive political systems when they legitimate subjugation. The ultimate object remains the same, though: power through force. As we have seen – by

[52] 'Chilcot Report: what Blair said to Bush in memos', *BBC*, 6 July 2016, available at www.bbc.co.uk/news/uk-36722312, accessed 18 May 2018.

[53] Ibid.

means of these plots – facts, myths, ideology, international crisis situations and hegemonic politics are brought together within an artificial unity in order to manufacture war. It is this synthesis of the heterogeneous the making available of complexity in a language that is approachable, which makes these plots so appealing and which brings them so close to politics and the public. By pulling together and integrating into one whole and complete unity complex and scattered issues, the right wing schematises and structures the direction of US foreign policy. This is especially pronounced and effective vis-à-vis an adversary such as Iran that has an underrepresented presence in the mainstream of US political culture, which in turn is due to the fact that (a) many analysts and journalists in the country have not moved beyond a largely perverted image of Iran and (b) the Iranian state continues to stymie Iranian civil society on a daily basis, which empowers the Iranian right wing that is similarly antagonistic to its US counterpart.[54]

A critical reading of these representations of Iran, which of course includes a critical view on what is being proposed in the present study, requires that we grasp the mechanism and operations that unify disparate issues for political ends. You may thus feel that it is useful to delve into the 'prehistory' of policy outcomes. The plots that I have tried to cover in this chapter in relation to Iran emerge from that background. With this emergence also comes to the fore the implied target, in our case the Islamic Republic. Understanding how this *target* is constituted as the prototypical *enemy* is central to understanding the manufacturing of war. Ideally, it would empower us to recognise 'an ideology as such, hence to pick it out from the properly argumentative modes, hence also to place it within the scope of a critique of ideology'.[55] It would equip me and you, in short, with a critical consciousness vis-à-vis the mechanisms of international security and global history.

The density of right-wing ideology engendered by the prolific actors mentioned above and carried into the public domain by a myriad of

[54] For an analysis of media misrepresentations of Iran see also Foad Izadi and Hakimeh Saghaye-Biria, 'A discourse analysis of elite American newspaper editorials: the case of Iran's nuclear program', *Journal of Communication Inquiry*, Vol. 31, No. 2 (2007), pp. 140–165.

[55] Paul Ricoeur, *Time and Narrative*, vol. 1, trans. Kathleen McLaughlin and David Pellauer, Chicago: University of Chicago Press, 1984, pp. 176–177.

think tanks and lobbying organisations does not mean, of course, that there are no competing narratives in the United States. I do not claim that the right wing has a total grip on the political culture of the country. This is quite impossible in a pluralistic political system, even when the United States has turned closer to being an illiberal democracy in terms of its mainstream political culture in recent years. There is no escaping the fact that the anti-Iranian right wing has had a strong influence on the levers of power in Washington DC. This has been repeatedly lamented by former high-ranking officials. For example, even Graham Fuller, a former vice-chairman of the National Intelligence Council for long-range forecasting at the CIA, concedes that 'efforts to portray Iran with some analytical balance have grown more difficult, crowded out by inflamed rhetoric and intense pro-Israeli lobbying against Tehran in Congress'.[56] That was in the 1990s. Today, that irrational hysteria about Iran is ring-fenced. Ultimately, right-wing ideology denotes the latest manifestation of the contemporary global leadership aspirations of the United States which have been seriously constrained by the reemergence of Russia and China as global powers. Hence some of the hysteria among the Trump administration and their allies.

This suitability of Iran as an object of war in the right-wing imagination is the overarching habitat I have explored in this chapter; the place where the image of Iran as an international threat is implanted. For what gives the country its negative image is not its own ontological content, not even the confrontational rhetoric of the Islamic Republic, but the act of institution, an installation, a consecration that gives significance to what has, in itself, a neutral content. It was within a comparable, very tight-knit, very ubiquitous cultural habitat that previous US-led wars were made possible and it is within a similarly pervasive *Kriegskontext* where the idea of military intervention against Iran is repeatedly cultivated. I hope that I have made it clear that right-wing ideology is central to this process, because it pulls together and integrates into one whole disparate issues, because it cuts down alternatives, because it reduces complexity, because it continuously works to quasi-legitimate its ultimate aim – war.

---

[56] Graham E. Fuller, 'Repairing US–Iranian relations', *Middle East Policy*, Vol. 6, No. 2 (1998), pp. 140–144.

What is at stake in revealing transnational right-wing propaganda is not to undifferentiate US foreign policies. I am suggesting no mono-causal link between this ideology, with all its contradictions and sub-groups, and hostility towards Iran, no automatism, no inevitable political outcome. Neither do I claim that Iranians are naive bystanders in all this. As indicated, there have been several public relations strat-egies that I have been involved in, in order to counter media distortions about Iran's nuclear file in particular and the foreign affairs of the country in general. Moreover, there is a global civil society and anti-war movement that has repeatedly been successful in preventing any movement towards war with Iran.

Yet the transnational right-wing media, many leading US politicians, the Israeli state, a whole range of activists and journalists and some academic experts continue to reify the general consensus that Iran is a threat to world order, if not to 'Western' civilisation. Now, this is not the same as saying that only deliberately subjective things are said about Iran. Neither does it mean, as Sadeq Zibakalam and Mashallah Shamsolvaezin noted after the first direct Iranian–American intergovernmental negotiations since the Islamic revolution, which focused on Iraq and were held in Baghdad on 28 May 2007, that Iran and the United States could not overcome their differences. They did under the Obama administration with reference to the nuclear issue, which was a tremendous achievement of international diplomacy. It does mean however, that the right wing and their allies will continuously and rather relentlessly exert pressures to derail any type of diplomatic resolution between the two states. So what I have hoped to explore in this chapter is the nihilistic international agenda right-wing ideology promotes; the social engineering of a militaristic discourse which has secured a place in that ferociously contested space that I have called 'international political culture' elsewhere.[57]

Ultimately, then, right-wing functionaries inscribe the narrative of war in international relations; they inscribe it in institutions (e.g. the Committee on the Present Danger), language (e.g. the 'axis of evil'), mindsets (e.g. 'Why do they hate us?') and policies (e.g. the doctrine of 'pre-emption', or the 'wars on terror'). This strategy transforms other countries into replaceable variables. To be more precise, pre-emption

---

[57] See further Arshin Adib-Moghaddam, *The International Politics of the Persian Gulf: A Cultural Genealogy*, London: Routledge, 2006.

and 'America First' doctrines are made into versatile ideological agents that can be employed to legitimate intervention *globally* – not only in the Iraqi, Syrian, Iranian, Venezuelan, North Korean or Cuban context, but also in other conflict scenarios, if necessary (China–Taiwan–Hong Kong, Russia–Chechnya–Ukraine etc.). From the right-wing perspective, Lebanon, Yemen, Palestine, Afghanistan, Venezuela, Iraq, Iran are just episodes in the same hegemonic project. This political strategy is reassuringly mimetic: once a specific imperial project has bedded in, its supposed chivalry is loudly trumpeted, bundled up in a morally righteous and infallible narrative – in essence the legitimation of hegemony or a new kind of imperialism – and stitched into the political fabric of the contemporary United States. It is in this sense that right-wing ideology all over the world reveals itself as war – a war continued by other means. The cynical irony of this ideology is that it makes some of us think that it serves the liberation of mankind.

The antidote to this global right wing is more scholarship, more activism premised on the truth and more emphasis on the commonality of cultures and peoples from different regions of the world – the ingredients of a cultural diplomacy that accentuates contacts between civil societies and not merely between states. By bringing the Iranian rapper Hichkas into this chapter, I have tried to demonstrate how such an approach can yield a common terrain where Iranians and US Americans can communicate without the impingement of ideological constructions. The language of music and art entails the aesthetics to embrace what seems 'alien' to us, no matter who the 'other' is. In this way, we can illustrate some indissoluble links between cultures, which is useful as a strategy to combat the venomous psycho-nationalism of states, and its detrimental impact on a better understanding of relations between nations in general and post-revolutionary Iran, the United States and Israel in particular.

As for the global right wing and their solutions coded in the language of neo-imperialism, sanctions, war: the lower-income strata of Iranian society have suffered due to US sanctions for a long time now. But the situation is less dire than the calamity of the people of Gaza and Afghanistan, the situation of Iraqis in the 1990s, or Syrians, Libyans and Yemenis today. This is one side of the spectrum. The other side is that sanctions simply don't work. They didn't work against Cuba, which has recently democratised its post-revolutionary polity with a new, rights-based constitution. They didn't work against revolutionary

China and they haven't worked against Iran. If anything, this 'isolation' has given impetus to an indigenous technological infrastructure that delivered the nuclear energy programme, the mass production of military hardware including stealth systems, drones, artificial intelligence induced biosecurity projects, long range ballistic missiles, a space programme and a 'Persian cyber army' that is repeatedly accused of hacking into US computer systems, which in itself is an admission of Iran's technological capabilities despite the sanctions.[58]

In political terms, the sanctions and the hysterical anti-Iranian propaganda did not yield 'regime change', but more defiance from Iran. In the words of Hichkas, there is an immense amount of social solidarity in the country, a civic consciousness that is geared to the ideals of justice, equality and independence that I set out in the previous chapters and that are also characteristic of major themes in Iranian rap music. Sanctions merely strengthen these bonds; they create a siege mentality that lends itself to divisive categorisations – us versus them. Lies go only so far, as Lawrence Wilkinson bravely opined, when he set out how he assisted then US Secretary of State Colin Powell to lie to the United Nations about Saddam Hussein's alleged weapons of mass destruction (WMD) arsenal in a warning about current US Secretary of State Michael Pompeo.[59] Then and now history has its own judgement and the truth always prevails as long as intellectuals are free to think and write, in some corner of the world.

As for the Israel factor, my research into Iranian politics does not indicate to me that the decision-makers of the country are united in any commitment to destroy Israel. The issue is Palestine, which acts as a Trojan horse for Iran's appeal in the Arab and Muslim world, as Ali Alavi rightly argues in his recent study of Iranian–Palestinian

---

[58] See Robert McMillan, 'Iranian hackers have hit hundreds of companies in past two years', *Wall Street Journal*, 6 March 2019, available at www.wsj.com/articles/iranian-hackers-have-hit-hundreds-of-companies-in-past-two-years-11551906036, accessed 12 April 2019. For an excellent analysis of the unilateral dimensions of the sanctions regime of the US see Hisae Nakanishi, 'The construction of the sanctions regime against Iran: political dimensions of unilateralism', in Ali Z. Marossi and Marisa R. Bassett (eds.), *Economic Sanctions under International Law: Unilateralism, Multilateralism, Legitimacy, and Consequences*, The Hague: Springer, 2015, pp. 23–41.

[59] Lawrence Wilkerson, 'Pompeo: the real threat to US national security', *LobeLog*, 19 February 2019, available at https://lobelog.com/pompeo-the-real-threat-to-u-s-national-security/, accessed 28 March 2019.

relations.[60] More specifically, Iranian decision-makers have various
positions on this issue: from calls for the demise of Israel by the right
wing of the country, to tacit accommodation by the centrists and
reformers. The latter approach has been repeatedly articulated when
the Iranian state felt at ease, that is during periods when it was
engaged diplomatically.

For instance, then-president Mohammad Khatami stated in an
interview with the *Financial Times* in 2006 that Iran would accept a
Palestinian state 'ready to live alongside Israel'.[61] When the Obama
presidency started to engage Iran, even Mahmoud Ahmadinejad confirmed the two-state solution. Asked if Iran would accept an agreement between Israel and Palestine, Ahmadinejad responded:
'Whatever decision they [Israeli/Palestinians] take is fine with us.
We are not going to determine anything. Whatever decision they
take, we will support that.'[62] At the time, his vice president Rahim
Mashaei even went as far as to say that 'Iran is a friend of the nation
in the United States and in Israel, and this is an honour. We view the
American nation as one with the greatest nations of the world.'[63] He
and President Ahmadinejad threatened Israel on other occasions, that
were rather more charged in terms of the international context, the
point being that Iran reacts to diplomacy, even on the contentious
issue of Israel.

Others such as Ayatollah Khamenei have called for a referendum,
after the return of Palestinian refugees, which would establish the future
of Israel/Palestine, in an obvious attempt to tilt the demographics in
favour of the Palestinians.[64] This view has been echoed very recently by
Hossein Amirabdollahian, the former deputy foreign minister for Arab
and African affairs in Iran's Ministry of Foreign Affairs: 'All people of
Palestine, including Muslims, Christians and Jews, will have the right to

[60] Alavi, *Iran and Palestine*.
[61] 'Iran "accepts two-state answer" in Mideast', *Financial Times*,
4 September 2006.
[62] 'Iran's President "would support two-state solution" for Israel', *The Telegraph*,
26 April 2009.
[63] 'Iranian VP: We are friends of the nation in Israel', *Ynet News*, 19 July 2008,
available at www.ynetnews.com/articles/0,7340,L-3570266,00.html, accessed
13 December 2019.
[64] 'Iran proposes referendum about Palestine', *Ynet, News*, 10 January 2011,
available at www.ynetnews.com/articles/0,7340,L-4129406,00.html, accessed
12 December 2019.

participate in the referendum.'[65] Under current circumstances, this approach is unlikely to garner much support in the region and beyond, partly because the Trump administration is firmly in line with Netanyahu's zero-sum approach to the conflict with the Palestinians, and in particular because of the recent peace deals between Israel on the one side and the UAE and Bahrain, on the other, which have somewhat 'normalised' the issue of Israel in the region. But at least the Iranian emphasis on the 'right of return' is consistent with several United Nations resolutions (i.e. 194 passed in December 1948 and 3236 in November 1974). The right of return was also considered in United Nations Security Council Resolution 242 which affirmed the necessity for 'achieving a just settlement of the refugee problem' which is why it became a major point of contention in the failed peace accords between Israelis and Palestinians. It continues to be the default position of all major Palestinian movements, including the PLO, irrespective of Iranian views about this matter. In terms of scholarship, the right of return is firmly in line with the research of the so-called New Historians, certainly Avi Shlaim and Ilan Pappe.[66] Khaled Hroub summarised the official Iranian position succinctly in a recently published analysis:

In reality, and contrary to the pomposity of 'erasing Israel', Iran's position on the Israel–Palestine conflict is ultimately to accept what the Palestinians would accept. In a nutshell, Iran accepts the two-state solution, much as the Arab states do, in accordance with the Arab Peace Initiative of 2002, which offered the recognition of Israel and a normalisation of relations in return for a Palestinian state along 1967 borders ... At the 2017 summit meeting of the Organisation of Islamic Co-operation in Istanbul, held in response to Trump's recognition of Jerusalem as the capital of Israel, Iran's president Hassan Rouhani and foreign minister Javad Zarif voiced no objection to a statement issued by the meeting that called for a two-state solution.[67]

The common thread running through the other scholarship on the subject, including the works of Trita Parsi and Haggai Ram (differences notwithstanding), is that the antagonism between Israel and Iran

---

[65] Hossein Amirabdollahian, 'Iranian proposal for a national referendum in the territory of Palestine', *Voltairenet.org*, 1 November 2019.

[66] For an overview see Michal Ben-Josef Hirsch, 'From taboo to the negotiable: the Israeli new historians and the changing representation of the Palestinian refugee problem', *Perspective on Politics*, Vol. 5, No. 2 (June 2007), pp. 241–258.

[67] Khaled Hroub, 'When blackmail becomes policy: for "Palestinian peace process" read "Iran war process"', *Qantara.de*, 13 May 2019.

can be mitigated.[68] The mistake is to fall into the trap of the 'global right wing', which I defined as a particularly patronising, angry, paternalistic, macho approach to politics in terms of strict boundaries between enemy and friend, self and other, which explains the title of this chapter and its reference to a 'global right wing'. For the Iranian right wing, demonising Israel is a straightforward weapon to subdue reform, diplomacy, democratisation. For the extremists in Israel, likening Iran to evil is a convenient tool to legitimate further suppression of Palestinian rights. In line with the 'post-national methodology' of this study, taking the Israeli–Iranian–Palestinian triangle out of this 'fake' habitat opens up a post-national tapestry that connects rather than divides, and it is within this truer context that the Israeli–Iranian conundrum appears resolvable and less charged. More recently, an excellent study by Lior Sternfeld demonstrates this rich dialectic and the shifting reaction in Iran to the question of Zionism, both in its political and religious manifestations, from the early twentieth century onwards. Sternfeld also shows how revolutionary Jewish organisations contributed to the success of the Iranian revolution of 1979, embedding this Jewish Iran even more firmly within a common narrative.[69]

So there is an emergent field dotted with post-nationalist ideas that could feed into an inclusive security architecture in the region which would address Israeli and Iranian concerns. One way of achieving this would be to offer Iran a non-aggression pact in return for a proactive role in Israeli–Palestinian peace negotiations, an improbable prospect largely because of the uncompromising stance of Israeli politicians such as Netanyahu who have deprived the national narrative in Israel of compromise and dialogue. As Yaacov Yadgar argued about Israel's identity politics in this book series: 'The Right's 'nationalisation' of Judaism/Jewishness tends to follow in recent decades the ideological drumbeat of religious Zionism.' This hold of the right wing on what it means to be Israeli and Jewish has serious consequences for the ability of the country to offer an alternative to the militarised foreign policy

---

[68] See Trita Parsi, *Treacherous Alliance: The Secret Dealings of Israel, Iran, and the United States*, London: Yale University Press, 2008; Haggai Ram, *Iranophobia: The Logic of an Israeli Obsession*, London: Stanford University Press, 2019.

[69] Lior B. Sternfeld, *Between Iran and Zion: Jewish Histories of Twentieth Century Iran*, Stanford: Stanford University Press, 2019.

prescribed by Netanyahu and others.[70] This idea of Israel negates hybridity and seriously minimises the 'Israeli self' to a gentrified territory that denies the rights of many 'others' including Israeli minorities.

To conclude with our musical piece and the genre that Hichkas represents, there is a narratological 'battle rap' at play whenever Iran and Israel engage each other which is reminiscent of the movie *8 Mile* starring the US rapper Eminem. In the movie the main protagonist engages in such battles of words where two rival MCs freestyle their rap on the same stage to find out who has the better verses. Despite the stringent efforts by the Israeli and Iranian states, or let's say MC Netanyahu and MC Khamenei, to treat the other side as an existential enemy with such recurrent wars of words, the two ideas remain intimately entangled. In the Iranian context this uneasy closeness is resolved by accentuating the ideological core of Israel as an idea and political reality: hence, the ad nauseam emphasis on the 'Zionist entity/regime'. In the official discourse of the Islamic Republic, even using the term Israel seems impossible. Israel has religious connotations, in a way that Zionism does not, at least from the perspective of Iranian officials and their underlying ideational persuasions. In this way, the 'Zionist regime' can be demonised in a way that 'Israel' cannot be. Using the term 'Zionist regime', then, is not only a straightforward challenge to the sovereignty of the Israeli state, but a rhetorical device to accommodate enmity towards it.

It takes two to battle-rap. From the Israeli perspective this uneasy if intimate war of words is resolved in a comparable way by emphasising the 'evil' nature of the Islamic Republic without any wholesale condemnation of Iranian-ness. Israeli discourse sometimes lapses into overt racism towards 'Arabs' in a way that it doesn't with reference to Iran. Such invented redefinitions of the 'other' along artificial political lines, rather than in light of historical truths, is an ideological device that makes the competition between Israel and Iran possible rhetorically, and by extension strategically. In this way, it is revealed that the competition is indeed political, geostrategic and without ideational depth. Unravelling this uneasy battle rap along those narratives, then, reveals that the ideas of Israel and Iran are historically intertwined. Peace becomes possible once this inevitable interdependence is accepted and turned into a politics of engagement. As a deeper analysis

---

[70] Yadgar, *Israel's Jewish Identity Crisis*.

of the battle rap demonstrates, the condemnation of the 'other' drives the rival MC into a defensive mode, thereby limiting the understanding of both self and other, and the enjoyment and serenity of the embrace that such an appreciation would bring about. What is provoked is an equally vociferous rap by the opposite side until one of the MCs steps down from the stage.

Let's bring all of this back to the current historical juncture. As long as the battle rap continues with such venom, the so-called resistance axis will continue to attract an audience. Rami Khoury, a reasonable voice for decades now, argues in a similar vein from Beirut, when he writes that the 'self-proclaimed "resistance axis" ethos is to defy foreign threats and refuse to bow to American [*sic*] and Israeli demands, even at the cost of war or debilitating sanctions'. Yet, he rightly adds that 'Iran's nuclear deal with the US, UK, Germany, France, China and Russia, and Hezbollah's indirect agreements and ceasefires with Israel show the resistance powers' willingness to engage their foes politically, but only based on equal respect for the rights of all sides.'[71]

Another unexplored avenue would be to establish a WMD-free zone in the region under the auspices of the United Nations, but that would require doing away with the nuclear hypocrisy that allows Israel to retain its arsenal without international supervision. The case for peace and reconciliation is there; what is missing is the political will to implement it. For that to happen, the us-versus-them mentality of the right wing has to be discarded. What we need is a philosophy of commonality, secular in approach, but appreciative of the ideational composition of this unique area of the world also in religious terms. Such a strong political culture, which is entirely possible and realisable because it is based on true bonds, promises to do away with the perils and false hopes of right-wing policies and their inhumane repercussions – that much is certain and that much is supported by a critical approach to Iran, Israel and the United States.[72]

---

[71] Rami G. Khoury, 'The battle of "resistance" versus "revolution" in the Middle East', *Al Jazeera*, 15 January 2020.

[72] See further Emanuel Stoakes, 'War on Iran: America's next catastrophe in the Middle East. An interview with academic and author Dr Arshin Adib-Moghaddam on the consequences of a future war with Iran', *Truthout*, 13 April 2012, available at https://truthout.org/articles/war-on-iran-americas-next-catastrophe-in-the-middle-east/, accessed 1 May 2012.

5 | *Eurasian Iran: 'Resistance' or a Persian Empire?*

Musical Piece:

'MOQAWEM'
(Resistance)
By: Julia Boutros (1968–)
Release Date: 2017

Adaptive (free) translation of lyrics:
Your glory was taint with humiliation and defeat
When the south stood up to resist.
The history of dignity is wide awake.
It's writing in our land stories of triumphs.

Your glory was taint with humiliation and defeat
When the south stood up to resist.
The history of dignity is wide awake.

I'm the definition of Will when the word is employed.
My sword hails your fall in every battle.
Every single soul in my nation embraces resistance.
Won't settle for less than glory.

Never bowed to humiliation, never bargained.
We triumphed despite your aggression.
Let the whole free world see,
How glory is made in nations.

Your glory was taint with humiliation and defeat
When the south stood up to resist.
The history of dignity is wide awake.
It's writing in our land stories of triumphs.

Arab Iran: Between Beirut and Riyadh

So far the present book has demonstrated how the meaning of Iran is engineered for ideological and psycho-nationalist purposes by influential stakeholders in the question 'what is Iran?'. These protagonists come from different directions and they include sections of the Iranian state itself, for instance the Iranian neo-conservatives as Anoushiravan Ehteshami and Mahjoob Zweiri rightly called them, and/or other right-wing movements.[1] Their common purpose is to engineer an image of Iran that is amenable to their political agenda.

This process of wilful distortion has not so much to do with a truer depiction of the country, even in terms of analysis that would be useful for proper policy decisions or governance, as many young US Americans, British, Iranians, Iraqis, Syrians, Afghans etc. have lost their lives for no good reason. Rather, it is meant to distract us from the real meaning of Iran which cannot be captured in grand narratives such as Islam, Shia, Persian etc. The truth of the country is lived by its people on a daily basis, by the teachers who go to work under dire financial circumstances, businessmen who have made a fortune in the reconstruction years, nurses and doctors who have put their lives at risk during Covid-19, youth activists who continue to be inspired by the siren song of freedom underlying the revolution of 1979 or Iranian women who resist the particularly drastic restrictions in the public sphere. This reality of Iran can only be seen and lived and it can't be defined by, or captured under, big headlines or 'tweets' which dominate our thinking about the country today, in this techno-political society of ours.

The previous chapters were centred around self-perceptions of Iran and views from the outside without an explicit focus on the regional context. In this chapter, I will complement my analysis with a focus on (West) Asia and North Africa, a particularly complex area of the world, into which the Iranian narrative is so intimately interwoven. It is impossible to imagine that region without an understanding of the Iranian presence and without the indissoluble effects that it has had on Iran itself.

To the purists among Iranian psycho-nationalists who would imagine the country as one-dimensionally 'Iranian', one can immediately reply

---

[1] Anoushiravan Ehteshami and Mahjoob Zweiri, *Iran and the Rise of its Neoconservatives: The Politics of Tehran's Silent Revolution*, London: I.B. Tauris, 2007.

that for over 800 years the seat of the 'Iranian–Iraqi' empires, Parthian and Sassanid, was in Ctesiphon which is in today's Iraq. The Cyrus Cylinder, discovered in the ruins of Babylon in Mesopotamia in 1879 and written in Akkadian cuneiform, is mythologised by these purists and anti-Arab ultra-nationalists as a distinctly 'Persian' advancement in human rights, rather than an expression of an empire, in this case Achaemenid, that didn't have a restrictive notion of (psycho-) nationalism, which only developed in modernity and which has led to a 'Persian' theft of the common historical archives that bind the peoples of the region together.

Likewise, in answer to the diversionist tendencies in Arab psychonationalism, one can easily point to the Abrahamic/Muslim hybridity that connects most peoples of this area, but also to secular interdependencies that transcend the Persian–Arab dichotomy that they have tried to uphold. Even a selective 'geography of the dead', that is a short itinerary of personalities enmeshed in the idea of Iran, transposes the country into the region and vice versa. There is a poetic latitude: the 'poet of love', Rumi, is buried in Konya, in the south central steppes of Anatolia in modern-day Turkey. There is a monarchical latitude: the tomb of the last shah of Iran, Mohammad Reza Pahlavi, is in the Al-Rifa'i Mosque in the Midan al-Qal'a, adjacent to the Cairo Citadel; the Al-Rifa'i mosque also acts as the royal mausoleum of Muhammad Ali's family and the burial place of King Farouk of Egypt. There is a clerical latitude: Grand Ayatollah Mirza Shirazi (1814–1895), the leader of the tobacco revolts of 1890, is buried in the Imam Ali Mosque in Najaf next to a range of other Grand Ayatollahs. And there is a 'republican' latitude: Ali Shariati was buried in Damascus, very close to the Sayyida Zaynab mosque in a ceremony (1977) that was led by the prominent Lebanese-Iranian cleric Musa al-Sadr, and attended by Mostafa Chamran and Ebrahim Yazdi, the first Iranian Provisional Revolutionary Government's defence and foreign ministers, respectively.

The musical piece that I have chosen for this chapter in order to illuminate this trans-spatial connectivity may seem controversial, especially to many readers in the United States and Israel, as it is an Arabic song titled 'Moqawem' praising the 'resistance' of Hezbollah against successive invasions of southern Lebanon by the Israeli Defence Forces (IDF).[2] It is performed by the Lebanese, Maronite-Christian singer

---

[2] Julia Boutros, 'Moqawem', 2017.

Julia Boutros whose husband is the current minister of defence and advisor to the Lebanese President Michel Aoun, himself an ally of Hezbollah.

The song that Boutros performs with great conviction and a powerful voice in her many live concerts shares a similarly dramatic drumbeat with some of the other musical pieces that I have chosen for this book. When she praises these 'holy warriors' for their 'dignity' when 'the south stood up to resist', Boutros uses similar idioms, imagery and symbols to those of the Iranian singers in order to convey an essentially ideological message, compounded by the beauty and charisma of her voice. Music as cultural translation functions here in a less antagonistic way despite politically emotive lyrics such as 'Every single soul in my nation embraces resistance. Won't settle for less than glory ... We triumphed despite your aggression ... You as you said are men of God on the battlefield.' What is important here is that Boutros conveys the sentiments of many Lebanese irrespective of their confessional background, which puts the political presence of Hezbollah and the contested alliance with Iran into a better context of the realities of the region and some of the perceptions permeating it. Many other Lebanese despise everything that the Islamic Republic stands for, of course. And their voice is amplified so that it overwhelms the other side that is sanctioned, marginalised, demonised and largely viewed as a temporary 'aberration'. A critical analysis must be nestled in the tensions that open up between these two attitudes vis-à-vis contemporary Iran, and this is something I will try to continue to pursue in this chapter.

The song is analytically useful to show, in particular to readers beyond the region, that there is a cultural constellation that binds separate actors together around a common cause, in this case the so-called resistance of Hezbollah supported by Iran, Hamas, Islamic Jihad, various Iraqi paramilitary units, Ba'athist Syria, Ansarallah in Yemen and others, against both Israeli ambitions and US foreign policies. This resembles a semiotic system, a regime of truth, or what I call a 'cognitology', which creates its own truth conditions with powerful psycho-political consequences on a continuous basis. Within this cognitological constellation, an Iran appears that is not considered to be alien, anti-Sunni or even anti-Arab. Iran is seen as a country that supports a common cause, an alliance against hegemony for many – which transpires into a quest for a new 'Persian empire', and against secular democracy, for others. The former is not the only depiction of the country, of course, but it is one that is repeatedly misunderstood. Therefore, it merits attention in this book.

Here, I did not choose this song of Boutros to make a point about its praise of the fighters of the so-called Party of God (Hezbollah). Once one steps out of the common narrative that this musical piece speaks to, Iran is perceived as a distinctly divisive actor in Lebanon and beyond, as I indicated throughout these pages. An identity revolution that created a state based on an interpretation of 'Islam' has its own limitations and contradictions that are unfolding themselves on a daily basis. But it will become clearer along the way that I will argue against the vogue to analyse the region in terms of 'sectarianism', less so in its scholarly manifestation which yields some useful insights as the urban-anthropological study of Joanna Randa Nucho shows, but much more in terms of its political appearance as a policy to externalise Iran as the ultimate 'other'.[3]

As such, it must be important to my discussion to indicate that this emotive alliance between Iran and Hezbollah goes beyond sectarian motives, that Hezbollah and Iran are fighting for what they consider to be a common strategic goal, that is to secure the southern border of Lebanon and to further Palestinian ambitions of statehood in support of Palestinian movements such as Hamas and Islamic Jihad, which is one of the many focal points of Amal Saad's impressive, fieldwork-driven scholarship about Hezbollah and its relationship with Iran and other like-minded actors in the region.[4] There seems to be quite an intimately interactive political and popular culture that carries this constellation into the mainstream.[5] As my colleague at SOAS, Dina Matar, together with Atef Alshaer and Lina Khatib correctly argue: 'Hizbollah has used culture and language as a dialectical relationship between system and practice,' using different public sites to

---

[3] See Joanna Randa Nucho, *Everyday Sectarianism in Urban Lebanon: Infrastructures, Public Services, and Power*, Princeton: Princeton University Press, 2016. On sectarianism see among others Toby Matthiesen, *The Other Saudis: Shiism, DIssent and Sectarianism*, Cambridge: Cambridge University Press, 2014; and Nader Hashemi and Danny Postel (eds.), *Sectarianization: Mapping the New Politics of the Middle East*, Oxford: Oxford University Press, 2017.

[4] See more recently Amal Saad, 'Challenging the sponsor-proxy model: the Iran–Hizbullah relationship', *Global Discourse*, Vol. 9, No. 4 (2019), pp. 627–650.

[5] On Iran and Lebanon see further Houchang E. Chehabi, *Distant Relations: Iran and Lebanon in the Last 500 Years*, London: I.B. Tauris, 2006.

communicate their message.[6] 'This type of branding has been helped by the charismatic authority and popularity of its leader Hassan Nasrallah, who tailors his speeches to appeal to different audiences within and outside Lebanon, while emphasising anti-sectarian rhetoric.'[7]

Ready to be unearthed, there is in this region an indissoluble Arab–Iranian (Turkish–Jewish–Kurdish etc.) dialectic, that is in many ways closer than anything that binds, for instance, Spain and Germany together before the idea of the European Community was engineered after the Second World War. There are common religious bonds, Islam, but also Judaism, Zoroastrianism and Christianity. There is a comparable 'ethnic' genealogy, a transnational Kurdish landscape, an Arabic alphabet and names such as Azin (the name of my sister), Hafiz, Maryam, Ibrahim, Mahmoud, Soraya, Shahin, Mohammad, Hossein and Ali, the common colonial experience, food culture, dance style and musical taste.

The politics of difference that has lent itself to analytically false notions of unbridgeable dichotomies between Persian and Arab, Sunni and Shia are political inventions, and nothing more, even in the Israeli–Iranian context as the last chapter showed. Beware: any individual who believes in such spatialisation based on 'identity' is either ideologically motivated or simply uneducated. The EU which happened between historically warring nations is the best contemporary example to demonstrate how such differences can be mitigated in support of peace.

To think in a direction of post-national politics requires this starting point: in the lived reality of the peoples of the region and beyond, national narratives are never immutable; they are impure, creolised phenomena, porous and polluted spaces that are open to interpretive manipulation. In order to govern that reality, psycho-nationalisms are socially engineered to simulate uniformity and positive distinction from the 'other'. In this sense, psycho-nationalism is a border-creating device, it is meant to create 'iron walls' staffed by intolerant gatekeepers. In its extremist manifestation psycho-nationalism provokes distinctly fascist politics. In Apartheid South Africa and in Israel among the right wing, it has informed policies of separation and oppression.

---

[6] Lina Khatib, Dina Matar and Atef Alshaer (eds.), *The Hizbullah Phenomenon: Politics and Communication*, London: Hurst, 2014, p. 8.

[7] Ibid., pp. 10–11.

This dangerous resurgence of the politics of identity is a global scourge. With reference to West Asia and North Africa, a quick perusal of current headlines such as 'ISIL massacres Shia in Iraq', 'Iran wants to Persianise the Arab world', 'Sunni extremist blows up Shia mosque in Kuwait' convey the impression that sectarian violence sparked by tempestuous ideologies is at the root of the region's conflicts. Identity is presented here as something primordial and seemingly monolithic, rather than invented and entirely permeable. Most of this journalism and analysis is simplistic and plainly wrong. Ultimately, it serves an age-old 'divide-and-rule' imperialism, that serves the interests of non-regional states.

The idea that Iran could be, or indeed is, interested in what King Abdullah of Jordan famously called 'A Shia crescent' in 2007 is as erroneous as the claim that movements such as Hezbollah, the 'Houthis' in Yemen, al-Wefaq in Bahrain or the Popular Mobilisation Forces of Iraq (Al-Hashd al-Sha'abi) are pawns in the hands of the Iranian state. Undoubtedly, there is an imperial impulse in some of Iran's foreign relations, a sense of Persian grandeur that is an ingredient in the psycho-nationalism of the modern Iranian state before and after the revolution. But the Iranian state is simply not in a position to dominate a region in which there are several other poles of power such as Turkey, Saudi Arabia, Iraq, Egypt and Israel. Comparable to the strategic theatre of South America where there is an inherent balance of power between different actors, the greater West Asian area, too, displays that inbuilt power balance.[8]

The primary material surveyed for this study speaks to this Iranian push for influence and control (and this holds true for Iranian foreign policies before and after the revolution of 1979). The rather more recent developments are a result of the US invasion of Iraq in 2003, which gave Iran the historic opportunity to bolster new political allies in Baghdad after the demise of Saddam Hussein and his brand of Ba'athism. Iran took full advantage of the new constellation, with two strategic aims in mind: to subdue so-called Islamic State (Daesh) and/or al-Qaeda to gain a foothold in Iraq and to prevent another 'Saddam Hussein phenomenon' in the region, as a broader strategy to ensure that Iran confronts challengers before they reach the Iranian borders.

---

[8] See further Anoushiravan Ehteshami, *Dynamics of Change in the Persian Gulf: Political Economy and Revolution,* London: Routledge, 2013, pp. 35ff.

After all, such movements were the first to directly target Iran's territorial integrity and the sovereignty of the state. As such, in January 2015, Daesh furthered the idea of 'Wilayat Khorasan' and 'Wilayat Arabistan' among other claims to Iranian territory, the former referring to the eastern provinces bordering Afghanistan, and the latter to the Iranian Khuzestan province which was also claimed by Saddam Hussein as a 'natural' part of the Arab world. Furthermore, on 7 June 2017, Daesh claimed responsibility for an attack on the Iranian parliament and the mausoleum of Ayatollah Khomeini in Qom, which left sixteen dead. For the Iranian state, then, engaging Daesh and its allies where they operated, that is in Syria and Iraq, and to a lesser extent along the Afghan–Pakistani border must have made strategic sense.

However, this expansion of Iranian activities has caused several dilemmas for the region and for Iran itself, because the newly emerging regional order has been baptised in blood, terror and trauma: The movements closely enmeshed in the 'resistance' narrative to which the musical piece of this chapter speaks, have been born within a distinctly violent context. The Iraqi Munazzama Badr (Badr Organisation) currently headed by Hadi Al-Amiri is a good example. The successor movement to the Badr Brigade emerged out of the Supreme Council for Islamic Revolution created in revolutionary Iran in 1982, that is during the terror of Saddam Hussein´s invasion of the country and his suppression of pro-Iranian movements in Iraq itself. The Badr organisation absorbed the tragedies of the devastating Iran–Iraq War as it fought alongside Iranian troops. Later on it continued as a military unit, during the devastating battles against Saddam Hussein's regime after Operation Desert Storm in 1991 and after the second US war against Iraq in 2003.

Hezbollah followed a similar trajectory. Established as a fighting unit in southern Lebanon shortly after the revolution in Iran, Hezbollah was baptised in blood during several military campaigns with Israel, as the song of Boutros captures so emotively. Hamas and Islamic Jihad in Palestine have been other members of the so-called *muqawama* axis that has been so patently affected by war, destruction and death.

The latest additions to this alliance that have been active in Syria, in particular in battles to safeguard the Sayyidah Zaynab Mosque in the southern suburbs of Damascus and in the fight against so-called ISIS with which Soleimani was so deeply involved, were also created as military/security organisations within a traumatic power-resistance dialectic. The Liwa Fatemiyoun (Fatimid banner), formed in 2014 primarily out of Afghan-Shia fighters; the Liwa Abu al-Fadhal al-Abbas formed in 2012 and staffed by Syrian- and Iraqi-Shia fighters; and the Liwa Zainebiyoun (Followers of Zainab Brigade) composed primarily of Shia from Pakistan – all of these movements, tied into the 'resistance narrative', as well as their nominal 'sponsor', the IRGC, absorbed trauma, death and destruction.

This history steeped in memories of violence and tragedy, makes it that much more difficult to turn such movements into organisations that operate in a politically benign or agonistic way. They are hence distinctly different compared to other 'Islamist' organisations such as Tunisia's Ennahda (Renaissance) party which aided and abetted the Tunisian democracy after the Arab Spring rather comfortably, because Ennahda never pursued a militant rationale and a 'guerrilla war' approach, which always also creates a garrison state mentality that is detrimental to democracy and peace. The resistance axis is a repository of the deadly struggles that this region of the world has had to endure for decades, now. As such, it can only stand for militarised resistance, rather than for democratic empowerment, at least at this violent juncture of the region's history.

Even long-standing political actors such as Hezbollah's 'Loyalty to the Resistance Bloc' which sits in the Lebanese parliament, have proven to be more comfortable with their 'brothers in arms', as states within states, and a clear challenge to the sovereignty of competing political institutions. The political establishment in Lebanon has to grapple with this institutionally abject situation, that there is a movement with a powerful army that repeatedly operates beyond the sovereignty of the elected institutions of the state. In Iraq, similar 'deep-state' outfits, such as the Popular Mobilisation Forces supported by Iran, pose a comparable dilemma, as they are not easily absorbed into the idea of inclusivity and pluralism in Iraq. And in Iran as well, the IRGC has repeatedly operated beyond government control, certainly as a challenge to the office of the presidency.

This situation is likely to affect the future of Syria, too, and it will continue to exacerbate suspicion towards Iran, as a sectarian or hegemonic force in the region and beyond. This essentially political problem cannot be resolved by these movements, precisely because they are infused with a military rationale. The *muqawama* narrative, then, was born in anarchy, within an environment of terror and destruction. The institutions that sustainin this 'resistance axis' are hard put to speak the language of peace, or to function in accordance with the demands of an increasingly vocal civil society throughout West Asia and North Africa, which explains the repeated demonstrations against 'sectarianism' and 'militancy' which are also directed against some of these actors and their policies.

The previous paragraphs explain why such advances into the Arab state system within a period of intense violence and destruction are perceived to make the Iranian state complicit in the tragedies of the Syrian, Yemeni and Iraqi populations. In addition, it tells us why Iran's geopolitical expansion along the narrative plane of the resistance axis has had its own backlash, most recently in the latter part of 2019, when massive demonstrations flared up in Beirut and Iraqi towns including the Shia centres of Najaf and Karbala, partially also directed against undue Iranian influence in Iraqi affairs. At the same time the ambitions of the Iranian state are tempered by the geopolitical balance of power, as indicated, and an influential strand in current Iranian foreign policy that accentuates diplomatic engagement and 'soft power' (i.e. *dawat* and *tabligh*) over military confrontation. Iran wants power, like any other state in the international system, but the ideas that inform how this power would be used are unrelated to a coherent doctrine of neo-imperialist expansion. The Iranian defence budget, for instance, is one of the lowest in the region, and the country's military forces have a defensive posture.[9] As a well-disposed foreign policy analyst in Iran correctly argues:

The debate about the emergence of a Shiite crescent has three dimensions: (1) it is an attempt by Iran to mobilize the masses, (2) it is an attempt by Iran to build an ideological belt of friendly Shiite governments, and (3) it is an attempt by Iran to expand its regional power ... Iran's aims are more defensive and pragmatic than expansionist. It is not attempting to become the only regional power through empowering the friendly Shiite factions in the region. Iran's aims are primarily oriented at building a secure environment at its immediate borders on the one hand and creating economic opportunities for strategic purposes on the other.[10]

---

[9] See 'Iran – Military Spending', *Globalsecurity.org*, available at www.globalsecurity .org/military/world/iran/budget.htm, accessed 11 September 2019.
[10] Kayhan Barzegar, 'Iran and the Shiite Crescent: Myths and Realities', *Brown Journal of World Affairs*, Vol. 15, No. 1 (2008), p. 97.

At the core of this argument, one has to place a rather more substantial point than mere geostrategic interests. Any interest of the state is informed by inventions of 'state identity' and the foreign policy culture translating it into policies. So interests do not emerge in a vacuum and mere references to power politics do not tell us much about how this power would be used, i.e. to what strategic ends. The strategic preferences of Iran, as demonstrated in the previous chapters, continue to be informed by some of the ideals of the revolution. At the root, of these preferences or 'state interests' is a very particular obsession with the region, almost a sense of entitlement to forge a new order in West Asia and North Africa that is amenable to the security concerns of the Iranian state and its aforementioned foreign policy culture which always also include references to Palestine, sometimes as a convenient Trojan horse to shore up support in Arab and Muslim-majority societies and/or out of a genuine sense of injustice committed by the Israeli state. The Iranian state does not have a similar 'obsession' with Central Asia and the Southern Caucasus, despite the intimate cultural and historical links that make Iran also a distinctly Eurasian country.

A second analytical point can be discerned here which can be located in the deep structural composition of this region of the world: there is no endemic pattern of hatred between Arabs, Persians, Sunni and Shia (nor between any of these invented categories and Jews); narratives based on sectarianism are unconvincing because of their problematic ideational presuppositions. These abstract national, religious or ethnic designations are far too undifferentiated to give us any analytical clues about the behaviour of regional states and societies. Serious research reveals that none of the traumas that the people of the region are experiencing can be explained simply in terms of a continuous conflict between Shia and Sunni and/or Arab and Persian. In fact, these categories are rather modern inventions imbued with the toxic venom of psycho-nationalism.[11]

Conversely, the song of Boutros that frames this chapter disturbs binary depictions in the name of a common cause, paradoxically one that has been the source of animosity towards Iran, even among learned people in the region, in Palestine, Lebanon and Iraq, exactly because the Iranian state is not seen as a model to be ameliorated. This

---

[11] See also Anoushiravan Ehteshami and Mahjoob Zweiri (eds.), *The Changing Nature of Shia Politics in the Middle East*, London: Ithaca Press, 2015.

is where the *Schadenfreude* comes from, whenever the Iranian security forces crack down on demonstrations in Iran: it demonstrates that this is not a system of governance, that can claim leadership or that can act as a model to the majority of the peoples of this region who are tired of ideology, and who are far more concerned with their livelihoods, human security and economic prosperity. Moreover, overt Iranian support to problematic militias in Syria, Iraq and elsewhere, as discussed, is a powerful contemporary driver for agitation against the country along ethnic and religious lines. This does not change the fact, of course, that such attitudes are based on false notions of 'identity', which is the main premise of my argument here. Criticising the policies of the Iranian state is one thing, assuming that the people of the country are fundamentally different and 'fanatical' is quite another.

My own 'genealogy' may serve as an example of the circularity of cultures and the permeability of 'identities' in this region of the world: Whereas my mother's family connects to Karim Khan-e Zand, the Kurdish-Lur ruler of Iran between 1751 and 1779, the genealogy of my paternal family encompasses the Hejaz in today's Saudi Arabia, Najaf in southern Iraq and Maragheh in Iranian Azerbaijan, which is heavily influenced by 'Turkic' traditions. Indeed, my grandfather was born in Iraq and he spoke primarily Arabic at the ancestral home in Ahvaz in the Iranian province of Khuzestan. Thanks to the trade routes being largely unimpeded by geographical and mental boundaries, my great-grandfather spoke Turkish, Arabic and Persian on a daily basis – they were merchants at a time when modern borders didn't exist. Their multilingual and multicultural day-to-day existence negates narrow-minded notions of nationality, ethnic 'origin' or religious 'roots'. Dig deep enough, and every reader of this book will unearth a comparably diverse background in their own personal history.

But there are also rather more direct analytical reasons to ignore this primitive and uneducated approach to the region, which reduces conflicts to sects or tribes. The emotive issue of the civil war in Syria is an obvious place to start to expose the flaws in the sectarian approach. Iran supports the Assad government, the argument goes, because the core of the Syrian state is Alawite, a branch of Shiism. But there are at least three reasons why the idea that a sectarian bond explains Iranian backing for Damascus is wrong. First, scholars are well aware that the Assad dynasty did not base its ideological legitimacy on religion or a sect. Under the Assads, the ideological foundation of the Syrian state was engineered around Ba'athism, a branch of secular Arab nationalism. Indeed, as members of a minority sect, the Assads were determined to flush out any sectarian references in the official discourse of the state. Syrian children were taught about the glories of Arab history, not the legitimacy of the Alawites or some kind of Shia brotherhood. The same is true for Iraq under Saddam Hussein, the other Ba'athist leader, whose state ideology was as much non-Sunni as the Assads' has been non-Shia.[12]

Second, Syria has been for Iran a strategic ally since the Iran–Iraq War (1980–1988), when Hafiz al-Assad was the only Arab leader to support the country against the invading armies of Saddam Hussein. So common interest and not sectarian allegiance is the reason for the Syrian–Iranian alliance. The point is echoed in the rhetoric of *muqawama* that links 'Sunni-Arab' Hamas in Palestine, to 'Arab-Shia' Hezbollah in Lebanon, to 'Persian-Shia' Iran via 'Secular-Arab' Syria. This Arab–Iranian axis is quite obviously interest-based, and cannot be explained along Shia/Sunni-Persian/Arab lines. The interests are informed by an ideational superstructure of course, i.e. Iran's strategic preference settings after the revolution which have been congruent with the strategic culture of Syria under the Assads and other movements in the region and beyond. For instance, there is a strong emphasis on a multipolar world order in Iranian foreign policy discourse, which is shared by China, Russia, Cuba, Venezuela, Nicaragua, Vietnam, Bolivia and even the EU, which explains some of the cooperation between Iran and these actors. Russia and Iran in particular worked closely together in Syria to buttress their interests, and Bashir al-Assad's apparent (pyrrhic) victory over so-called ISIS/Daesh and other challengers to his rule would not have been possible without Iranian and Russian support to that end.

Third, even a Syrian state composed of 'socialist atheists' would not have caused a problem to Iranian decision-makers seeking to build a trusted alliance. For the same reason, Iran can have strong relations with socialist leaders in Cuba and Bolivia, Daniel Ortega in Nicaragua and Nicolas Maduro in Venezuela. If any ruler has a foreign policy conducive to Iran's agenda, he or she can be embraced as much as the most pious, god-loving but (essentially) pro-Iranian Shia. Conversely,

---

[12] See further Nadia von Maltzahn, *The Syria–Iran Axis: Cultural Diplomacy and International Relations in the Middle East*, London: I.B. Tauris, 2015.

if a Shia movement is opposed to the Iranian state, it will be challenged. The thousands of Iranian exiles and secular Shia groups can testify to this delineation between friend and foe: one based on its stance vis-à-vis the Iranian system, rather than a Shia or Iranian 'identity'.

A comparable logic applies to Iraq. There, Ayatollah Ali Sistani is not only a Shia but a *Marja-e taghlid*, a source of emulation constituting the highest clerical rank in the Shia hierarchy. His religious credentials outweigh even those of Iran's supreme leader, 'Ayatollah' Ali Khamenei. But Sistani adheres to the quietist tradition of the late Ayatollah al-Khoei (and Ayatollah Boroujerdi in Iran), while Khamenei is heir to Ayatollah Khomeini's doctrine of *Velayat-e faqih* which compels clerics to be political leaders and ideological prophets. There is no theological congruence between them or their followers. They tolerate each other, but they operate at different ends of the Shia political spectrum.[13]

Similar dynamics operate in other realms of Iraqi politics. Iranian clerics and their Iraqi Shia counterparts organised around Moqtada al-Sadr could not agree, but for the opposite reason – i.e. because for a long time Sadr was not someone that Iran favoured although he had studied in Iran's clerical 'Vatican', Qom. Moqtada al-Sadr is the son-in-law of Ayatollah Muhammad Baqir al-Sadr, who was one of the main Iraqi supporters of Khomeini and his *Velayat-e faqih* paradigm (leadership of the Supreme Jurisprudent). A *Marja-e taghlid* (Source of Emulation) in his own right, Muhammad Baqir al-Sadr and his sister Bint al-Huda were killed on the orders of Saddam Hussein, a few months before Hussein invaded Iran in September 1980. Today, a main expressway in Tehran is named after Muhammad Baqir al-Sadr.

In Lebanon, Hezbollah is in Iran's foreign policy orbit not because they are Shia but on account of the movement's allegiance to Khomeinism, even if it has turned into a decisively national movement dedicated to changing the politics of Lebanon.[14] The late cosmopolitan superstar of Lebanese Shiism, Musa al-Sadr (who was 'Iranian'), would have been seen in a very different light by today's leaders in Tehran compared to the combatant Hassan Nasrallah (who is

---

[13] See further Adib-Moghaddam (ed.), *A Critical Introduction to Khomeini*.

[14] For comprehensive, recent studies see Aurelie Daher, *Hezbollah: Mobilisation and Power*, Oxford: Oxford University Press, 2019; and Adham Saouli, *Socialisation and Its Tragic Ironies*, Edinburgh: Edinburgh University Press, 2019.

'Arab-Lebanese'). Again, the issue is not Sunni versus Shia or Arab versus Persian, but shared geostrategic preferences. In the case of Iraq and Lebanon, these interests are defined by creating a common front against Israel; in the case of the Iraqi state by finding reliable allies in the fight against Daesh (or ISIL/'Islamic State') and to stabilise the central government against disintegration of the Iraqi nation-state (which also implies preventing an independent Kurdistan on Iraqi territory).

The clerical lines of 'descent' and 'origin' are further blurred in political terms by the fact that the most important source of emulation in modern Iraq, Ayatollah Khoi, was 'Iranian'. Yet as indicated he was apolitical, following the quietist tradition in Shia theology, rather then the doctrine of Ayatollah Khomeini. Conversely, Mohammad Sadiq al-Sadr, the father of Muqtada al-Sadr, was born in Iraq, yet he was sympathetic to the revolution in Iran and supported Ayatollah Khamenei after he became the Supreme Leader in 1989. The late Ayatollah Muhammad Baqir al-Hakim was also nominally Iraqi. Yet, he created the Supreme Council of the Revolution in Iraq (SCIRI) and its military wing the Badr Brigade when he was in exile in neighbouring Iran, and modelled the movement after the Iranian blueprint. A main express highway running through central Tehran is named after him.

In the opposite direction, Ayatollah Mahmoud Shahroudi, who was born in Najaf and created the Dawa party in Iraq, became a powerful politician in Iran. As every aspiring Shia scholar must go through the Hawza system in Najaf, Ali Khomeini, who is the grandson of Ayatollah Khomeini, is currently studying in the Iraqi seminaries. Furthermore, the official representative of Ayatollah Sistani in Iran is Jawad Shahristani who is also his son-in-law. This is important for our analysis because the daughter of Shahristani is married to the son of the current Iranian Supreme Leader Ayatollah Khamenei. This is nothing but an intimately connected and integrated clerical social class, that is distinctly transnational.

More recently, this transnational interdependence was discernible from the mourning ceremonies for the Iranian General Soleimani and the Iraqi commander of the Hezbollah Brigades Abu Mahdi al-Muhandis, who were killed by a US drone strike in January 2020, as discussed. All the major clerics and political figures in Iran and Iraq were either directly present or sent their condolences to both families.

The ceremonies for their deaths encompassed both Iranian and Iraqi towns, in an obvious attempt to further a common Iraqi–Iranian historical space. The list of intimate interdependencies goes on and on and it negates the simplistic accounts framed in terms of Arab versus Persian (or Shia versus Sunni).

Yemen is another example for that facile analysis, as my distinguished SOAS colleague Gabriele vom Bruck demonstrates in her comprehensive research about the country.[15] The Zaydi *Ansarallah* (or 'Houthis') may have overlapping Shia beliefs with Iran, which is a majority Twelver Shia country, but this far from explains the link between the two which is rooted in a common strategic vision that is shared by Hezbollah, the Iranian state, Syria and dominant factions in Iraq. In a rare interview, the leader of *Ansarallah*, Sayyid Abdul-Malik Badreddin al-Houthi, made this connection clear:

Our position and announcement about our readiness to send fighters to engage in any Israeli war against Lebanon and Palestine is a responsible, serious and honest position and a position that comes from our principles. This is also a very natural position ... Had our country been geographically located directly on the borders with Lebanon or Palestine, we would have not hesitated to participate in the fighting alongside the Lebanese or Palestinian Resistance. Our Yemeni people are very well engaged in the causes of their nation and fully aware of the Israeli threat against the entire nation. Inshallah, the circumstances will help them to play a large part in supporting and assisting their brothers in the nation ... We believe that the responsible and natural position ... is for everyone to come together and to cooperate. We believe that the Islamic unity and brotherhood constitute an Islamic duty. The right situation is for all the populations of our nations to be brothers and to cooperate thus achieving their real interests ... Hezbollah [is the party of] the brothers who obtained the honour of liberation and who raised the nation's flag in the face of the American hegemony. They took an honest stand by the side of the Palestinian people at one of the most important and most dangerous phases. This is the reason why some sides are so hostile to them.[16]

The ongoing Saudi-led military intervention in Yemen which started in 2015 has less to do with the danger of an expanding Persian empire, and much more with the threat of a Yemeni government independent

---

[15] See Gabriele vom Bruck, *Islam, Memory and Morality in Yemen: Ruling Families in Transition*, London: Palgrave, 2005.

[16] *Mideastwire*, 27 March 2018, available at https://mideastwire.com/page/articleFree.php?id=6633327, accessed 12 January 2019.

of Saudi patronage and aligned to a common regional strategy with Iran that would disturb the status quo ante, including in Palestine. In the intra-Arab 'cold war' of the 1960s, a similar factor compelled King Saud to intervene in Yemen (then under British leadership) in order to thwart the influence of Nassir's powerful pan-Arab nationalism. In Oman in the same period, the shah of Iran – equally opposed to the ambitions of Egypt's leader – sent troops to quell a Marxist rebellion in the country's Dhofar region (1972–1975) in order to preserve the status quo.[17] King Saud and the shah, 'objective' allies against Nasserism, were following their own interests and not any sectarian motif. Then and now, the interests of states or non-state movements override sectarian allegiances: If it were otherwise, Saudi Arabia ('Hanbali-Sunni-Wahhabi') would be allied to al-Qaeda, and Iran ('Persian-Twelver Shia') would not support Armenia ('Christian-Orthodox') in its conflict with Azerbaijan ('Shia-Muslim' majority). Creating difference is a psycho-national strategy – in reality the peoples in this area of the world and indeed around the world are far more connected than some politicians allow them to accept.

The Cold War between Iran and Saudi Arabia

Overarching the myth of an endemic Persian–Arab, Sunni–Shia conflict is the so-called cold war between Saudi Arabia and Iran which flares up every now and then, for instance after the execution of the Shia cleric Sheikh Nimr al-Nimr in Saudi Arabia in January 2016 which triggered a predictable diplomatic crisis.[18] Iran immediately condemned the move, the Saudi embassy in Tehran was attacked by angry demonstrators, the Tehran City Council named a street after him, and Saudi Arabia then severed diplomatic ties with the country. Almost immediately, Bahrain, Sudan and the UAE followed suit. Yet despite the war of words, it is important to remember that this crisis is merely a microcosm of a wider geostrategic chess game between Saudi Arabia and Iran. Saudi Arabia must have known that the execution of a senior Shia cleric would exacerbate existing grievances, especially with Iran.

---

[17] See further James F. Goode, 'Assisting our brothers, defending ourselves: the Iranian intervention in Oman, 1972–1975', *Iranian Studies*, Vol. 47, No. 3 (2014), pp. 441–462.

[18] See Dilip Hiro, *Cold War in the Islamic World: Saudi Arabia, Iran and the Struggle for Supremacy*, Oxford: Oxford University Press, 2019.

After all, both countries claim leadership within the region and beyond. But the truth is that these new developments are more about cognitological manipulation than some kind of primordial battle between Sunni and Shia.

Historically, Iran and Saudi Arabia have generally had cordial relations, precisely because both recognise and act in accordance with their national interests – the two countries are not ideologically blinded, and have tended to be driven by their own interests rather than emotion. For example, Saudi Arabia vehemently opposes the Muslim Brotherhood, ostensibly one of the biggest 'Sunni' political organisations in the Arab world. Iranian leaders, meanwhile, rarely talk about Shia supremacy because, as a minority in the Muslim world, such a strategy would limit the country's foreign policy options.[19]

Still, the US invasion of Iraq in 2003 fundamentally changed the view from Saudi Arabia, because for the first time in modern history, Iran began to cultivate friendly relations with Baghdad. Immediately, King Abdullah of Jordan admitted his 'real problem with certain Iranian factions' political influence inside Iraq'. For him, 'Iraq [was] the battleground, the West against Iran.'[20] A similar statement was made by Prince Saud al-Faisal in 2005. According to him, 'Iraq was effectively handed over to Iran', which provoked the then Iraqi interior minister Bayan Jabr to call him a 'Bedouin on a camel', depicting the al-Saud family as 'tyrants who think they are king and God'.[21]

Similar views on Iran were expressed during this period after the Iraq War in 2003 by Ehud Olmert, members of the Bush administration, Hosni Mubarak, Ayman al-Zawahiri, Osama bin Laden and others with political constituencies in the region and beyond.[22] Indeed, suspicion about Iranian designs has motivated

---

[19] See further Mohammad Soltaninejad, 'Iran and Saudi Arabia: emotionally constructed identities and the question of persistent tensions', *Asian Politics and Policy*, Vol. 11, No. 1 (2019), pp. 104–121.

[20] 'King Abdullah II, "Iraq is the battleground – the West against Iran"', *Middle East Quarterly*, Vol. 12, No. 2 (2005), available at www.meforum.org/688/king-abdullah-ii-iraq-is-the-battleground, accessed 8 November 2020.

[21] 'Iraqi minister lashes out at Saudi Arabia over rumours', *Daily Star* (Beirut), 3 October 2005.

[22] For a symbiotic view see Matein Khalid, 'Persian undercurrent in Islamic civilisation', *Khaleej Times*, 29 November 2006.

Saudi Arabia, the UAE and Bahrain to open up an implicit dialogue with Israel. Reflecting the necessity of such collusion against Iran, Ahmad al-Jarallah, editor-in-chief of the *Arab Times* wrote a strongly worded editorial supporting a Saudi dialogue with Israel during the war in Lebanon in 2006. According to him,

> this attitude of Saudi Arabia, which has been doing all it can to protect the Arab world from Israeli aggression, is enough to unmask the adventurers, who have violated the rights of their own countries and tried put their people under the guardianship of foreign countries like Iran and Syria. A battle between supporters and opponents of these adventurers has begun, starting from Palestine to Tehran passing through Syria and Lebanon. This war was inevitable as the Lebanese government couldn't bring Hezbollah within its authority and make it work for the interests of Lebanon. Similarly leader of the Palestinian Authority Mahmoud Abbas has been unable to rein in the Hamas Movement. Unfortunately we must admit that in such a war the only way to get rid of 'these irregular phenomena' is what Israel is doing. The operations of Israel in Gaza and Lebanon are in the interest of people of Arab countries and the international community.[23]

So 2003 was crucial, as the ill-fated US invasion of Iraq exacerbated existing grievances about Iranian alliances in the Arab world. Iran already had good relations with Syria and access to Lebanon via its strong alliance with Hezbollah. So the idea of an axis connecting Tehran and Baghdad in the Persian Gulf to Damascus and Beirut in the Levant would likely have been seen as unacceptable to Saudi Arabia. Compounding current Saudi frustrations is the fact that its military intervention against the Ansarallah movement has failed to bring about any serious, long-term gains, while its announcement of an Islamic Military Counter Terrorism Coalition – another effort to marginalise Iran – fell flat.

Moreover, at the time of writing, the Saudi crown prince, Muhammad Bin Salman, has picked up two prominent depictions of Iran that this study already carved out. The first is the analogy to Hitler that I dissected in the previous chapter:

> I believe that the Iranian supreme leader makes Hitler look good ... Hitler didn't do what the supreme leader is trying to do. Hitler tried to conquer Europe. This is bad ... But the supreme leader is trying to conquer the world.

---

[23] Ahmad al-Jarallah, 'No to Syria, Iran agents', *Arab Times*, 17 July 2006.

He believes he owns the world. They are both evil guys. He is the Hitler of the Middle East. In the 1920s and 1930s, no one saw Hitler as a danger. Only a few people. Until it happened.[24]

In another interview, on this occasion with the *New York Times*, the Saudi crown prince reiterated this comparison between Khamenei and Hitler: 'He wants to create his own project in the Middle East very much like Hitler, who wanted to expand at the time,' Bin Salman stated. 'Many countries around the world and in Europe did not realize how dangerous Hitler was until what happened. I don't want to see the same events happening in the Middle East.'[25]

The second theme that Bin Salman accentuated is equally prominent and links up to the narratives of the global right wing that I laid out in the previous chapter. From this perspective, Iran is represented as an irrational Juggernaut, and the leaders of the country are typically depicted as apocalyptic and partially insane. According to Bin Salman, the 'Iranian regime ... wants to spread their ... extremist Shiite ideology. They believe that if they spread it, the hidden Imam will come back again and he will rule the whole world from Iran and spread Islam even to America.'[26] This is a reference to the Twelfth Imam in Shia eschatology who is said to be hidden until Judgement Day when he would return with Jesus to create a just world order. For Bin Salman and others this cultural idea provides a ready-made propaganda tool to depict the Iranian state as genocidal.

This is not a new strategy. As early as 2005, the prominent and widely read *Washington Post* columnist Charles Krauthammer wrote the following with reference to the former Iranian president Mahmoud Ahmadinejad: 'So a Holocaust-denying, virulently anti-Semitic, aspiring genocidist, on the verge of acquiring weapons of the apocalypse ... believes that the end is not only near but nearer than the next American presidential election ... This kind of man', Krauthammer continued,

[24] Jeffrey Goldberg, 'Saudi Crown Prince: Iran's Supreme Leader "makes Hitler look good"', *The Atlantic*, 2 April 2018, available at www.theatlantic.com/international/archive/2018/04/mohammed-bin-salman-iran-israel/557036/, accessed 4 May 2019.

[25] Ben Hubbard, 'Saudi Crown Prince likens Iran's Supreme Leader to Hitler', *New York Times*, 15 March 2018, available at www.nytimes.com/2018/03/15/world/middleeast/mohammed-bin-salman-iran-hitler.html, accessed 12 February 2019.

[26] Ibid.

'would have, to put it gently, less inhibition about starting Armageddon *than a normal person.*'[27]

'There is a radical difference between the Islamic Republic of Iran and other governments with nuclear weapons,' Bernard Lewis agreed at the time. 'This difference is expressed in what can only be described as the apocalyptic worldview of Iran's present rulers ... Mr. Ahmadinejad and his followers clearly believe', Lewis emphasised, 'that the terminal struggle has already begun ... It may even have a date, indicated by several references by the Iranian president to giving his final answer to the US about nuclear development by Aug. 22 [2006] ... This year,' we were told, 'Aug. 22 corresponds, in the Islamic calendar, to the 27th day of the month of Rajab of the year 1427. This, by tradition,' Lewis claimed, 'is the night when many Muslims commemorate the night flight of the prophet Muhammad on the winged horse Buraq, first to the "farthest mosque," usually identified with Jerusalem, and then to heaven and back (cf, Koran XVII.1)'. Lewis delved even deeper into the realms of cognitological mythology when he warned that 'it would be wise to bear the possibility in mind' that 22 August 'might well be deemed an appropriate date for the apocalyptic ending of Israel and if necessary of the world'.[28] The same theme was picked up by Kenneth Timmerman: 'As the world prepares to confront an Iranian regime that continues to defy the International Atomic Energy Agency over its nuclear programs,' he warned, 'we must listen to what Iran's leaders say as we watch what they do. A religious zealot with nuclear weapons is a dangerous combination the world cannot afford to tolerate.'[29]

Krauthammer and Lewis referred to some of the statements of the former president of Iran, Mahmoud Ahmadinejad, a rather belligerent decision-maker with a limited understanding of politics and international diplomacy. Ahmadinejad made repeated references to the return of the twelfth imam (or Imam Mahdi) in order to appeal to the right wing of the Iranian political establishment, and in particular conservative clerics in Qom, the religious 'Vatican' of the country.

[27] Charles Krauthammer, 'In Iran, arming for Armageddon', *Washington Post*, 16 December 2005, emphasis added.

[28] Bernard Lewis, 'August 22: Does Iran have something in store?', *Wall Street Journal*, 8 August 2006.

[29] Kenneth R. Timmerman, 'Is Iran's Ahmadinejad a messianic medium?', *Daily Star* (Beirut), 30 December 2005.

Such millenarian talk about an impending apocalypse which would bring about a new world order has a long history in world politics, especially during times of crisis. The end of the world was proclaimed at the end of each Christian millennium. In Russia, religious zealots thought Napoleon was the Antichrist and during the Bolshevik revolution the same role was designated to Lenin. There is also a cultural element here: in Persian and Arabic references to the 'Hidden Imam' are cultural expressions that predate the establishment of the Islamic Republic.

There is a lot of psycho-nationalist venom in some of these concepts in the political jargon of the country, largely reserved to the right wing as indicated. This political language is quite comparable to the disposition of some of the extremist evangelicals in the United States and their emphasis on some future, godly ordained world order. In fact, the religious right has much in common, both in Iran and the United States. Senator Lindsey Graham may think that the leadership in Iran can be compared to the Nazis, but his righteous and arrogant religious ideology is not entirely different from the views of the Iranian right wing that he so vehemently detests.[30] For the religious right wing anywhere, psycho-nationalist pretensions about an impending new world order (under their leadership) always also cater for domestic consumption in order to shore up destructive sentiments of national pride during times of crisis. But it is one thing to use such language for the purpose of politics, it is something very different to assume that such proclamations would be translated into Armageddon.

It should not come as a surprise that there is such close affinity between the views of the right wing in the United States and Israel and the statements of Crown Prince Bin Salman. The driving force of this machinery of falsehoods is a particularly aggressive form of gunboat diplomacy, combined with propaganda, for instance to stress the importance of Saudi Arabia in the face of Iranian 'hegemony', which allows the country to gain access to US military technology. In an audacious new study, Tim Anderson rightly argues that Iran is a target, not because Iran is a 'real' threat, but because the Iranian state gives impetus to the idea of independence and opposition to US interests. It is

---

[30] Tal Kopan, 'Lindsey Graham: "There are religious Nazis running Tehran"', *CNN*, 8 September 2015, available at https://edition.cnn.com/2015/09/08/politics/lindsey-graham-iranians-nazis/index.html, accessed 3 February 2018.

this insistence on independence, according to Anderson, that turns the country into a target of hybrid warfare by its enemies which utilise propaganda offensives, economic sanctions, terrorist proxies, direct invasions and military occupations followed by repression via client states, in order to keep such resistance fragmented.[31]

Anderson's argument resembles what Alastair Crooke pointed to a decade ago: that some of the Islamist resistance is fostering a political consciousness geared to independence, which is opposed by conservative monarchies in the region and their extra-regional patrons.[32] Secular 'anti-colonialists' who resisted imperial policies in the name of national independence were similarly subdued: from Nassir in Egypt, Guevara in Latin America, Nkrumah in Ghana, Lumumba in the Congo, Fanon in Algeria, to Mossadegh in Iran. The problem for Empire has always been resistance in the name of 'independence', as thought and practice, no matter if it is Islamic, Marxist, nationalist or intellectual for that matter.

The second and more important factor for such moves against regional autonomy advocated by Iran and its allies is money or the capitalist superstructure governing today's international political economy which facilitates the payment of millions of dollars to US-based lobbying organisations by the Saudi state. In this regard, the *New York Times* reported in May 2018 that Saudi Arabia and the UAE have been repeatedly using think tanks in the United States as part of an extensive lobbying effort to shore up their support from Donald Trump, who has been seen as a strong supporter of Crown Prince Muhammad Bin Salman.[33] In response to the killing of the Saudi dissident Kamal Khashoggi (the CIA made Bin Salman responsible), Trump made it explicit that the relationship between the al-Saud and his government is purely driven by economic interests. The statement given in November 2018, and which was meant to be in response to the allegations that Bin

---

[31] Tim Anderson, *Axis of Resistance: Towards an Independent Middle East*, London: Clarity Press, 2020.

[32] See Alastair Crooke, *Resistance: The Essence of the Islamist Revolution*, London: Pluto Press, 2009.

[33] See David D. Kirkpatrick and Mark Mazzetti, 'How 2 Gulf monarchies sought to influence the White House', *New York Times*, 21 March 2018, available at www.nytimes.com/2018/03/21/us/politics/george-nader-elliott-broidy-uae-saudi-arabia-white-house-influence.html, accessed 12 January 2019.

Salman personally ordered the murder of Khashoggi, starts with an anti-Iranian tirade in order to remind the audience who the real enemy is:

The country of Iran, as an example, is responsible for a bloody proxy war against Saudi Arabia in Yemen, trying to destabilize Iraq's fragile attempt at democracy, supporting the terror group Hezbollah in Lebanon, propping up dictator Bashar Assad in Syria (who has killed millions of his own citizens), and much more. Likewise, the Iranians have killed many Americans and other innocent people throughout the Middle East. Iran states openly, and with great force, 'Death to America!' and 'Death to Israel!' Iran is considered 'the world's leading sponsor of terror.'[34]

So rather than starting to talk about the main issue of the speech, Trump used the occasion to identify his real target, i.e. Iran. He then moved on, in his quintessentially simplistic manner, to set out the reasons for the unwavering alliance between the United States and Saudi Arabia:

After my heavily negotiated trip to Saudi Arabia last year, the Kingdom agreed to spend and invest $450 billion in the United States. This is a record amount of money. It will create hundreds of thousands of jobs, tremendous economic development, and much additional wealth for the United States. Of the $450 billion, $110 billion will be spent on the purchase of military equipment from Boeing, Lockheed Martin, Raytheon and many other great US defense contractors. If we foolishly cancel these contracts, Russia and China would be the enormous beneficiaries – and very happy to acquire all of this newfound business. It would be a wonderful gift to them directly from the United States!

... We have already sanctioned 17 Saudis known to have been involved in the murder of Mr Khashoggi, and the disposal of his body ... After the United States, Saudi Arabia is the largest oil producing nation in the world. They have worked closely with us and have been very responsive to my requests to keep oil prices at reasonable levels – so important for the world. As President of the United States I intend to ensure that, in a very dangerous world, America is pursuing its national interests and vigorously contesting countries that wish to do us harm. Very simply it is called America First![35]

The US secretary of state, Mike Pompeo, reiterated the same message in November 2018, when he spoke of Saudi Arabia as a 'powerful

---

[34] 'Statement from President Donald J. Trump on Standing with Saudi Arabia'. *The White House*, 20 November 2018, available at www.whitehouse.gov/briefings-statements/statement-president-donald-j-trump-standing-saudi-arabia/, accessed 4 December 2018.

[35] Ibid.

force for stability in the Middle East'. In this view, being a force for stability translates into keeping 'Baghdad tethered to the West's interests, not Tehran's'. Almost identical to the syntax of the Trump statement quoted above, Pompeo went on an angry tirade against Iran:

Is it any coincidence that the people using the Khashoggi murder as a cudgel against President Trump's Saudi Arabia policy are the same people who supported Barack Obama's rapprochement with Iran – a regime that has killed thousands world-wide, including hundreds of Americans, and brutalizes its own people? Where was this echo chamber, where were these avatars of human rights, when Mr Obama gave the mullahs pallets of cash to carry out their work as the world's largest state sponsor of terrorism? Saudi Arabia, like the US – and unlike these critics – recognizes the immense threat the Islamic Republic of Iran poses to the world. Modern-day Iran is, in Henry Kissinger's term, a cause, not a nation. Its objectives are to spread the Islamic revolution from Tehran to Damascus, to destroy Israel, and to subjugate anyone who refuses to submit, starting with the Iranian people. An emboldened Iran would spread even more death and destruction in the Middle East, spark a regional nuclear-arms race, threaten trade routes, and foment terrorism around the world.[36]

In the face of the murder charges against him, Trump and Pompeo tried to rationalise the support for Muhammad Bin Salman with economic and geostrategic reasons. Yet studies into the claims of the president showed that Trump was wrong to suggest that he has US\$110 billion in military orders from Saudi Arabia. A much smaller amount in sales was actually signed. The US State Department also estimated far fewer jobs in the United States than Trump's figure of 500,000 to 600,000, projecting merely 'tens of thousands'. The Congressional Research Service described the package as a combination of sales that were already pursued under the Obama administration and discussed with Congress, and new sales still being developed.[37] This combination of blatant lies and the lack of strategic acumen explains why Saudi Arabia and the United States have been marginalised from the events in Syria, Iraq, Palestine, Libya, Lebanon

---

[36] Mike Pompeo, 'The US–Saudi partnership is vital', *Wall Street Journal*, 27 November 2018, available at www.wsj.com/articles/the-u-s-saudi-partnership-is-vital-1543362363, accessed 5 December 2019.

[37] See further Hope Yen and Calvin Woodward, 'AP fact check: Trump inflates jobs impact of Saudi arms deal', *Associated Press*, 20 October 2018, available at www.apnews.com/59efe0a1b2b8444b9d83b49c925f6e84, accessed 3 January 2019.

and elsewhere in West Asia and North Africa. This is a simple analytical point, yet it signals a radically different dynamic in the international politics of this region which favours, at least at this moment, Iranian interests and far more fundamentally, Russian and Chinese influence.

Space Wars: Iran as the 'Other'

There is a another narrative that is pushed by Bin Salman and his supporters which has an equally long pedigree among right-wing circles as the other ones that I have attempted to deconstruct in order to reveal their questionable analytical value for a better understanding of Iran and the international politics of West Asia and North Africa. Bin Salman repeatedly placed Iran in a so-called triangle of evil, which resembles the 'axis of evil' rhetoric of George W. Bush in 2003. According to Bin Salman, Iran is joined in this triangle by 'the Muslim Brotherhood, which is another extremist organisation ... and al-Qaeda, ISIS that want to do everything with force'. Furthermore, 'this triangle is promoting an idea that God and Islam are not asking us to promote. Their idea is totally against the principles of the United Nations and the idea of different nations having laws that represent their needs.'[38] In another obvious echo, in May 2018, US President Donald Trump linked Iran to al-Qaeda when he stated that the 'Iranian regime is the leading state sponsor of terror. It exports dangerous missiles, fuels conflicts across the Middle East, and supports terrorist proxies and militias such as Hezbollah, Hamas, the Taliban, and al Qaeda.'[39] This same narrative was then pushed by his secretary of state, Pompeo: 'Today, we ask the Iranian people: Is this what you want your country to be known for? For being a co-conspirator with Hezbollah, Hamas, the Taliban, and al-Qaeda?'.[40]

[38] Goldberg, 'Saudi Crown Prince: Iran's Supreme Leader "makes Hitler look good"'.
[39] 'Remarks by President Trump on the Joint Comprehensive Plan of Action', *The White House*, 8 May 2018, available at www.whitehouse.gov/briefings-statements/remarks-president-trump-joint-comprehensive-plan-action/, accessed 6 May 2019.
[40] 'Mike Pompeo gives a silly speech on Iran', *Washington Post*, 21 May 2018, available at www.washingtonpost.com/news/global-opinions/wp/2018/05/21/mike-pompeo-gives-a-silly-speech-on-iran/?noredirect=on&utm_term=.424605c817f2, accessed 3 May 2019.

Even someone with a limited knowledge of world politics knows that Iran fought the Taliban in Afghanistan together with Russia and India in support of the Northern Alliance at a time when the United States abandoned many of its former allies in the Mujahideen who had fought the Soviets so successfully during the heyday of the Cold War. In addition, the involvement of Iran and Hezbollah fighters in Syria had also to do with the threats to Shia shrines there and the virulently anti-Iranian, anti-Shia ideology underlying movements such as al-Qaeda and ISIS who were responsible for the bombing of several mosques in Iraq and Syria and several campaigns of ethnic cleansing. Al-Qaeda and the Taliban routinely targeted Shia minorities in Afghanistan (in particular the Hazara community) and Pakistan. A quick perusal of their references to what they consider to be 'Persians' (which includes Arab Shias) reveals terms such as 'pest of the East', 'Safavids', 'Fire worshippers' 'kaffirs' (unbelievers) etc. The Taliban has somewhat evolved from such narratives, but al-Qaeda type movements continue to propagate hate and terror towards Shia and Iranians all over the world, including in some Saudi-sponsored mosques in European and North American capitals and throughout Asia and Africa.

Here, as well, we can find a link to a pre-existent narrative, one that was promoted by Saddam Hussein and his followers, who himself was wrongly indicted to be allied to al-Qaeda in order to justify the US/UK invasion of Iraq in 2003. Psycho-nationalism, in the case of Saddam Hussein, implied advancing the myth that there has been a perennial conflict between Persians and Arabs.

The Ba'athist leadership soon realised that the fact that Arabs and Iranians have shared long periods of common history on both sides of the Shatt-al Arab required a systematic effort to invent strict cognito-logical boundaries. Central to this strategy was (a) accentuating the 'racial' composition of Iran, which was pursued by referring to the country as Persia; (b) historicising the challenge of the Persians which was pursued by projecting the conflict back to the reign of the Persian king Cyrus, who gave refuge to the Jews when they were persecuted by the Babylonian king Nebuchadnezzar in the sixth century BC; (c) stressing the intrinsic hostility of Iranians which was the central argument of state-sponsored poems, books, pamphlets etc. such as *Al-Madaris al-Yahudiyya wa-l-Iraniyya fi-l-'Iraq* (Jewish and Iranian schools in Iraq) published in 1980 by Fadil al-Barrak; and *Al-Harb al-sirriyya, khafaya al-dawr al-Isra'ili fi harb al-khalij* (The secret war: the mysterious role of Israel in the [First]Gulf War) by Sa'd al-Bazzaz. The former deals with the 'destructive' and 'dangerous' impact of Jewish and Iranian schools on Iraqi society. The latter outlines how Israel and Iran conspired to combat Iraq, with special reference to the destruction of the nuclear reactor in Osirak by the Israeli air force in June 1981; and (d) emphasising the 'cultural' and 'racial' inferiority of the 'Persian race' by similar means, for instance in the writings of Khairallah Talfah and his *Three Whom God Should Not Have Created: Persians, Jews and Flies*, or serials entitled *Judhur al-'ada al-Farsi li-l-umma al-'Arabiyya* (The roots of Persian hostility toward the Arab nation), and proverbs such as *Ma hann a'jami 'ala 'Arabi* (An *ajam* or Persian will not have mercy on an Arab).[41]

Yet the effort to historicise the myth of seemingly endemic Persian–Arab enmity was not sudden or merely in response to the revolution in Iran or Khomeini's repeated diatribes against Saddam Hussein (and the al-Saud monarchy for that matter), for it was not only power politics that propelled Saddam Hussein to demonise Persia. Arab psycho-nationalists have singled out Iranians as a main source of anti-Arab conspiracies at least since the writings of Michel Aflaq and Sati Khaldun al-Husri. Both were instrumental in the institutionalisation of Ba'athist psycho-nationalism in Iraq. The former – who had founded the Ba'ath party in the 1940s – because of his decision to side with the Iraqi Ba'ath of Saddam Hussein against the Syrian branch of Hafiz al-Assad in the early 1970s, the latter because of his educational posts between 1921 and 1941.[42]

Ultimately, the reification of this norm under Saddam Hussein's rule, central as it was to the nation-building process pursued by the state, was not entirely unrelated to the identity politics of the Pahlavi monarchs with its emphasis on Iranian-Aryan racial superiority towards the 'Semitic' Arabs, the support of Iraqi-Kurdish movements by the shah in close collaboration with the United States and Israel from the late 1960s until the Treaty of Algiers in 1975, and Khomeini's

---

[41] See Khairallah Talfah's *Three Whom God Should Not Have Created: Persians, Jews and Flies*, or serials entitled *Judhur al-'ada al-Farsi li-l-umma al-'Arabiyya* (The roots of Persian hostility toward the Arab nation), and proverbs such as *Ma hann a'jami 'ala 'Arabi* (An *ajam* or Persian will not have mercy on an Arab).

[42] See further Adib-Moghaddam, *The International Politics of the Persian Gulf*, ch. 2.

antagonism to Saddam Hussein and his calls for the 'export of the revolution' to Iraq.

Declassified US State Department documents and the Duelfer Report presented by US chief arms inspector in Iraq, Charles Duelfer, provide further evidence for the Ba'athist obsession with Iran. The Duelfer Report confirms the centrality of the 'Persian menace' to Ba'athist threat perceptions: 'From Saddam's viewpoint', the author argues, 'the Persian menace loomed large and was a challenge to his place in history.' Moreover, the report suggests that Iran (not the United States) was the 'pre-eminent motivator' of Saddam's WMD programme. 'All senior level Iraqi officials', the interrogations revealed, 'considered Iran to be Iraq's principal enemy in the region.'[43] The Duelfer Report also revealed that Saddam Hussein used the United Nations–managed oil-for-food programme to provide millions of dollars in subsidies to the aforementioned MKO (which was supported by Bolton and other members of the Trump administration). The armed military wing, which was headquartered in Iraq until 2003 but disarmed and confined to one location by the US military until the base was dismantled by the Iraqi government, launched several terrorist attacks inside Iran between 1988 and 2002.

Indeed, this obsession with Iran can also be discerned from Saddam Hussein's comments during the war crimes trial against him. He would take responsibility 'with honour' for any attacks on Iran using conventional or chemical weapons during the 1980–1988 war, he proclaimed on 18 December 2006, a week before his lawyer's appeal against the death penalty was rejected by the Iraqi High Court. Hussein even blamed 'Iranian agents' (and the United States) for the death penalty itself.[44] Undoubtedly, from the perspective of Saddam Hussein, Iran *was* a threat to Ba'athist rule both before and after the revolution much in the same way as the al-Saud are concerned about Iranian influence today.

---

[43] 'Comprehensive Report of the Special Advisor to the DCI on Iraq's WMD', 30 September 2004, www.cia.gov/library/reports/general-reports-1/iraq_wmd_2004/, accessed 8 November 2020. See Michael Isikoff and Mark Hosenball, 'Shades of gray: the Duelfer report alleges that Saddam gave funds to a listed terror group, but the claim does little to advance the White House case for war', *Newsweek*, 13 October 2004.

[44] 'Saddam proud of any Iran gas attack', *Gulf Times*, 19 December 2006.

On top of the material already marshalled, more primary documents reconfirm this comparable attitude in Saudi views about Iran. In a meeting between US officials and the former Saudi king Abdullah in 2008, the Saudi representatives made repeated reference to the necessity to keep 'Iraq's Arab identity and resist Iranian influence'.[45] Another cable from 2008 shows how the Saudi ambassador to the United States, Adel al-Jubair, told a diplomat about King Abdullah's 'frequent exhortations to the US to attack Iran and so put an end to its nuclear weapons program ... he told you to cut the head off the snake'. Another cable from 2009 quotes King Hamad bin Isa al-Khalifa of Bahrain calling 'forcefully for taking action to terminate [Iran's] nuclear program, by whatever means necessary'.[46]

It is obvious that the reification of a cognitologically powerful discourse that identifies Iran as the biggest enemy of the Arab world is a space-making device to fortify the 'Arab' realm against Iranian intrusions. This was the rationale behind the rhetoric of Saddam Hussein and the current statements and policy of the Saudi leadership. As it is a cognitological system, a regime of truth, this idea of Iran as a perennial traitor engenders its own pseudo-reality. Such an idea of Iran not only guides people towards what *ought to be* – it also tells them what '*is*'. In Ba'athist Iraq as in Saudi Arabia today, a whole cultural apparatus was put into operation in order to tell us that Iran *is* the eternal enemy of Arabs, that Persians *are* partially racists, that they *are* different etc. As this is a pseudo-reality, concocted and full of flaws, it didn't override the hybridity of the Iraqi–Iranian narrative, which re-emerged from the rhizome of its Arab–Iranian genealogy, immediately after the downfall of the Ba'athist state in Baghdad. Lies have short legs, which explains why Iranian and Arab psycho-nationalists have found it so hard to separate what it means to be coherently 'Arab' or 'Iranian' in the first place. To accept that these inventions are meaningless is the first step towards a mindset that fosters regional peace.

---

[45] 'Saudi King Abdullah and senior princes on Saudi policy towards Iraq', 20 April 2008, *Public Library of US Diplomacy*, available at https://wikileaks.org/plusd/cables/08RIYADH649_a.html, accessed 12 January 2009.

[46] See Dan Murphy and Laura Kasinof, 'How WikiLeaks trove will affect US–Arab cooperation on Iran, Yemen', *Christian Science Monitor*, 29 November 2010, available at www.csmonitor.com/World/Middle-East/2010/1129/How-WikiLeaks-trove-will-affect-US-Arab-cooperation-on-Iran-Yemen, accessed 2 April 2011.

Admittedly, compared to the discourse propounded by Saddam Hussein there is less psycho-nationalist venom in the current narratives about Iran among Saudi leaders. Yet, the intention is comparable: to delineate the Arab world from this alien Iranian 'other', to undermine transnational sentiments expressed in the song of Boutros that informs this chapter. As Amin Saikal has recently argued: 'This situation has pleased the forces of the Right in the United States and Israel ... which has helped to forge an unprecedented degree of cooperation [even] between Saudi Arabia and Israel,' although largely behind the scenes.[47]

As indicated, the Iranian state has aided such sentiments by its 'over-expansion' into the Arab state system. At the same time, the fact that these sentiments exist in the Arab world itself, and that songs such as the one by Boutros are a part of a cultural context that cannot be simply cleansed from the Iranian presence, routinely defy such dichotomisations, even if the song is also imbued with problematic identitarian baggage. Yet the song of Boutros is analytically valuable for the conceptual message of this chapter: cleansing a supposed 'self' from an equally invented 'other' does not work in a region where connections are so obviously intimate that even contemporary DNA research fails to distinguish anyone along racial or ethnic lines. The recipe for regional peace lies in acknowledging this inherent hybridity which speaks to a post-national future, based on a past that was not dissected by psycho-nationalism and seemingly clearly delineated 'lines in the sand', that created the contemporary nation-states in this region and in other parts of the colonised global south.

Turkic Iran: Precedents for Peace[48]

With an eye on future developments, it is well worth advancing ideas about what 'thinking' might yield movement towards the communitarian end of international life in this region, i.e. *change* of the culture

---

[47] Amin Saikal, *Iran Rising: The Survival and Future of the Islamic Republic*, Princeton: Princeton University Press, 2019.

[48] This section has been adopted from Arshin Adib-Moghaddam, 'After the Middle East: Turkey and Iran in a new region', *JETRO-IDE ME Review*, Vol. 6 (2018–2019), pp. 1–7. The article benefited from several keynote lectures and conversations with Prof. Hitoshi Suzuki at IDE-JETRO in Tokyo, Prof. Hisae Nakanishi at Doshisha University in Kyoto and Prof. Satoshi Ikeuchi at the University of Tokyo.

of distrust towards amicable relations, or what theorists of security call 'a security community'. In their seminal work Karl Deutsch and his associates defined a security community as a group that had gone down the path of integration to the degree that there is 'real assurance that the members of that community will not fight each other physically, but will settle their disputes in some other way'.[49] They differentiated between two variants: an 'amalgamated security community', defined as the 'formal merger of two or more previous units into a single larger unit, with some type of common government after amalgamation';[50] and a 'pluralistic security community' which preserves the formal independence of autonomous governments.

Communication processes and transaction flows between peoples are central to the emergence of a pluralistic security community, something that I consider inherent to the deep civil structure in West Asia and North Africa, due to common historical narratives and other bonds, despite the emphasis on 'difference' held up by regional states. Migration, tourism, cultural and educational exchanges help to create a reflexive social fabric which appreciates process on both the elite and societal levels. The transaction and communication processes, Deutsch argued, instil the sense of community, which turns into a 'matter of mutual sympathy and loyalties; of "we feeling", trust, and mutual consideration; of partial identification in terms of self-images and interests; of mutually successful predictions of behaviour'.[51] Security communities can be achieved along a three-tiered process which moves the level of interaction from institutionalised cultural exchanges to semi-governmental forums to traditional interstate security considerations.

If we are to modify the theory of Deutsch for our purposes, an important emphasis has to be given to understanding, trust and empathy, the central concepts that I have carved out in this study, as imperative to understand Iran. These sentiments are nestled in the deep structure of any functioning relationship. I borrow from 'post-structural' notions here, highlighting that the origin of an agent – individual or state – is inextricably linked to the differentiation between self and other. Such self–other dialectics are central to 'critical Iranian studies' and we have benefited from this in the present book, whether in our

---

[49] Karl Deutsch et al., *Political Community and the North Atlantic Area*, Princeton: Princeton University Press, 1957, p. 5.
[50] Ibid., p. 6.   [51] Ibid., p. 36.

emphasis on notions of Iranian superiority inherent in Iranian psycho-nationalist discourse, the equally invented myth of the 'Persian' threat to the Arab *umma* in some Arab psycho-nationalist writings, Islamist politics, or the issues surrounding the global right wing. The point is that individuals and societies are bound together by a 'common fate', only denied by psycho-nationalist politics that is meant to erase such immanent commonality simulating the false notion that 'your' security can be achieved at the expense of 'mine'. In today's interdependent world order, there will always be some form of blowback to any war. There is hence an inbuilt common fate in the relation between states which demands self-restraint because any act of violence is likely to have repercussions for both the other *and* the self. This is particularly apparent in densely interdependent regions such as Eurasia. The emphasis on human security, rather than merely national security, was largely absent in previous, state-centric security orders that failed to pacify the region.[52]

It is analytically crucial to understand here that such peaceful interaction does not require the total alignment of interests, neither are mere economic transactions enough. Business is a part of the mix, and does not deliver long-term peace on its own. The relationship between Turkey and Iran, divergent on many issues, yet structurally peaceful, is a case in point. In the past decade, relations between the two countries have stabilised along three themes of mutual concern: economic transactions, opposition to separatist movements and, to a lesser extent, support for a Palestinian state. Despite their competition and disagreements, in particular over Syria, central Asia and Turkey's NATO membership, these three themes have contributed to cordiality, amidst occasional outbreaks of intense rivalry, between the two countries. Therefore, Turkish–Iranian relations could act as a template to resolve rather more problematic interstate relations in the region, in particular between Saudi Arabia and Iran.

Much ink has been spilled over an enduring competition between Iran and Turkey, presumably linked to a seemingly insurmountable legacy of Ottoman–Safavid antagonism or even less persuasively to a Sunni–Shia split engulfing the region, as I challenged above. Analyses that cut and paste history onto contemporary world politics without

---

[52] Mehran Kamrava, *Troubled Waters: Insecurity in the Persian Gulf*, London: Cornell University Press, 2018.

critical acumen mimic ideology, and are not scholarship. Turkey and Iran operate on the basis of their perceived state interests which are processed within the realities of the contemporary world order. This is also because that history, once divested of its ideological pretensions, offers an intensely intimate, common cultural geography.[53]

It is true that modern relations between the two countries have been beset by occasional outbreaks of rivalry and suspicion, for instance immediately after the revolution in Iran in 1979, when there was intense ideological friction between the secular, Kemalist state in Turkey and the Shia revolutionary Islamic Republic. Iran before the revolution, especially under the reign of the first monarch of the Pahlavi dynasty, Reza Shah (1878–1941), was emulating the Turkish model – Pahlavi Iran and Kemalist Turkey were close ideational bed-fellows, as they were both secular, nationalist and followed a model of modernity premised on European notions of 'progress'.[54] After the revolution in Iran in the name of a Shia-Islamic order, the ideological affinity evaporated, but relations between the two countries did not deteriorate into active aggression. Turkey managed to stay relatively neutral during the Iran–Iraq War (1980–1988) and refrained from being dragged into the complex politics of West Asia and North Africa. For Iran, Turkey was not a major factor given that the country was focused, ideationally and strategically, on Europe and the 'West'.

The dynamics changed drastically in 2002 with the ascendancy to power of the Islamic Justice and Development Party (AKP). Iran already figured rather more prominently on the radar screen of the first generation of Turkish 'Islamists' who took power and who reorientated Turkish foreign policy more firmly towards West Asia and North Africa. Necmettin Erbakan, who came to power in 1996 as the first prime minister of the country with politico-Islamic persuasions, chose Iran as his first destination for a foreign visit, a great affront to the pro-Western elite in the country for whom the Islamic Republic represented everything Turkey should not be (he visited again in 2009 after an eleven-year-long ban on his participation in Turkish politics). Whilst in Tehran, in July 1996, Erbakan concluded a US$23 billion deal for the delivery of natural gas from Iran over twenty-five

---

[53] See further Marianna Charountaki, *Iran and Turkey: International and Regional Engagement in the Middle East*, London: I.B. Tauris, 2019.
[54] See further Touraj Atabaki (ed.), *The State and the Subaltern: Modernisation, Society and the State in Turkey and Iran*, London: I.B. Tauris, 2007.

years. He also facilitated with Iran the establishment of the so-called Developing Eight (D-8) comprising Malaysia, Indonesia, Egypt, Bangladesh, Pakistan and Nigeria.[55]

But Erbakan's power base was not strong enough to resist the opposition of the anti-Islamist elite and in particular the staunchly secular higher echelons of the Turkish military that were endowed with the constitutional mandate to uphold the Kemalist system in the country. At the National Security Council meeting on 28 February 1997, the generals of the Turkish national army imposed their views on separating Islam from the politics of the government in line with the laicity principle institutionalised since the establishment of contemporary Turkey by Mustapha Kemal ('Ataturk'). Consequently, Erbakan had to retreat. In a further escalation between June 1997 and early 1998, Turkish courts declared Erbakan's Refah (Welfare) party illegal and forced him out of office.

The reformist core of the party reorganised first as the Virtue Party, which was banned in 2001, and then under the banner of the Justice and Development Party (Adalet ve Kalkinma Partisi, or AKP), whereas the rather more Islamist wings merged into the Felicity Party (Saadet Partisi) which was created in 2001. The AKP captured the imagination of the new middle class in Turkey and the party won the parliamentary elections in 2002, forming the Turkish government. Since then, Iranian–Turkish relations have re-stabilised, despite the push of Turkey into the Arab state system, and repeated disagreements with Iran about strategic issues. My point is that Iran and Turkey worked around these grievances, along a positive-sum rationale that has benefited both countries.

Erbakan was heavily criticised for his charm offensive towards Iran, precisely because this policy was turned into a question of 'identity' and 'loyalty' for the secular political elites, that were quickly losing their grip over the levers of power in Ankara. As one commentator in *Today's Zaman* put it: 'I wanted to understand, for example, why Erbakan had a soft spot for no-good neighbour Iran ... I was surprised ... to see him making a difficult trip in a wheelchair to attend a National Day reception for Iran in the Swissôtel Ankara in

---

[55] For the dialectic of Islam and politics, with a particular emphasis on reform, see among others Günes Murat Tezcür, *Muslim Reformers in Iran and Turkey: The Paradox of Modernisation*, Austin: University of Texas Press, 2010.

2010 while opting out of other countries' receptions.'[56] There is no doubt that the second-generation Islamists in Turkey learned their lessons from the backlash against Erbakan. They have been far more prudent and diligent in their dealings with Iran.[57]

And yet, Erdogan also continued to strengthen ties with the Islamic Republic, not least in order to satisfy the energy demands of Turkey's booming economy. As indicated, shortly after taking office, Erbakan concluded a US$23 billion deal for the delivery of natural gas from Iran over twenty-five years. In February 2007, under the AKP government, Turkey and Iran agreed to seal two additional energy deals: one allowing the Turkish Petroleum Corporation (TPAO) to explore oil and natural gas in Iran and another for the transfer of gas from Turkmenistan to Turkey (and on to Europe) through a pipeline in Iran. This pipeline deal was at odds with Washington's preference for avoiding Iran by transporting the gas through the Caspian Sea, and added a new element of friction to US–Turkish relations.[58]

Despite the fluctuations that I will get to, it is indicative of the depth of the Turkish–Iranian relationship that the two countries are also cooperating in the realm of national security. If relations were merely pragmatic, based on short-term economic gain and tactical man-oeuvres, it would be unlikely that Ankara and Tehran would trust each other enough to cooperate on internal matters with transnational security implications such as the issue of Kurdish separatism. The breakthrough on this front came during Prime Minister Erdogan's visit to Tehran in July 2004, when Turkey and Iran signed a security cooperation agreement that branded the PKK a terrorist organisation. Since then, the two countries have stepped up cooperation to protect their borders. Similar to Turkey, Iran faces security problems in its Kurdish-populated areas: In particular between 2004 and 2010, an Iranian group affiliated with the PKK, the Party for a Free Life in Iranian Kurdistan (PJAK), launched attacks against Iranian security

---

[56] Abdullah Bozkurt, 'Erbakan's legacy and gas deal with Iran', *Today's Zaman*, 18 May 2012.

[57] On 'Islamism' in Turkey see among others William Hale and Ergun Özbudun, *Islamism, Liberalism and Democracy in Turkey: The Case of the AKP*, London: Routledge, 2009.

[58] For an interesting take on the Turkey–Iran–US triangle see Stephen Kinzer, *Reset: Iran, Turkey and America's Future*, London: Times Books, 2010.

officials. Tehran reacted by shelling PKK bases in the Kandil Mountains in close liaison with the Turkish military. While Iran condemned rather more overt Turkish military operations against Kurdish groups in northern Iraq and Syria, the two countries have continued their strategic dialogue about Kurdish separatism.[59]

At least until the uprising in Syria which started in 2011, Iran also facilitated closer Syrian–Turkish relations. Strained in the 1980s and early 1990s, they reached a crisis point in October 1998, when Turkey threatened to invade Syria if Damascus did not cease supporting the PKK. In the face of Turkey's overwhelming military superiority, Damascus backed down, expelling the PKK leader Öcalan, to whom it had given safe haven, and closing PKK training camps. The shift in Syrian policy opened the way for a gradual improvement in relations. This rapprochement was underscored by Syrian President Bashar al-Assad's visit to Ankara in January 2005 – the first trip by a Syrian president to Turkey since Syria's independence in 1946. Despite Turkey's initial support for the opposition to Assad's rule, which put it in direct confrontation with the policies of Iran, it is revealing that this competition over Syria did not undermine the central signposts of Iranian–Turkish relations.

As indicated, the Iranian leadership views the battle in Syria as crucial in order to keep one of the constituent members of the 'resistance' axis in power, and to ensure that Syria does not turn into a US satellite. Thus, Iranian foreign policy elites have deemed Syria a valuable ally in the Arab world, and a convenient conduit to Hezbollah in Lebanon, ever since the Iran–Iraq War when Hafiz al-Assad was the only regional leader supporting Iran. Thus, the Ba'athist secular state in Damascus is not a 'Shia' ally of the Islamic Republic, as I have argued above. But Syria and Iran have shared a common vision of regional affairs and have pursued their *muqawama* policy towards Israel and in support of Palestine, as discussed.

The fact that the Khaled Meshaal wing of Hamas broke with Assad at the height of the Syrian civil war in 2013 and shifted their headquarters away from Damascus was a significant blow to this 'axis of resistance', but since then relations between Iran and Hamas have

---

[59] For these security interactions see Suleyman Elik, *Iran–Turkey Relations, 1979–2011: Conceptualising the Dynamics of Politics, Religion and Security in Middle-Power States*, London: Routledge, 2013.

bounced back. Turkey, on the other side, became increasingly aware
that it can't take the Iran factor out of the regional equation, so the
AKP has trodden carefully when it comes to the Syrian crisis, aiming to
reassure Iran that Turkey is not acting on behalf of the United States
and Israel in opposing Assad. In fact in early 2018, Turkey broke with
the United States more openly in the build-up to the Afrin military
campaign against the US-backed 'Syrian Democratic Forces' and the
country has established closer relations with Russia in recent years,
including in the contested realm of military technology.

The oppositional politics in Syria may have halted a decade of
deepening engagement between Turkey and Iran and set the limits
for closer relations in the future. Yet, at the same time the fallout has
been contained. There have been no public recriminations about each
other's motives in Syria, in itself an indicator that neither country was
willing to jeopardise relations, even over such an emotive issue as the
civil war that has ravaged Syria in the past years. Iran is interested in a
Syrian government that is independent, does not fall into the strategic
sphere of the United States and continues to support the Palestinian
case for statehood via Hezbollah. Turkish motives were not necessarily
seen as being in opposition to those aims, which explains why both
countries co-organised several talks about Syria together with Russia.

From the perspective of the political elites in Iran, Turkey's tentative
move away from a strategic alliance with Israel towards rather more
pro-Palestinian policies was welcomed as a firm indicator of the shift in
Turkey's strategic preferences in West Asia. Erdogan has been openly
critical of Israeli policy in the West Bank and Gaza, repeatedly likening
Israeli military campaigns to acts of state terrorism. At the same time,
Erdogan has established closer ties to the Palestinian leadership and
this as well was largely welcomed in Tehran.

The pro-Palestinian turn has been apparent for over a decade now.
A few weeks after the elections in the Palestinian territories in January
2006, Erdogan hosted a high-ranking Hamas delegation, led by
Khaled Meshaal, in Ankara. Erdogan was hoping that the visit would
highlight Turkey's ability to play a rather more prominent diplomatic
role in the region. Indicative of the future direction of Turkish foreign
policy, the meeting was arranged without consulting the United States
and Israel and irritated both governments, which wanted to isolate
Hamas. Likewise, Turkey adopted a position at odds with Israeli
policy during the crisis in Lebanon in 2006 which was supported by

Iran. Erdogan sharply condemned the Israeli attacks, and in several major Turkish cities there were large-scale protests and burnings of the Israeli flag, pictures that were enthusiastically broadcast by Iran's state-owned media conglomerate.

Turkish NGOs have also condemned Israel's policies in Lebanon and the Palestinian territories, culminating in the 'flotilla crisis' which was defused by an Israeli offer to compensate the families of Turkish nationals killed during raids on ships in May 2010. While Ankara and Tehran have not been willing to coordinate their policies on Palestine, from the Iranian perspective Turkey's pro-Palestinian stance is indicative of the changes within the country. The issue of Palestine has been at the heart of the revolutionary rhetoric of the Islamic Republic since 1979, and while Iran is not willing to concede its claim to regional leadership in that regard, it routinely displays an automatic proclivity towards countries that embrace the cause of Palestinian statehood.

If Syria exemplified Turkey's new-found self-confidence as a regional power in West Asia and North Africa, its wholehearted embrace of the opposition to Bashir al-Assad's rule in Syria fanned its rivalry with Iran which acts upon a similar claim and which has firmly supported Assad's rule for the strategic reasons mentioned above. Tensions between the two countries were further exacerbated in 2012, when Turkey agreed to station a NATO missile defence shield in eastern Anatolia, which was sold by successive administrations in the United States as a deterrent to Iran's burgeoning missile capability.[60] The Iranian military establishment reacted nervously, prompting one general of the Islamic Revolution Guard Corps, to warn, 'Should we be threatened, we will target NATO's missile defence shield in Turkey and then hit the next targets.'[61]

At the same time and rather typically, both countries were quick to contain the fallout: The then foreign minister of Turkey, Ahmet Davutoglu, reassured his Iranian counterpart Ali-Akbar Salehi during a joint news conference in Tehran in January 2012 that Turkey 'would

---

[60] See 'Part of NATO missile defense system goes live in Turkey', *CNN*, 16 January 2012, available at http://edition.cnn.com/2012/01/16/world/europe/turkey-radar-station/index.html, accessed 14 April 2013.

[61] Ali-Akbar Dareini, 'Iran threatens to hit Turkey, if US, Israel attack', *Associated Press*, 26 November 2011, available at http://news.yahoo.com/iran-threatens-hit-turkey-us-israel-attack-153655802.html, accessed 18 April 2013.

never take any step that could negatively affect our relations with our neighbour ... We would never accept any attack on any of our neighbours from our soil. We don't want such a perception of threat to exist, especially against Iran.' In return, Salehi put the remarks of the IRGC general in context underlining that 'some people, knowingly or not, express views without much knowledge and by stepping beyond their responsibilities, and it causes misunderstandings'.[62]

Turkey is increasingly caught between US dictates and securing its own interests in the region; it is negotiating, in many ways, the 'burden' of being a NATO partner on the one side and its geostrategic position in Eurasia which does not readily yield to claims to US hegemony, on the other. The nuclear issue and the sanctions regime is a case in point. Caught between US demands to tighten sanctions against Iran and safeguarding its own economic interest, Ankara reduced oil imports from Iran by 20 per cent when the sanctions regime was reinforced in 2012.[63] These measures were complemented when Turkey agreed to cease to act as a financial intermediary – through the state-owned Halk bank – to process Iran's lucrative oil trade deals with countries such as India – in effect, contributing to the economic warfare on Iran led by the United States. However, the AKP has been reluctant to enforce unilateral sanctions by the EU and the United States beyond the measures contained in UN Security Council Resolution 1929, despite repeated demands to that effect, most recently by the Trump administration.

Moreover, AKP officials have repeatedly signalled that they won't support any military action against Iran and that they are supportive of Iran's civilian nuclear energy programme. This explains why President Erdogan has tried to act as a mediator in the nuclear issue, culminating in the Tehran agreement which was successfully negotiated with Brazil's then-president Lula and Mahmoud Ahmadinejad in May 2010.[64] The initiative was eventually shot down by the EU and the United States, but the fact that Erdogan (and Lula) was willing to

[62] 'Turkey gives assurances to Iran on NATO missile shield', *Today's Zaman*, 5 January 2012.

[63] See further 'Turkey says no new US request to cut Iranian crude', *Today's Zaman*, 5 December 2012.

[64] For the full text see 'Text of the Iran–Brazil-Turkey deal', *The Guardian*, 17 May 2010, available at www.guardian.co.uk/world/julian-borger-global-security-blog/2010/may/17/iran-brazil-turkey-nuclear, accessed 22 April 2013.

spearhead a major diplomatic campaign, and thereby knowingly cut across US demands to determine diplomacy on the Iranian nuclear file, indicated Turkey's newly acquired assertiveness in international affairs. More recently, and in response to the US withdrawal from the JCPOA in May 2018, the spokesman of the Turkish government reiterated this position: 'While there is no evidence that Iran is violating the agreement, the US taking this decision means to take the exact opposite position of its allies.'[65]

Turkey and Iran have tried to mitigate the vicissitudes of a radically fluctuating international environment which is creating a fundamentally new order in West Asia and North Africa. Yet despite the turmoil that has engulfed the region, in particular after the Arab Spring, both countries have retained cordial relations interspersed with occasional outbreaks of crisis that are quickly contained and ameliorated through diplomatic channels. Crucially, both states act in support of each other's national sovereignty and stability. When demonstrations broke out in Iran in January 2018, Turkey was quick to voice its support for the government of Iranian President Hassan Rouhani and Iran opposed the coup attempt in Turkey in July 2016.

Analytically, this proclivity towards diplomacy over the rhetoric of threats indicates that there is a strategic consensus among the political elites currently ruling both countries that they have to act as neighbours and can't afford to jeopardise relations, even over rather more contentious issues such as Syria and Iraq. In many ways, Turkey and Iran are too embedded within each other to be separated or to act antagonistically. This is a crucial point because this interdependence is not merely apparent in terms of mutual security concerns that a common border inevitably brings about, it is also lodged in the cultural tapestry that holds the Iranian–Turkish dialectic together. After all, these two successor nation-states to dynastic empires have interacted with each other over millennia. This is why today there are millions of Turkish-speaking Iranian-Azeris that have natural ties to Turkey and one hears Persian widely spoken in Istanbuli quarters such as Laleli. Persia and Turkey, in short, share too much to be thought of in distinct and antagonistic terms. Ultimately, similar interdependencies can be unearthed between the other countries of the region and they could act

<hr>

[65] 'Turkey: US decision on Iran deal unfortunate step', *Anadolu Agency*, 9 May 2018.

as ingredients for a new form of peace diplomacy, around a positive-sum calculus, and around a security paradigm that is appreciative of cultural interaction and historical understanding.

Eurasian Futures

Iranian–Turkish relations are a good example for a partnership built on relative trust, at least at the time of writing. If our knowledge about the 'other' is central to our understanding of each other's intentions, dialogue, transactions and cultural communication become the necessary tools to create such trust and to avoid misperceptions. Here, instituting communicative action and institutionalising regional forums for dialogue ensure that diplomacy evolves as the only permissible 'language' of interstate interaction in the region. To that end, the involvement of Asian powers such as China, Japan, India and Pakistan who have a pronounced interest in stability in WANA is an important option, increasingly contemplated by critical national security theorists in eastern and western Asia.

Certainly, within a wider multipolar security paradigm, Asian countries have a distinct interest in creating a security architecture that prohibits war. There are profound cultural, ideational, economic and political interdependencies between these countries, and their security cannot be safeguarded separately from each other. The evolving institutional framework is already being developed with China as a potent engine: most obviously in the Shanghai Cooperation Organisation (SCO) which now comprises China, Russia, Kazakhstan, Kyrgyzstan, Tajikistan, Uzbekistan and, since 2017, Pakistan and India; Iran has observer status and Turkey is a partner for dialogue. The international system is swiftly moving to a multipolar order, where the United States must be considered one among many factors. The SCO is an institutional manifestation of this emerging new world order. For several decades successive US governments had their chance to contribute to regional peace – it is time to look for other options.

The SCO is flanked by two major economic projects that bind 'Eurasia' closer together. The first is the International North South Transport Corridor (INSTC) signed into action by Russia, India and Iran in May 2002. The INSTC is a 7,200 km long infrastructure project that connects the shipping, rail and road routes of Iran, India, Russia, Central Asia and Europe. As such, it creates a major transit route that functions to facilitate the transfer of goods from Mumbai in India to Helsinki in Finland, using Iranian ports and railroads, which Iran is connecting to those of Azerbaijan and Russia and its Baltic ports.

The second major economic initiative is the Belt and Road initiative, the contemporary Silk Road, spearheaded by China. Apart from instituting a 'unified large market', the Belt and Road initiated by President Xi Jinping has a strong cultural component as it sponsors exchanges and integration, 'to enhance mutual understanding and trust of member nations, ending up in an innovative pattern with capital inflows, talent pool, and [a] technology database'.[66] Even as an authoritarian state, ruled by a one-party system with a regressive notion of totalitarian sovereignty that has been repeatedly violent in enforcing its power, the current approach of China to West Asia is not constituted by imperial interference or one-dimensional domination. There is a cultural language that is carefully calibrated along narratives of dignity, respect and common bonds, almost entirely absent from the current US approach to the region. As a young postgraduate student at the University of Tehran commented in the *China Daily* with reference to the 'Asian Civilisation Conference',

The conference suggests China's great role not only on an economic level but also on a cultural one. In fact, the Chinese stance in this conference echoed the words of Zhao Tingyang, one of China's leading contemporary philosophers: 'Maximizing cooperation is even more important than minimizing conflict.' It is only through cooperation that we could decrease conflicts and accelerate the momentum of building trust.[67]

The long-term aim of all of this feeds exactly into the idea of a pluralistic security community, that I summarised above and which would safeguard a formal respite from war in Asia and beyond. The

---

[66] 'Full text: Action plan on the Belt and Road Initiative', *The State Council The People's Republic of China*, 30 March 2015, available at http://english.www .gov.cn/archive/publications/2015/03/30/content_281475080249035.htm, accessed 12 November 2018. In terms of useful secondary literature see Anoushiravan Ehteshami and Niv Horesh (eds.), *China's Presence in the Middle East: The Implication of the One Belt and One Road Initiative*, London: Routledge, 2017.

[67] Behzad Abdollahpour, 'Asian civilization conference: a chance for prosperity, stability', *China Daily*, 16 May 2019, available at www.chinadaily.com.cn/a/ 201905/16/WS5cdccceea3104842260bbfe7.html, accessed 12 June 2019.

practical pathways to that end can be chartered along two concepts: cultural diplomacy and trans-identitarian politics carried by an inclusive discourse that is non-sectarian and subdues psycho-nationalist narratives that are based on antagonism and hate. In an increasingly networked and interlinked world, the security of state A in West Asia and North Africa can't be treated in isolation from the security of state B in East Asia or Europe. The initiatives mentioned above have an underlying rationale that appreciates such factors. What I am referring to is a shift away from a zero-sum game i.e. a situation in which one participant's gains result only from another participant's equivalent losses, to a positive-sum game: no one wins at someone else's expense – indeed the sum of positives and negatives (wins and losses) is positive.

Secondly, security can't be achieved merely between states. A functioning security paradigm has to be built upon people-to-people contacts as the Belt and Road initiative seems to appreciate. Once institutionalised further, such a Eurasian paradigm centred around human security (rather than merely state security) would act as a major anchor for regional peace in West Asia and North Africa. As my friend and colleague Prof. Hisae Nakanishi recently stated in a short analysis, what is needed is a human security approach that appreciates 'vernacular security' for the people of the region, 'as a perspective to capture the reality of those who are under siege', in order to be able to 'address actual situations and conditions of the marginalized people: women, religious and ethnic minorities and those who are impoverished'.[68] In this regard, this grass-roots approach offers a richer understanding of 'security' compared to state-centred models, that have dominated thinking about security, both in scholarship and political practice, in this region and beyond.[69]

---

[68] Hisae Nakanishi, 'Human security and political violence in the Middle East: views from security-development nexus perspective', *Advances in Social Science, Education and Humanities Research (ASSEHR)*, vol. 138, International Conference on Contemporary Social and Political Affairs, 2017, p. 40.

[69] For the conceptual underpinnings of the human security approach beyond the vast UN literature see further Giorgio Shani, 'Human security as ontological security: a post-colonial approach', *Postcolonial Studies*, Vol. 20, No. 3 (2017), pp. 275–293; Philip Darby, 'Recasting Western knowledges about (post)colonial security', in Damian Grenfell and Paul James (eds.), *Rethinking, Insecurity, War and Violence*, London: Routledge, 2009, pp. 98–110; Edward Newman, 'Critical human security studies', *Review of International Studies*, Vol. 36, No. 1 (2010), pp. 77–94.

Efforts between the GCC states and Iran in the 1990s have demonstrated that even a 'communitarian Gulf' does not have to remain a remote utopia. Even Saudi Arabia and Iran repeatedly found ways to transcend their insecurities in the past, as indicated, extending their dialogue into the contested realm of religion.[70] Despite their rivalry, Iran and Saudi Arabia have no interest in fighting each other, exactly because of the symbolic importance that both countries claim in the Muslim world and beyond.

The recent skirmishes between Iran and Saudi Arabia have not changed this reluctance to turn a rivalry over influence into a hot war. Despite divergent agendas in Iraq, Yemen, Syria, Bahrain and the Lebanon, Saudi Arabia and Iran have maintained diplomatic contacts, sometimes direct and if necessary through mediators. Indeed, despite the anti-Iranian vitriol in some quarters of the Saudi media, even the then Iranian president Mahmoud Ahmadinejad, who was not a reformist, was invited by King Abdullah to attend an extraordinary meeting of the Organisation of the Islamic Conference (OIC) on Syria in Medina (August 2012). Iranian–Saudi relations may have their ups and downs, but they have never really degenerated into anything but rivalry. In fact, the patterns of the past demonstrate that the current dearth in relations is likely to change for the better in the near future.[71]

The emergence of a sense of community in the Persian Gulf commands restraint, promotes non-violence, requires a degree of solidarity and prohibits the use of war in the conduct of interstate affairs. Once these principles are digested and institutionalised, we may even be able

---

[70] There have been several examples of such a dialogue. In 1997, Iran's ambassador to Saudi Arabia, revealed that he had met with the Kingdom's top cleric and arbiter of Wahhabism, General Mufti Shaykh 'Abdallah Bin Baz, and other members of the Saudi Council of Senior 'Ulama (*Al-Sharq al-Awsat*, 4 July 1997); a year later, protests expressed by the head of Iran's hajj delegation, Ayatollah Reyshari, led to the dismissal of the popular but anti-Shia imam of the Medinite sanctuary, Shaykh Ali Abdal-Rahman al-Hudhayfi (see *Summary of World Broadcasts*: ME/3183 Med/17, 24 March 1998 and ME/3186 MED/15, 27 March 1998). In a remarkable step in July 2003, both countries signed a judiciary cooperation deal during the visit to Riyadh of Iran's then minister of the judiciary, Ayatollah Mahmoud Hashemi-Shahroudi ('Saudi Arabia, Iran sign judicial cooperation deal', *AFP*, 11 July 2003). The exchanges extend to the societal level as well, exemplified by increasing numbers of Saudi tourists spending their vacation in Iran. See 'Letter from Saudi Arabia: Iran current hot tourist spot for Saudis', *Gulf News*, 4 August 2003.

[71] 'Ahmadinejad arrives in Saudi Arabia for Islamic Summit', *Daily Star* (Beirut), 13 August 2012.

to admire the song of Boutros at a concert in Jeddah or Dubai just as a musical piece, and not as ideological incitement. We would connect to the pain and suffering that underlies the political message, even when Boutros glorifies something we detest. As human beings we are coded to feel the same sentiments vis-à-vis forms of domination, after all. We shan't answer righteousness, with anger. In this way, the musical piece for this chapter is a litmus test of our tolerance for a message that we may disagree with. Despite of all the horrible things that have happened in the last decades, I am hopeful that, through education, a radical change toward more empathy can be achieved in a relatively short period of time.

The current trends may indicate the contrary, but at the time of writing, decision-makers on both sides of the Gulf appear to feel relatively reassured that they will not fight each other in the near future. Respite from war has not been guaranteed by the heavy US military presence in the Persian Gulf and beyond, but through diplomatic channels and human-to-human interactions. If anything, the United States has proven to be a source of instability, not least because there are movements and states that oppose the militarisation of the region by external powers, that will always clash with the US presence there. Certainly, the US military bases have not resolved the security dilemma in the deep structure of this regional system which is why new alliance patterns are taking over.

Furthermore, and in terms of 'internal', regional dynamics, once we accept the analytical truth that the geography of violence in this region is largely built on the psycho-nationalist myths of 'origin' and separation, a prerequisite for a peaceful future emerges. Sustainable peace in West Asia and North Africa can only be achieved when at the root of the structural composition of this area, psycho-nationalist inventions and their cognitological systems are unearthed and destroyed once and for all, which is a major prerequisite for a functioning 'pluralistic security community'. At that point in time, being Jewish, Muslim, Christian, Sunni or Shia becomes secondary to being human, a member of Bani Adam (humankind) to use Sa'adi's beautifully embracive words that I will conceptualise as a recipe for peace and understanding in the epilogue. On that basis, difference is minimised, self and other are liberated from the unrewarding politics of identity, 'our' fate folds into 'theirs'. Locating this interconnectivity in theory and practice has been the common conceptual thread holding together the tectonic plates undergirding this book.

There must be room to think in terms of such humanistic ideas, even in the sinister and cynical world of regional politics, and the hyper-macho language that permeates the writing and discourse of the raft of think-tank analysts that cover what is being said about the region with such vehement 'realism', that is devoid of an approach to security that puts the individual at its centre. A template for peace is available, a humanistic tradition that appreciates 'human security' is discernible, a philosophy of peace is realisable – What we need are competent politicians to do their job and to turn this post-identarian vision into reality. So far, the governments of this region of the world have failed the people, certainly on this account.

Epilogue: A Symphony of Flowers

A Conversation between the Shah, Khomeini (and Oriana Fallaci)

I have written as a political philosopher, perhaps even as a critical theorist and sometimes as a theoretician of global thought and international relations. Only intermittently did I allow for an artistic interpretation of Iran in order to add further perspectives to my own views. Undoubtedly, for anyone who wants to know Iran and especially for those readers who want to see Iran as a model for pluralism, peace, democracy, social equality and independence, the psycho-nationalistic depictions of the country by the political classes are not only utterly frustrating, they are simply untrue. Moreover, to the detriment of Iranians and the world, there is convergence in the way the reality of Iran has been manipulated by successive states ruling the country. In terms of an authoritarian approach to the way Iran should be interpreted, and in the way the meaning of the country is narrowed down to fit cloistered political ideologies filled with problematic notions of identity, the periods before and after the revolution are surprisingly consistent.

In order to finalise my diagnosis and as a means to summarise my prescriptions that could put Iran at peace, at least in my humble view, I would like to compare two interviews conducted by the aforementioned Oriana Fallaci. Fallaci was in many ways the *enfant terrible* of global journalism for decades until she passed away in 2006. Assertive and charismatic, she became viciously anti-Muslim firmly in line with the trend of Islamophobia after the al-Qaeda terror attacks on the United States in September 2001. When Fallaci interviewed the shah in December 1973, at a time when he was at the zenith of his power, the monarch displayed exactly the authoritarian approach to Iran that I alluded to in order to ease us into this chapter. For Fallaci the insecure shah was easy prey, and it didn't take long until she entangled him in his own contradictions and dilemmas: 'A monarchy is the only possible means to govern Iran,' the shah replied to a question from Fallaci about the challenges of being a king.[1] 'If I have been able to do something, a lot, in fact, for Iran, it is owing to the detail, slight as it may seem, that I'm its king.'[2] And then the shah adds a revealing point in his mode of argumentation: 'To get things done, one needs power, and to hold onto power one mustn't ask anyone's permission or advice . . . I ought to say that your regimes won't last and mine will.'[3]

The shah speaks of Iran and its inhabitants as if they were his property. But it is not only this dictatorial aspect that is analytically valuable. He presents himself as the only capable leader of the country, not even *primus inter pares*, no – *primus* full stop. The monarchy is pushed forward as a Trojan horse to legitimate his all-encompassing power as the one and only capable king. It should be obvious to readers of this book that the meaning of Iran is contracted to the degree that it can easily be placed in the hands of the monarch. The scientific rule that we can deduce is simple: states that create a mythology that is very far from the reality of the country that they rule will be destroyed. Efficient governance requires convergence between the interpretation of the state and the reality as it is lived by society. The Iran in the imagination of the shah was not the real Iran. It was a figment of his desire, an ideological construct that could not gain traction because it was not deeply anchored in a legitimacy that needed to be conveyed by the Iranian people. Such a constellation destroys the sovereignty of the state, even if the state uses the most systematically repressive measures. None of the contemporary polities in Iran seems to understand this basic rule.

Let me hold on to this authoritarian appropriation of Iran by the country's leaders for a moment. In the discourse of Ayatollah Khomeini, there was a comparable theft of the meaning of Iran that has repeatedly opened up opposition to the state to this day. The revolution was a cosmopolitan event, global in its scope and internationalist in its ambition. It was imbued with currents from Central and South America – certainly Simon Bolívar, Che Guevera and Castro; Francophone philosophy – definitely Sartre, Fanon and Foucault; German critique – Marcuse and Adorno; leftist

---

[1] Oriana Fallaci, 'The Shah of Iran: an interview with Mohammad Reza Pahlavi', *New Republic*, 1 December 1973, available at https://newrepublic.com/article/92745/shah-iran-mohammad-reza-pahlevi-oriana-fallaci, accessed 23 August 2018.
[2] Ibid.   [3] Ibid.

internationalism, from Mao to Marx; Irish Republicanism – the legend of Bobby Sands; and Muslim anti-imperialism – the ideas and activism of Muhammad Ali, Malcolm X, Muhammad Iqbal and Sayyid Qutb. The Iranian movement was fostered in the age of revolution, the distinctly modern twentieth-century zeitgeist that created these tectonic shifts in world politics.

The impetus to the revolution, then, was global. The rule of the shah, at that moment of history, was considered to be decadent, dictatorial, even fascistic, not only by most Iranians themselves, but by other movements around the world, especially among the left, Islamists and in anti-colonial settings. This globality of the revolution explains why there were demonstrations against the shah wherever he went: most infamously in West Germany in June 1967, when he attended Mozart's *The Magic Flute* at the Deutsche Oper in Berlin during his state visit to the country. When the protest turned violent after clashes with pro-shah supporters, aided and abetted by intelligence officers of the shah's secret service SAVAK, Benno Ohnesorg was shot by a German police officer named Kurras.[4] His death became a tragic symbol of resistance to the state for the student movement in West Germany, especially in the 1970s.

Other examples of the global anti-shah movement were equally revealing, for instance in November 1977, when the shah visited Washington DC and his welcome at the White House was disrupted by protests led by Iranian students. In an iconic moment in the build-up to the revolution, the tear gas used by the US police to dispel the demonstrators drifted to the White House lawn, where the shah and President Carter had to dab their eyes as the wind turned against them (literally). Even after the shah was deposed, the demonstrations against him continued beyond Iran, for example in Panama, where the shah and his family sought refuge in December 1979. The *New York Times* reported at the time that hundreds of leftist students in Panama voiced their opposition to the shah's presence: 'Panama has become the political trash can of the United States', one opposition paper head-lined.[5] Indeed, there is increasing evidence of, and compelling research

---

[4] It was later revealed that at the time of the events Kurras was an informal collaborator with the East German secret police (Stasi), and a long-time member of the Socialist Unity Party of Germany, the ruling East German Communist party.

[5] 'Panama suppressing protests over shah', *New York Times*, 20 December 1979.

into, the global networks of the student movements and their support for the Iranian revolution, in Europe, the United States, Latin America and beyond.[6]

The age of revolution. The previous paragraph was meant to demonstrate that the Islamised version in Iran was merely another manifestation of this passage of global history which was geared to utopian notions of total change that were not meant to contain and confine, but to transcend and liberate. But in this interview with Khomeini none of these aspects of the reality of 1970s Iran, nor its global context, are represented or acknowledged. Like the shah, Ayatollah Khomeini dotted his conversation with Fallaci with restrictions, boundaries, walls, narrowing down the meaning of Iran. The present book is exactly about movements of meanings in order to demonstrate that an authoritarian approach towards Iran restricts the country's ability to be free. This particularly revealing conversation with Khomeini took place in September 1979, when the revolution had swept away the shah and when the discourse of Khomeini was significantly different from the rather more inclusive approach that he had proclaimed in exile. Now that he had triumphed, Khomeini must have thought, it was time to stand firm: In response to a question about his authority over the state, Khomeini replied to Fallaci: 'Since the people love the clergy, have faith in the clergy, want to be guided by the clergy, it is right that the supreme religious authority should oversee the work of the Prime Minister or of the President of the republic'.[7] This is to ensure that 'they don't make mistakes or go against the law: that is, against the Koran'.[8]

In a similar fashion to the shah who pushed the monarchy forward to justify his special role within the state, Khomeini mentions Islam as the 'institution' that gives him the right to rule. In this way, sovereignty is taken out of the hands of the people and placed far away in the realm of an abstract institution of which the speaker, in this case Khomeini, is the central representative. 'The turban for the crown', in the poignant

---

[6] See further Susannah Aquilina, 'Common ground: Iranian student opposition to the shah on the US/Mexico border', *Journal of Intercultural Studies*, Vol. 32, No. 4 (2011), pp. 321–334.

[7] Oriana Fallaci, 'An interview with Khomeini', *New York Times*, 7 October 1979, Section SM, p. 8, available at www.nytimes.com/1979/10/07/archives/an-interview-with-khomeini.html, accessed 23 August 2018.

[8] Ibid.

words of Said Amir Arjomand.[9] For sure, Khomeini's position as Supreme Leader was eclipsed by the other institutions of the state, which is why his rule, unlike the shah's, was not a one-man dictatorship. Neither was he corrupt, he didn't take power to enrich himself and his family, and he certainly had very firm principles geared to notions of national independence and individual piety. This is a clear difference to the shah. But Khomeini did reserve a very special, even divine, status for the representatives of his idea of Iran. In such a constellation, the people are relegated to objects of power to be ruled, and not subjects of their own political preferences.

It is not that Khomeini and the shah didn't care about being perceived as unjust. They were simply contracting the space for those Iranians who disagreed with them, thus creating a hierarchy at the top of which they put the sovereignty that they claimed for their constituency, wider in Khomeini's case, and rather more oligopolistic in the case of the shah. This is why both the shah and Khomeini considered themselves to be benevolent leaders. They were really convinced that their form of governance was just. In the words of Khomeini: 'I cry I laugh, I suffer. Do you think I am not a human being? With regard to forgiving: I pardoned the majority of those who caused us harm ... But for those that we discussed before, there is no pardon, there is no pity.'[10] The shah created an equally egocentric scenario, where it is taken for granted that his judgement is not only just, but forgiving: 'I've always granted a pardon to those who attempted to assassinate me, but I've never shown the slightest mercy to the criminals you call guerrilla fighters or to traitors to the country. They're people we must eliminate.'[11]

In their responses to questions about their treatment of the opposition, an equally arbitrary attitude to governance reveals itself: According to the shah: 'It depends on what you mean by political prisoners. If it's Communists you mean, for instance, I don't consider them political prisoners because communism is against the law. It follows that a Communist is ... a common criminal.'[12] Khomeini criminalised the opposition in very similar terms: In his reply to Fallaci he said: 'You even presume that I should permit the plots of those who want to bring the country to anarchy and corruption – as

---

[9] Said Amir Arjomand, *The Turban for the Crown: The Islamic Revolution in Iran*, Oxford: Oxford University Press, 1989.
[10] Fallaci, 'An interview with Khomeini'.   [11] Fallaci, 'The Shah of Iran'.
[12] Ibid.

though freedom of thought and of expression were the freedom to plot and to corrupt.'[13] For Khomeini, as well, 'communists' were the primary target: 'If they were arrested [it] was because they were serving a foreign interest, like the phony Communists who act on behalf of America, and of the Shah.'[14]

When Fallaci pressed them on the issue of freedom and democracy, their angry and short-tempered reactions reveal the contradictions in their mode of argumentation, so typical of an authoritarian personality: The shah: 'But I don't want that kind of democracy! Haven't you understood that? I don't know what to do with that kind of democracy! I don't want any part of it, it's all yours, you can keep it, don't you see?'[15] And Khomeini: 'To begin with the word Islam does not need adjectives such as democratic. Precisely because Islam is everything, it means everything. Besides, this democracy, which you love so much and that you consider so valuable, does not have a precise meaning ... If you foreigners don't understand, too bad for you. It's none of your business ... If some Iranians don't understand it, too bad for them.'[16] Their illiberal interpretation of Iran can even be gathered from their anger when Fallaci pressed them on the issue of individual rights – Khomeini: 'This is none of your business. Our customs are none of your business.'[17] And the shah: 'Freedom of thought, freedom of thought! Democracy, democracy! With five-year-olds going on strike and parading the street. Is that what you call democracy? Freedom?'[18]

No wonder, then, that the shah and Khomeini were particularly territorial and opinionated when it came to the status of women. Their macho interpretation of Iran was built on the psycho-nationalist notion that they played the role of the benevolent, ultimately wise father of the nation. Both the shah and Khomeini were ageist and patriarchal. When confronted by Fallaci about their views on women and their status in Iran they became defensive, even angry: The shah: 'Equality you say? ... I don't want to seem rude but ... You may be equal in the eyes of the law, but not I beg your pardon for saying so, in ability ... You [women] have produced nothing great, nothing! Tell me how many women capable of governing have you met ...?'[19] For Khomeini, it was equally natural to speak on behalf of Iranian women as if they were his

[13] Fallaci, 'An interview with Khomeini'.   [14] Ibid.
[15] Fallaci, 'The Shah of Iran'.   [16] Fallaci, 'An interview with Khomeini'.
[17] Ibid.   [18] Fallaci, 'The Shah of Iran'.   [19] Ibid.

property. Just before Fallaci lost her temper and removed her headscarf, shouting 'I'm going to take off this stupid medieval rag right now. There. Done.',[20] Khomeini attacked her for being dressed like 'coquettes who put on makeup and go into the streets showing off their necks, their hair, their shapes ... If you do not like Islamic dress you are not obliged to wear it. Because Islamic dress is for good and proper young women.'[21] The shah, to be fair, didn't have anything against such 'coquettes'.

The point of simulating a conversation between the shah, Khomeini and Oriana Fallaci is not to explain all of their political attitudes in terms of their responses or even their personality. Obviously, the shah instituted a set of women's rights during the so-called White Revolution of 1963, ushering in their right to vote which was criticised by the orthodox clergy, including Khomeini, who in turn advocated the same right as a part of the revolution of 1979. The point of my comparison is to demonstrate that both the shah and Khomeini were divisive politicians. Especially with the mandate of the revolution that brought him to the fore, Khomeini had the 'divine' blessing of history to become a Mandela or a Gandhi. Instead, he chose to become a Lenin, admittedly with less bloodshed in terms of the revolutionary excesses, but with a similarly dichotomic conception of politics. With it came contempt for the political enemy, and his destruction, if necessary.

The shah, in turn, could have governed as a constitutional monarch as the Iranian constitution stipulated. He had the backing of the United States; his state was not threatened from the outside. All he had to do was to understand his country. He failed dismally. Instead, both the shah and Khomeini established boundaries between 'good' Iranians, largely those that agreed with them, and the rest. There was no compromising conception of the political opponent as a legitimate competitor that needed to be folded into the political process in order to ensure a consensus and harmony within society. Hence the divisive political landscapes among Iranians to this day, and hence also the binary between *khodi* (those that belong to us) and *gheyre khodi* (those that do not) in the Persian political lexicon and in the reality of Iranian lives. A people interrupted, as Hamid Dabashi rightly termed it.[22]

Our concepts help us to understand all of this even better now. I conceptualised psycho-nationalism as a space-creating device, a

---

[20] Fallaci, 'An interview with Khomeini'.   [21] Ibid.
[22] Hamid Dabashi, *Iran: A People Interrupted*, New York: The New Press, 2008.

boundary that marks the strictly enforced delineation between 'us' and 'them', friend and foe, *khodi* and *gheyre khodi*. The wide parenthesis that opens up after the term Iran in order to give it meaning is narrowed down to a few ideological precepts which are meant to fix the boundary between those who are right and those who are wrong. The criminalisation of the latter is exactly the reason why before and after the revolution so many Iranians and non-Iranians were killed and maimed by the state.

Philosophy and its derivative, political science, a much neglected and maligned discipline in any authoritarian setting, give us all the answers to comprehend this tragedy. In Iran, the real meaning of the country, which can only be captured in a sophisticated symphony, has been crushed under the heavy weight of ideological cacophony. Yet, where there is power, there is always resistance. The pendulum of state power that swings against resistance will always provoke a reaction in much the same way as the law of equation in physics. At the point of impact, the pendulum weight provokes a regular back and forth. This is the power–resistance dialectic that has punctured contemporary Iranian history. If this had not been the order of things in Iran, all the upheavals that I have covered in this book would not have happened. The politico-scientific rule is simple: if legitimacy is simply asserted, and not engineered; if it is not based on a meaning of Iran that is wide enough to accommodate that diverse and inherently complex composition of Iranian society, it *will* fail.

No ideological hocus-pocus can change reality long-term. Stripped of its nefarious pretensions, the Iranian state would have to do what the revolution promised: deliver social justice, political empowerment, independence from authoritarianism and forms of hegemony, both in terms of Iran's external relations and domestic politics. The state would finally have to perform for society and not the other way around. The hocus-pocus is but a bad trick to shirk these responsibilities, and not a long-term formula for governance. Many sectors of the political classes in Iran have understood this fundamental dilemma, but they lag behind in institutionalising solutions.

It may be clear by now that psycho-nationalism is about a dangerous transmission belt, exactly that hocus-pocus that I have just been referring to – black magic, a devil's trick that leaves the stench of sulphur wherever it shows up in the world. It traces the way politics manipulates our genuine feelings for the nefarious purpose of worshipping the state, killing and dying for it. As opposed to traditional nationalism studies, psycho-nationalism focuses on the cognitive effects of this form of mental abuse. So psycho-nationalism really presents a psychology of the way the idea of the nation-state is continuously invented and introjected into our thinking as something worth killing and dying for. It is not a natural, innate human desire to enter this one-sided, abusive relationship. Psycho-nationalists act as narcissistic bullies who push and shove their objects into submission for the pure purpose of power/control. Psycho-nationalism is alive and well exactly because this psychology to create boundaries between 'us' and 'them' has been cognitively anchored in our minds for a long time now through a process of mental introjection.

But contrary to its institutionalisation, the Iranian revolution itself was a hybrid, cosmopolitan and libertarian event. The revolutionaries were not nationalists in the traditional sense of the term. Of course, Ayatollah Khomeini was against the forms of Persian ultra-nationalism espoused by the monarchy. And yet, the Iranian state, as it was institutionalised after the revolution, couldn't fully escape the legacies of psycho-nationalism in the country. The political formula for power remained similar until gradual reforms were implemented as part of the pluralistic momentum driving the dialectic between state and society. Yet, there continues to be a rather stringent boundary between the sanctioned ideology of the state and those placed outside of it. The state continues to claim a sacrosanct hegemonic position that demands the sacrifice of the populace for the sake of the nation, repeatedly codified in terms of Iranians close to the ideology of the state more specifically. Of course, the tropes and metaphors have changed from the shah's orthodox Persian nationalism and they took on a rather more potent religious, theocratic and explicitly transcendental colouring after the revolution. But the divisive friend–enemy dichotomy continues to be enforced, to the detriment of rather more symbiotic and peaceful state–society relations.

Therefore, this emphasis on the nation as a sacred project continues to hamper a process of national reconciliation, exactly because it does not correspond to the reality of Iran's manifold identity set and in particular its cosmopolitan, globally constituted historical consciousness. The state remains the sanctioned ideal that everyone should be cognitively obliged to. This is psycho-nationalism par excellence because it is based on the irrational notion that this claustrophobic interpretation of Iran can be force-fed to Iranians, if only they would understand that this Shia-Islamic-clericalised idea of the country is the one and only acceptable representation. Yet at the same time there is a nuanced difference in attitude from that of the right wing in Europe and North America who subscribe to a similarly authoritarian depiction of their countries as monolithic and one-dimensional. In Iran, psycho-nationalism is not imbued with a systematic grammar of racism, despite the informal and formal discrimination enforced by some sections of the state. This genealogical and biological emphasis on difference, that was developed in the laboratories of the European Enlightenment, never really turned into a systematic movement in Persia, not least because Muslim political thought and philosophy is – at its ideational epicentre – incompatible with scientific racism.

An Artist's Impression: Iran As a Global Symphony[23]

It is helpful to the flow of my analysis that the seventeenth-century German composer Johann Sebastian Bach, a true genius of classical music, appears twice in the interviews with which I started this epilogue: First, in the response of the shah, when he pointed out to Fallaci that women never produced a Bach. And second, in her question to Khomeini when she asked if the music of Bach would be forbidden in Iran. We can use this lucky coincidence to connect rather neatly to the functions of music (and art) in the methodological framework of this study – our discursive musicology.

First and foremost, all three of our protagonists failed to point to music as an art form that could open up a symphony of dialogue and empathy between cultures, a West–Eastern Divan, in the words of Goethe that inspired the initiative of Daniel Barenboim and the late Edward Said.[24] This is contrary to the effort in this book to introduce music as a *via media* in order to tease out a different sensation in the reader's imagination. Fallaci herself revealed an ignorant and arrogant streak in her personality when she presumed that a seventy-eight-year

23 Parts of this section are taken from an interview with David Orsi. See 'Interview – Arshin Adib-Moghaddam', *E-International Relations*, 26 July 2018, available at www.e-ir.info/2018/07/26/interview-arshin-adib-moghaddam-2/, accessed 24 June 2019.
24 See further 'West–Eastern Divan Orchestra', available at www.barenboim-said.es/en/west-eastern-divan-orchestra/, accessed 12 September 2019.

old revolutionary cleric had to know Bach. Obviously, she wanted to portray Khomeini as an ignorant reactionary, but in the way she posed her questions even to the rather more bourgeois shah, she entrenched the false notion that there is some kind of inevitable dichotomy between her enlightened and democratic 'West' and the backward 'East'.

Fallaci could have asked Khomeini or the shah about the doyens of 'Persian-Muslim' poetry, art and philosophy, such as Rumi (Mowlana Balkhi), Hafiz, Sa'adi or Omar Khayyam. But that would have disturbed her mission to suggest that East–West binary, as these Muslims led a rather hedonistic and bohemian lifestyle, sweetened by a lot of wine, that should have appealed to her gusto. If she was really interested in understanding Persia, she could have prompted Khomeini to comment on the famous poem of Rumi called 'One Song', which chimes with my appreciation of music as a *via media* for tolerance. 'What is praised is one,' Rumi brings together, 'so the praise is one too, many jugs being poured into a huge basin. All religions, all this singing, one song.'[25] What would have been the reaction of Khomeini if he had been confronted with a libertarian anecdote taken from his own cultural milieu? Fallaci would have none of it. Self-righteous in her Eurocentric and discriminatory feminist fundamentalism, her interviews reveal a divisive and opinionated form of journalism without much cultural empathy or understanding. As such, her hatred for Muslims and migrants, expressed at a later stage of her life, should not come as a surprise.

I have argued that the immersion of Iran in the world is the inevitability that defies Iranian governments that are based on confined interpretations of the meaning of the country. Only a state that accepts the reality of the immensely complex and intricate tapestry that makes up the Iranian body politic will have a syncretic relationship to it and a democratic wellspring of sovereignty and legitimacy. This is because global history is immanent to Iran, as some of my evidence demonstrated, certainly in the prologue that we are connecting with now. After all it was no one less than the doyen of modern philosophy, and seminal influence on Karl Marx, the German Georg Wilhem Friedrich Hegel (1770–1831), who singled out the Zoroastrian-Persian empire

---

[25] Craig Considine, 'Rumi and Emerson: a bridge between the west and the Muslim world', *Huffington Post*, 14 October 2013. See further Cyrus Masroori, 'An Islamic language of toleration: Rumi's criticism of religious persecution', *Political Research Quarterly*, Vol. 63, No. 2 (2010), pp. 243–256.

of the Achaemenids as 'strictly the beginning of world history'.[26] In a sweeping historical analysis and obviously under the influence of Goethe, Hegel considered Persian Muslim poetry, in particular that of Hafiz, as a sublime art form that realises the freedom of the artist from external constraints. This distinctly libertarian sublimity of 'Mohammedan-Persian' poetry, that he dissects in his monumental *Aesthetics: Lectures on Fine Art*, turns any object into more than its components, and certainly more than a mere metaphor for God. The rose, for instance, 'appears to the poet as ensouled, as an affianced beloved, and with his spirit he is engrossed in the soul of the rose'.[27]

We have seen how the humble red tulip was turned into a metaphor for sacrifice after the revolution in Iran. Conversely, Hegel connects to the role of flowers in general, and red roses in particular, in Persian philosophy, art and poetry – flowers as a metaphor for equilibrium, freedom, peace. These themes inspired the Russian composer Nikolai Andreyevich Rimsky-Korsakov to write his famed symphonic suite *Sheherzadeh* in 1888, named after the equally famous female character and storyteller in the frame narrative of *One Thousand and One Nights*. The rose, in particular, played a crucial role in his *Four Cycles*, in which he named song number 2 'The Nightingale and the Rose'. This metaphor of *gol-o-bolbol* (rose and nightingale) has had a prominent presence in Persian literature, the poetry of Rumi and Hafiz, and even in architecture as a decorative theme promoted in particular by the Zand dynasty (1750–1779) in their capital Shiraz. The tileworks and marble dados of the *haft tan* (the grave of seven mystics), for instance, were decorated with a design of the rose and the nightingale in the typical Zand style.[28]

The same theme provided the title of Oscar Wilde's (1854–1900) classic book. We now know that Wilde had access to the poems of Hafiz as part of his small collection of books in prison.[29] In these global manifestations of art, we find a wellspring of a dialogical,

[26] Georg Wilhelm Friedrich Hegel, *Lectures on the Philosophy of History*, London: Henry G. Bohn, 1861, p. 174. See further the comprehensive study by Lori Khatchadourian, *Imperial Matter: Ancient Persia and the Archaeology of Empires*, Oakland: University of California Press, 2016.

[27] Georg Wilhelm Friedrich Hegel, *Aesthetics: Lectures on Fine Art*, vol. 1, Oxford: Oxford University Press, 1985, p. 370.

[28] See further 'Gol o bolbol', *Encyclopaedia Iranica*, available at www.iranicaonline.org/articles/gol-o-bolbol#prettyPhoto, accessed 12 August 2019.

[29] See Alex Johnson 'The book list: what was in Oscar Wilde's prison library', *The Independent*, 20 March 2018, available at www.independent.co.uk/arts-

universalistic spirit that connects, rather than divides, includes, rather than rejects, and embraces, rather than separates. In light of these dialogical connections, the answers of the shah and Khomeini with which we started this chapter must seem primitive and politically naive. How can you assume that the meaning of Iran can be contracted to a set of ideological platitudes without opening up an unbridgeable chasm, and without that abyss staring back at you?

Flowers as symbols for philosophy, diplomacy, global history? Certainly, the rose garden of the famed Persian-Muslim poet Sa'adi, one of the genius prodigies of the Shiraz school in thirteenth-century Persia, believed in this 'flower power' when he set up the rose garden (or *golestan*) as a metaphor for paradise (derived from the Persian *pardis*), envisaged as an attainable place of inner and outer peace to which every individual could venture. This well-known verse of Sa'adi which is part of chapter 1, story 10 of his world-famous *Golestan* is woven into an immensely beautiful carpet in the UN headquarters in New York, and connects rather neatly to this beautifully universalistic spirit that is central to my argument here:

> Human beings are members of a whole,
> In creation of one essence and soul.
> If one member is afflicted with pain,
> Other members uneasy will remain.
> If you have no sympathy for human pain,
> The name of human you cannot retain.

Flower power indeed. This humanistic tradition in Persian-Muslim poetry, which can be discerned from ancient Zoroastrian sources as well, was taken as an entry point for the diplomacy that delivered the JCPOA, when President Obama quoted the verse in his videotaped new year (*Nowrouz*) message to Iran in March 2009, opening up a new chapter in US–Iranian relations: 'But let us remember the words that were written by the poet Sa'adi, so many years ago,' Obama said. '"The children of Adam are limbs to each other, having been created of one essence."'[30] Sa'adi's 'Bani Adam' adorns the United Nations

entertainment/books/features/oscar-wilde-prison-library-a-book-of-book-lists-reading-gaol-a8265866.html, accessed 15 September 2019.

[30] 'Remarks of President Obama marking Nowruz', *The White House*, 20 March 2010, available at https://obamawhitehouse.archives.gov/realitycheck/the-press-office/remarks-president-obama-marking-nowruz, accessed 4 September 2019.

building in New York (the British band Coldplay also made it the name of a song on their album *Everyday Life*). Obama connected to this radiant universal tradition in Iran that is inextricably entangled with global history. Sa'adi extracted a rich political theory of statecraft out of his life-affirming, humanistic and cosmopolitan poetry. For instance, in chapter 1 of *Bustan*, he recounts following counsel in support of good, effective and ethical governance:

Cherish the poor, and seek not thine own comfort. The shepherd should not sleep while the wolf is among the sheep. Protect the needy, for a king wears his crown for the sake of his subjects. The people are as the root and the king is as the tree; and the tree, O son, gains strength from the root. He should not oppress the people who has fear of injury to his kingdom. Seek not plenteousness in that land where the people are afflicted by the king.[31]

In turn, the problem of governance in the modern history of Iran is largely due to a highly ideological negation of that global spirit, inclusive approach, and mutually beneficial social contract between the state and society, that Sa'adi understood as necessary in order to rule legitimately, even in the thirteenth century. Hence the ongoing clashes between state and society, exactly at the rhizome where the modern Iranian state claims its legitimacy, before and after the revolution of 1979.

Some of this poetic flower power continues to live on in the work of contemporary Iranian artists, such as Lida Sherafatmand whose world-renowned 'florescentist' style, that adorns the cover of this book, uses flowers as a tapestry for objects, defying narrow conceptions of identity.[32] Instead, her work speaks to a universalistic language of hope, seldom spoken in the heavy and unimaginative world of politics. Her art is another example of the location of Iran on a global map that this book has tried to navigate. It resembles a life-affirming universe made up of attainable dreamworlds. Gentle brushstrokes adorn a canvass that speaks to our common humanity and the peace and love deeply embedded therein. This is art beyond identity, and it is an

---

[31] David Rosenbaum (ed.), *The Bustan or Orchard of Sa'di*, trans. E. Hart Edwards, London: Omphaloskepsis Books, 2010, p. 9. See also Alireza Shomali and Mehrzad Boroujerdi, 'On Sa'di's Treatise on Advice to the Kings', in Mehrzad Boroujerdi (ed.), *Mirror for the Muslim Prince: Islam and the Theory of Statecraft*, Syracuse, NY: Syracuse University Press, 2013, pp. 45–81.

[32] See further her official website www.lida.gallery/, accessed 11 August 2018.

appropriate artistic manifestation of the post-national methodology underlying this study. To my mind, Lida sits in the same garden as Sa'adi; astounded by the same beautiful symphony of flowers. They meet beyond time and space, exactly where the historical reality of Iran *should* be situated. Her painting explodes, not in order to destroy, but to invite us into a different expression of understanding, much like the 'dawn motif' propounded by the brass fanfare in the composition of Strauss that I used for Chapter 1. Art and music conducted in this mode give us profound insights that appear ideologically neutral, yet are philosophically overwhelming.

Such syncretism is inscribed in the fabric of Iran. From Alexander 'the Great' to Pablo Picasso, whose masterpieces are kept in the Iranian Contemporary Art Museum, together with an incredibly fascinating collection of artists such as Monet, Warhol (his lithography of Mick Jagger), Van Gogh, Edvard Munch, Henry Moore and Alberto Giacometti: Iran transcends. There is also this Occident in the DNA of contemporary Persia, that can be pinned down in the inspirational story of Howard Baskerville, another personality who is 'present' in Iran, whether some of the hard-line factions in the country want it or not. Baskerville connects the history of US 'rebels' to Iranian resistance to tyranny, through his active support of the constitutional revolt in 1907 which brought about major democratic reforms in the country. When Baskerville was shot on a sortie in support of the constitutional-ists a couple of years later, the legendary hero of the constitutional revolt, Sattar Khan, sent a poignant telegram to Baskerville's parents: 'Persia much regrets the honourable loss of your dear son in the cause of liberty, and we give our parole that future Persia will always revere his name in her history like Lafayette and will respect his venerable tomb.'[33] There is a beautifully crafted bronze bust of Baskerville in the constitutional house of Tabriz in north-western Iran where he is buried. In this way, he has become another inerasable nodal point of Iran's dialectic with global history, in this case with the United States.

'Layla', the iconic song by Eric Clapton, connects to the Iranian dialectic with the world from a similarly intimate angle and gives us the perfect endnote to our 'global symphony' of Iran. Clapton adopted

---

[33] Mark F. Bernstein, 'An American hero in Iran', *Princeton Exchange*, 9 May 2007, available at https://paw.princeton.edu/article/american-hero-iran, accessed 8 November 2020.

the song from the romantic poem *Layla and Majnun*, written in the twelfth century by the Persian-Muslim Sufi master Nizami Ganjavi (1141–1209), who adopted it from a long history of Arabic anecdotal writings.[34] Clapton wrote it for his future wife who was married to George Harrison at the time the song was released in 1971. Ganjavi's poem had been given to him by Ian Dallas, the Scottish playwright and actor, who had embraced Islam and became a Sufi sheikh with a global following in 1967 (one decade before Yusuf Islam (Cat Stevens) embraced Sufism). But the important point for my musings is that this romantic poem, that every Iranian that I have encountered knows, and that Lord Byron aptly called 'The Romeo and Juliet of the East', has a special place in popular music. This is yet another example of the global connections that the Persian presence in the world created and that Hegel singled out with reference to what he called 'Mohammedan-Persian' poetry, despite his Eurocentric conception of history. This global consciousness will always be there, because it is inscribed onto such a vast array of world culture, which continuously radiates back onto the meaning of Iran.

However, it is not enough to assert, as the contemporary Iranian philosopher Abdolkarim Soroush famously did, that Iran shares a Muslim, Persian *and* Western identity because of some of these global entanglements.[35] Recent scholarship has shown that being 'Muslim' or 'Western' are themselves problematic generalisations that need to be broken down, and lodged into their global context, which gives their origins meaning and sustenance. Critical Iranian studies has attempted to smash these constructs into infinitesimally small pieces in order to enable a wider meaning of Iran which can accommodate those who are regularly excluded from big identity concepts. Iran cannot be captured by platitudes, indeed no country can. The reality of contemporary

---

[34] See further Ali Asghar Seyed-Gohrab, *Laylī and Majnūn: Love, Madness and Mystic Longing in Nezāmi's Epic Romance*, Leiden: Brill, 2003.

[35] See further 'Soroush: pedar chande-ye eslah talaban nistam [Soroush: I am not the godfather of the reform movement]', *Shargh*, 29 Mordad 1385; Abdolkarim Soroush, *Reason, Freedom & Democracy in Islam: Essential Writings of 'Abdolkarim Soroush*, trans. and ed. Mahmoud Sadri and Ahmad Sadri, Oxford: Oxford University Press, 2000; and Abdolkarim Soroush, 'Scientific development, political development', *Kian Monthly Review*, Vol. 10, No. 54 (2000), available at www.drsoroush.com/English/By_DrSoroush/E-CMB-19990500-Seminar_on_Tradition_and_Modernism_held_in_Beheshti_University.html, accessed 8 November 2020.

Persia must also be captured from the perspective of its minorities –
from the Mandeans, followers of John the Baptist who have been
living in Ahvaz for thousands of years, to the descendants of African
slaves in rural and urban communities in the provinces of Sistan and
Baluchistan, Hormuzgan, and Khuzestan who inject a distinctly
African tradition into the meaning of Iran. This fascinating
African-Iranian canvas connects to a political economy of slavery
that extends to Africa in the west and India in the east, to Russia and
Turkmenistan in the north, and to the Arab states in the south and
of course to the pain and suffering that the slave trade brought
about in the Americas.[36]

The level of freedom in any country must be judged by the minorities, who are always the first to bear the brunt of any authoritarian
setting. We have to ask the queer Iranian, the Arab-Iranian, the
African-Iranian community in the country, the Kurd, Baluchi and
Sunni Iranian, the Baha'i and Buddhist, are you free, do you feel
emancipated? If the answer by a majority of the respondents is yes,
then we can start speaking of a success of the revolution and the state
that was built upon it.[37]

Recent research is exploring this global Iran.[38] We are, thanks to our
biological composition, trained to think logically, which is exactly why
the political systems around us attempt to target our rationality on a
continuous basis – and now increasingly with the help of machine

[36] See Behnaz A. Mirzai, *A History of Slavery and Emancipation in Iran, 1800–1929*, Austin: University of Texas Press, 2017. The research of Pedram Khosronejad has touched upon related subjects. See his *Re-imagining Iranian African Slavery: Photography As Material Culture*, North Charleston, SC: Create Space Independent Publishing Platform, 2018.

[37] The problematic relationship between the Iranian state and the minorities in the country is explained in Alam Saleh, *Ethnic Identity and the State in Iran*, London: Palgrave, 2013; and Rasmus Christian Elling, *Minorities in Iran: Nationalism and Ethnicity after Khomeini*, London: Palgrave, 2011.

[38] See for instance Hamid Dabashi, *Persophilia: Persian Culture on the Global Scene*, Cambridge, MA: Harvard University Press, 2015; Hamid Dabashi, *Reversing the Colonial Gaze: Persian Travellers Abroad*, Cambridge: Cambridge University Press, 2019; Golbarg Rekabtalaei, *Iranian Cosmopolitanism: A Cinematic History*, Cambridge: Cambridge University Press, 2018; Jason Bahbak Mohaghegh, *Insurgent, Poet, Mystic, Sectarian: The Four Masks of an Eastern Postmodernism*, New York: State University of New York Press, 2015; and Lucian Stone (ed.), *Iranian Identity and Cosmopolitanism: Spheres of Belonging*, London: Bloomsbury, 2014.

learning and artificial intelligence. The effort has been resisted precisely because it goes against nature. This is why none of the totalitarian systems in human history survived. They are literally unnatural. Neuroscientists have long established that the human brain is biologically coded for abstraction and logical thinking; that it is instrumental in mapping our world, that it corrects the errors of our other senses in order to logically interpret our surrounding habitat. This is why you can read the following sentence: *Yuo aer noet a dgorp in teh ocaen. Yuo aer teh entrie oeacn in a drgop. In raeedinng this poem wittren by Rumi, the olny naccassrey tihng is taht the frist and lasat ltteer be at the rghiet pclae. yuor mnind spleles the wrods form tohse cuees alnoe.*

Ultimately, a morally conscious, scientific approach to politics can only emerge out of that firm trust in our ability to think logically and critically. A global caste of thinkers continues to write and educate to that end, united in our cause for relative freedom and relative world peace without hysterical calls for revolution. As a part of this mission, a critical engagement with the state is necessary. One shouldn't shirk that responsibility out of ideological aversion to any kind of political system. After all, it is the political class that is in need of education about the world of politics and society. If a concerned intellectual doesn't go to the meetings, a right-wing think-tank activist will happily take his or her place and make the case for war. I have experienced this in my own activism against a war with Iran, Iraq, Venezuela or a range of other countries which have been on the target list.

As a part of that activity, I have talked to civil rights activists, NGO leaders, prime ministers, presidents, ambassadors and of course with scholars all over the world. They included sceptics about Iran's role in the world, such as the former chairman of the Arab League Amr Moussa, Malcolm Rifkind, who held ministerial posts in successive Conservative governments in the United Kingdom and several ministers and ambassadors of the Gulf Cooperation Council, at the Doha Forum in Qatar. Other interlocutors included British journalists such as Jon Snow and Lindsey Hilsum at SOAS and Chatham House respectively; former Iranian president Mohammad Khatami at Oxford University; Lamberto Dini in Sicily; ministers and high-ranking army officials in India and from Pakistan and many other countries; senior diplomats in Japan, Armenia, South America, the United States and the EU; and Britain's former ambassador to the UN, Sir Jeremy

Greenstock, in Whitehall, to name but a few.[39] I believe that in the end the argument for peace and diplomacy was stronger and that the audiences at these events came out with a different view about the possibility of dialogue, with Iran and other target countries. In addition, I have signed dozens of letters including to the United Nations' Secretary General António Guterres, the high representative of the EU's foreign affairs and security policy and vice-president of the European Commission, Frederica Mogherini, even Ayatollah Khamenei and Donald Trump.[40] I mention these activities merely to encourage a dialogue with the new generation of scholars focusing on Iran and the region, that is emerging with force all over the world – a 'tweet' is not a substitute for speaking truth to power in the 'belly of the beast', if necessary. After all, we *do* know better than many politicians and most other people, because it is our job to do so. It is detrimental to the cause of peace to confine this painfully earned knowledge to the ivory tower. It is as simple as that.

As a result of this joint effort by many concerned peace activists all around the world we have so far succeeded in making a case against yet another tragedy in West Asia because we were present in the corridors of power in order to speak the truth, which is part of our job in a democratic society. One's overall responsibility, then, is to be present as a critical 'locus' for ideas in the relevant realms of society, the media, government, the educational sector etc. Admittedly, one has to be humble. But the overall aim is rooted in the same realistic utopia that the good guys in human history have striven for since the beginning of

---

[39] A lot of these events are publicly accessible on the internet. See, for instance, 'NATO Parliamentary Assembly: Joint Seminar of the Mediterranean and Middle East Special Group (GSM), the Sub-Committee on East–West Economic Co-operation (ESCEW), and the Sub-Committee on National Partnerships (PCNP)', Catania, Italy, 8–10 October 2012, available at www.google.cm/url? sa=t&rct=j&q=&esrc=s&source=web&cd=5&ved= 2ahUKEwj4hMHQ4rzkAhXGShUIHYveBCEQFjAEegQIBRAC&url=http% 3A%2F%2Fwww.congreso.es%2Fbackoffice_doc%2Finternacional% 2Fviajes_orden_dia%2Fanexoot13.pdf&usg= AOvVaw22KMIYdPsEaQEptJLbHV1p, accessed 1 September 2019; or Global Strategy Forum, 'The January 2012 Debate: "Iran and the West: Is War Inevitable?"', available at www.globalstrategyforum.org/events/the-january-debate-iran-and-the-west-is-war-inevitable/, accessed 21 January 2018.

[40] These letters are archived here: https://en-gb.facebook.com/pages/category/ Writer/Professor-Arshin-Adib-Moghaddam-1046158852061511/, accessed 11 August 2019.

time: freedom and world peace within the possibilities that we have. Today, more than ever, we are in need of intellectual contributions to that end. *We* have a clear conscience, after all. The dystopian alternative held up by the resurgent global right wing promises nothing but a bleak abyss of harm, abuse and aggression. The world certainly doesn't need any more of that. I, for one, happily subscribe to the flower power of Sa'adi instead. The rose as a metaphor for peace – for the world and Iran as a petal of it. Imagine that!

Bibliography

Abdollahpour, Behzad, 'Asian civilization conference: a chance for prosperity, stability', *China Daily*, 16 May 2019. Available at www.chinadaily.com.cn/a/201905/16/WS5cdccceea3104842260bbfe7.html, accessed 12 June 2019.

Abedi, M. and G. Leggenhausen (eds.), *Jihad and Shahadat: Struggle and Martyrdom in Islam*, Houston: Institute for Research and Islamic Studies, 1986.

Abrahamian, Ervand, *Khomeinism: Essays on the Islamic Republic*, London: I.B. Tauris, 1993.

The Coup: 1953, the CIA, and the Roots of Modern US–Iranian relations, New York: The New Press, 2013.

Adelkhah, Fariba, *Being Modern in Iran*, trans. Jonathan Derrick, London: Hurst & Company, 1999.

Adib-Moghaddam, Arshin, 'Global intifadah? September 11th and the struggle within Islam', *Cambridge Review of International Affairs*, Vol. 15, No. 2 (2002), pp. 203–216.

The International Politics of the Persian Gulf: A Cultural Genealogy, London: Routledge, 2006.

'The pluralistic momentum in Iran and the future of the reform movement', *Third World Quarterly*, Vol. 27, No. 4 (2006), pp. 665–674.

'The Whole Range of Saddam Hussein's war crimes', *Middle East Report*, No. 236 (2006), pp. 30–35.

'Manufacturing war: Iran in the neo-conservative imagination', *Third World Quarterly*, Vol. 28, No. 3 (2007), pp. 635–653.

'Discourse and violence: the friend–enemy conjunction in contemporary Iranian–American relations', *Critical Studies on Terrorism*, Vol. 2, No. 3 (2009), pp. 512–526.

On the Arab Revolts and the Iranian Revolution: Power and Resistance Today, New York: Bloomsbury, 2013.

(ed.), *A Critical Introduction to Khomeini*, Cambridge; Cambridge University Press, 2014.

'Global grandeur and the meaning of Iran: from the shah to the Islamic Republic', in Henner Fürtig (ed.), *Regional Powers in the Middle East:*

New Constellations after the Arab Revolts, London: Palgrave, 2014, pp. 43–58.

Psycho-nationalism: Global Thought, Iranian Imaginations, Cambridge: Cambridge University Press, 2017.

'Inventions of the Iran–Iraq War', in Nargues Bajoghli and Amir Moosavi (eds.), *Debating the Iran–Iraq War in Contemporary Iran*, London: Routledge, 2018.

'After the Middle East: Turkey and Iran in a new region', *JETRO-IDE ME Review*, Vol. 6 (2018–2019), pp. 1–7.

'People of region yearn for democracy, human rights, social equality', *Mehr News Agency*, 12 April 2019. Available at https://en.mehrnews.com/news/143871/People-of-region-yearn-for-democracy-human-rights-social-equality, accessed 3 June 2019.

Alavi, Seyed Ali, *Iran and Palestine: Past, Present, Future*, London: Routledge, 2019.

Al-e Ahmad, Jalal, *Plagued by the West (Gharbzadegi)*, New York: Caravan, 1982.

'The outline of a disease', in Lloyd Ridgeon (ed.), *Religion and Politics in Modern Iran: A Reader*, London: I.B. Tauris, 2005.

Alemzadeh, Maryam, 'The Islamic Revolutionary Guards Corps in the Iran–Iraq War: an unconventional military's survival', *British Journal of Middle Eastern Studies*, Vol. 46, No. 4 (2019), pp. 622–639.

Algar, Hamid, *Constitution of the Islamic Republic of Iran*, trans. Hamid Algar, Berkeley: Mizan Press, 1980.

Alimagham, Pouya, *Contesting the Iranian Revolution: The Green Uprisings*, Cambridge: Cambridge University Press, 2020.

Alvandi, Roham, *Nixon, Kissinger and the Shah: The United States and Iran in the Cold War*, Oxford: Oxford University Press, 2014.

Anderson, Tim, *Axis of Resistance: Towards an Independent Middle East*, London: Clarity Press, 2020.

Aquilina, Susannah, 'Common ground: Iranian student opposition to the shah on the US/Mexico border', *Journal of Intercultural Studies*, Vol. 32, No. 4 (2011), pp. 321–334.

Arjomand, Said Amir, *The Turban for the Crown: The Islamic Revolution in Iran*, Oxford: Oxford University Press, 1989.

Ashley, Richard K., 'Foreign Policy as Political Performances', *International Studies Notes*, 1998, pp. 51–54.

Atabaki, Touraj (ed.), *The State and the Subaltern: Modernisation, Society and the State in Turkey and Iran*, London: I.B. Tauris, 2007.

Barzegar, Kayhan, 'Iran and the Shiite crescent: myths and realities', *Brown Journal of World Affairs*, Vol. 15, No. 1 (2008), pp. 87–99.

Batmanghelidj, Esfandyar and Abbas Kebriaeezadeh, 'As Coronavirus spreads, Iranian doctors fear the worst', *Foreign Policy*, 3 March 2020. Available at https://foreignpolicy.com/2020/03/03/iran-corona virus-spreads-sanctions-covid19-iranian-doctors-fear-worst/, accessed 16 March 2020.

Bajoghli, Nargues, 'The hidden sources of Iranian strength', *Foreignpolicy. com*, 15 May 2015. Available at https://foreignpolicy.com/2019/05/15/ the-hidden-sources-of-iranian-strength, accessed 12 August 2019.

Iran Reframed: Anxieties of Power in the Islamic Republic, Stanford: Stanford University Press, 2019.

Bajoghli, Nargues and Amir Moosavi (eds.), *Debating the Iran–Iraq War in Contemporary Iran*, London: Routledge, 2018.

Beeman, William O., *The Great Satan vs. the Mad Mullahs: How the United States and Iran Demonize Each Other*, Chicago: Chicago University Press, 2008.

Bennett, Brian, Elaine Shannon and Adam Zagorin, 'A web of intrigue: inside the Israel espionage investigation', *Time*, 5 September 2004.

Bernstein, Mark F., 'An American hero in Iran', *Princeton Exchange*, 9 May 2007. Available at https://paw.princeton.edu/article/american-hero-iran, accessed 8 November 2020.

Browning, Christopher R., 'The suffocation of democracy', *New York Review of Books*, 25 October 2018. Available at www.nybooks.com/ articles/2018/10/25/suffocation-of-democracy/, accessed 1 September 2019.

Bruck, Gabriele vom, *Islam, Memory and Morality in Yemen: Ruling Families in Transition*, London: Palgrave, 2005.

Chan, Stephen, *Out of Evil: New International Politics and Old Doctrines of War*, London: I.B. Tauris, 2004.

Charountaki, Marianna, *Iran and Turkey: International and Regional Engagement in the Middle East*, London: I.B. Tauris, 2019.

Chehabi, Houchang E., *Distant Relations: Iran and Lebanon in the Last 500 years*, London: I.B. Tauris, 2006.

'Chilcot Report: what Blair said to Bush in memos', *BBC*, 6 July 2016. Available at www.bbc.co.uk/news/uk-36722312, accessed 18 May 2018.

'Comprehensive Report of the Special Advisor to the DCI on Iraq's WMD', 30 September 2004, www.cia.gov/library/reports/general-reports-1/iraq_ wmd_2004/, accessed 8 November 2020.

Conduit, Dara and Shahram Akbarzadeh, 'The Iranian reform movement since 2009', in Conduit, Dara and Shahram Akbarzadeh (eds.), *New Opposition in the Middle East*, London: Palgrave, 2018, pp. 119–149.

Crooke, Alastair, *Resistance: The Essence of the Islamist Revolution*, London: Pluto Press, 2009.

Dabashi, Hamid, *Iran: A People Interrupted*, New York: The New Press, 2008.

Persophilia: Persian Culture on the Global Scene, Cambridge, MA: Harvard University Press, 2015.

Reversing the Colonial Gaze: Persian Travellers Abroad, Cambridge: Cambridge University Press, 2019.

Daher, Aurelie, *Hezbollah: Mobilisation and Power*, Oxford: Oxford University Press, 2019.

Darby, Philip, 'Recasting Western knowledges about (post)colonial security', in Damian Grenfell and Paul James (eds.), *Rethinking, Insecurity, War and Violence*, London: Routledge, 2009, pp. 98–110.

'Darius iii, Darius I, the Great', *Encyclopaedia Iranica*. Available at www.iranicaonline.org/articles/darius-iii, accessed 11 May 2019.

Darwich, May and Juliet Karboo, 'IR in the Middle East: foreign policy analysis in theoretical approaches', *International Relations*, Vol. 34, No. 2 (2020), pp. 225–245.

Davari, Arash, 'A return to which self? Ali Shariati and Frantz Fanon on the political ethics of insurrectionary violence', *Comparative Studies of South Asia, Africa and the Middle East*, Vol. 34, No. 1 (2014), pp. 86–105.

Deutsch, Karl et al., *Political Community and the North Atlantic Area*, Princeton: Princeton University Press, 1957.

Ebtekar, Massoumeh, *Takeover in Tehran: The Inside Story of the 1979 US Embassy Capture*, Vancouver: Talon Books, 2000.

Ehteshami, Anoushiravan, *Dynamics of Change in the Persian Gulf: Political Economy and Revolution*, London: Routledge, 2013.

Ehteshami, Anoushiravan and Raymond Hinnebusch: *Syria and Iran: Middle Powers in a Penetrated Regional System*, London: Routledge, 2002.

Ehteshami, Anoushiravan and Niv Horesh (eds.), *China's Presence in the Middle East: The Implication of the One Belt and One Road Initiative*, London: Routledge, 2017.

Ehteshami, Anoushiravan and Mahjoob Zweiri, *Iran and the Rise of Its Neoconservatives: The Politics of Tehran's Silent Revolution*, London: I.B. Tauris, 2007.

Ehteshami, Anoushiravan and Mahjoob Zweiri (eds.), *The Changing Nature of Shia Politics in the Middle East*, London: Ithaca Press, 2015.

Elik, Suleyman, *Iran–Turkey Relations, 1979–2011: Conceptualising the Dynamics of Politics, Religion and Security in Middle-Power States*, London: Routledge, 2013.

Elling, Rasmus Christian, *Minorities in Iran: Nationalism and Ethnicity after Khomeini*, London: Palgrave, 2011.

Fallaci, Oriana, 'An interview with Khomeini', *New York Times*, 7 October 1979, Section SM, p. 8. Available at www.nytimes.com/1979/10/07/archives/an-interview-with-khomeini.html, accessed 23 August 2018.

'The Shah of Iran: an interview with Mohammad Reza Pahlavi', *The New Republic*, 1 December 1973. Available at https://newrepublic.com/art icle/92745/shah-iran-mohammad-reza-pahlevi-oriana-fallaci, accessed 23 August 2018.

Farabi, Abu Nasr, 'kitab al-jam 'bayn ra'yay al-hakimayn, Aflatun al-ilahi wa Aristu (Reconciliation of the two sages spiritual Plato and Aristotle)', in Hossein Nasr with Mehdi Aminrazavi, *An Anthology of Philosophy in Persia* vol. 1, Oxford: Oxford University Press, 1999, pp. 110–118.

Fisk, Robert, *The Great War for Civilisation: The Conquest of the Middle East*, London: Harpers Perennial, 2006.

Forozan, Hesam, *The Military in Post-revolutionary Iran: The Evolution and Roles of the Revolutionary Guards*, London: Routledge, 2016.

'Full text: Action plan on the Belt and Road Initiative', *The State Council The People's Republic of China*, 30 March 2015. Available at http://english.www.gov.cn/archive/publications/2015/03/30/content_281475080249035.htm, accessed 12 November 2018.

'Full text: Netanyahu's speech on Iran in Munich', *Haaretz*, 18 February 2018, available at www.haaretz.com/middle-east-news/full-text-neta nyahu-s-speech-on-iran-in-munich-1.5826934, accessed 2 August 2019.

Fuller, Graham E., 'Repairing US–Iranian relations', *Middle East Policy*, Vol. 6, No. 2 (1998), pp. 140–144.

Gasiorowski, Mark J. and Malcolm Byrne (eds.), *Mohammad Mosaddeq and the 1953 Coup in Iran*, London: Syracuse University Press, 2004.

Ghaffari, Soudeh, 'From religious performances to martial themes: discourse of Shi'a musical eulogies, war and politics in Iran', *Journal of Language and Politics*, Online first 27 June 2019. Available at https://benjamins .com/catalog/jlp.18059.gha, accessed 24 July 2019.

Ghamari-Tabrizi, Behrooz, *Foucault in Iran: Islamic Revolution after the Enlightenment*, Minneapolis: University of Minnesota Press, 2016.

Gharayagh-Zandi, Davoud, *Nahadha-ye madani va hoviyat dar Iran* [Civil groupings and identity in Iran], Tehran: Entesharat-e tamadon-e Iran, 1380 (2001).

Golchin, Husein, *Namazi dar atash va khun* [A prayer in the midst of fire and blood], Tehran: Cultural Centre for Islamic Propaganda, 1372 (1993).

Goodarzi, Jubin, *Syria and Iran: Diplomatic Alliance and Power Politics in the Middle East*, London: Bloomsbury, 2006.

Goode, James F., 'Assisting our brothers, defending ourselves: the Iranian intervention in Oman, 1972–1975', *Iranian Studies*, Vol. 47, No. 3 (2014), pp. 441–462.

Habermas, Jürgen, 'Three normative models of democracy', in Ronald J. Terchek and Thomas C. Conte (eds.), *Theories of Democracy: A Reader*, Oxford: Rowman & Littlefield, 2001, pp. 236–243.

Hagan, John, Joshua Kaiser and Anna Hanson, *Iraq and the Crimes of Aggressive War*, Cambridge: Cambridge University Press, 2015.

Haghighi, Shahrokh, *Gozar az moderniteh? Nicheh, Fuko, Liotar, Derida* [Beyond modernity? Nietzsche, Foucault, Lyotard, Derrida], Tehran: Agah, 1380 (2001).

Hale, William and Ergun Özbudun, *Islamism, Liberalism and Democracy in Turkey: The Case of the AKP*, London: Routledge, 2009.

Haque, Amber, 'Psychology from Islamic perspective: contributions of early Muslim scholars and challenges to contemporary Muslim perspective', *Journal of Religion and Health*, Vol. 43, No. 4 (2004), pp. 357–377.

Hashemi, Nader, and Danny Postel (eds.), *Sectarianization: Mapping the New Politics of the Middle East*, Oxford: Oxford University Press, 2017.

Hegel, Georg Wilhelm Friedrich, *Lectures on the Philosophy of History*, London: Henry G. Bohn, 1861.

Aesthetics: Lectures on Fine Art, vol. 1, Oxford: Oxford University Press, 1985.

Hiro, Dilip, *Cold War in the Islamic World: Saudi Arabia, Iran and the Struggle for Supremacy*, Oxford: Oxford University Press, 2019.

Hobsbawm, Eric J., *Nations and Nationalism since 1780: Programme, Myth, Reality*, 2nd ed., Cambridge: Cambridge University Press, 1992.

'Human development reports', *United Nations Development Programme*, Available at http://hdr.undp.org/en/composite/HDI, accessed 12 August 2019.

Ibn Sina, 'Mantiq al-mashriqiyyin', in Seyyed Hossein Nasr with Mehdi Aminrazavi, *An Anthology of Philosophy in Persian*, vol. 1, Oxford: Oxford University Press.

'Individuals using the internet', *The World Bank*, 2019. Available at https://data.worldbank.org/indicator/IT.NET.USER.ZS?locations=IR, accessed 19 May 2019.

Iqbal, Zafar, *Islamophobia: History, Context and Deconstruction*, London: Sage, 2020.

'Iran and Global Scientific Collaboration in the 21st Century', *Association of Professors and Scholars of Iranian Heritage*, 3 September 2011. Available at www.apsih.org/index.php/news/english-news/275-iran-and-global-sci entific-collaboration-in-the-21st-century, accessed 18 June 2018.

Izadi, Foad and Hakimeh Saghaye-Biria, 'A discourse analysis of elite American newspaper editorials: the case of Iran's nuclear program', *Journal of Communication Inquiry*, Vol. 31, No. 2 (2007), pp. 140–165.

Jannessari, Sohail and Darren Loucaides, 'Spain's Vox Party hates Muslims – except the ones who fund it', *Foreignpolicy.com*, 27 April 2019. Available at https://foreignpolicy.com/2019/04/27/spains-vox-party-hates-muslims-except-the-ones-who-fund-it-mek-ncri-maryam-rajavi-pmoi-vidal-quadras-abascal/, accessed 12 May 2019.

Kadkhodaee, Elham and Zeinab Ghasemi Tari, 'Otherising Iran in American political discourse: case study of a post-JCPOA senate hearing on Iran sanctions', *Third World Quarterly*, Vol. 40, No. 1 (2019), pp. 109–128.

Kamrava, Mehran, *Troubled Waters: Insecurity in the Persian Gulf*, London: Cornell University Press, 2018.

Karimi-fard, Hossein, 'Siasat-e taneshsodai-ye Rouhani dar ghabal-e Amrika: Ahdaf va mavaneh', *Faslname-ye Siasat*, Faculty of Law and Political Science: University of Tehran, Vol. 49, No. 1 (1398) (2019), pp. 205–224. Available at https://jpq.ut.ac.ir/article_70954.html, accessed 16 July 2019.

Keshavarzian, Arang, *Bazaar and State in Iran: Politics of the Tehran Marketplace*, Cambridge: Cambridge University Press, 2007.

Khatami, Mohammad, *Islam, Dialogue and Civil Society*, Canberra: Centre for Arab and Islamic Studies, 2000.

Khatchadourian, Lori, *Imperial Matter: Ancient Persia and the Archaeology of Empires*, Oakland: University of California Press, 2016.

Khomeini, Ruhollah, 'We shall confront the world with our ideology', *Middle East Report*, June 1980, pp. 22–25.

Sahifey-e nur, Vol. 18, Tehran: Vezarat-e Ershad, 1364 (1985).

Islamic Government: Governance of the Jurist, Qom: The Institute for Compilation and Publication of Imam Khomeini Works, 1379 (2000).

'The failure of the US Army in Tabas', 25 April 1980. Available at http://en.imam-khomeini.ir/en/NewsPrint.aspx?ID=7819, accessed 12 April 2012.

Khosronejad, Pedram, *Re-imagining Iranian African Slavery: Photography As Material Culture*, North Charleston, SC: Create Space Independent Publishing Platform, 2018.

Kinch, Penelope, *The US–Iran Relationship: The Impact of Political Identity on Foreign Policy*, London: I.B. Tauris, 2016.

Kinzer, Stephen, *Reset: Iran, Turkey and America's Future*, London: Times Books, 2010.

Lawson, Fred. H., 'From here we begin: a survey of scholarship on the international relations of the Gulf', *British Journal of Middle Eastern Studies*, Vol. 36, No. 3 (2009), pp. 337–357.

Leigh, David, 'Britain's security services and journalists: the secret story', *British Journalism Review*, Vol. 11, No. 2 (2000), pp. 21–26.

Leslie, Jonathan Gerwin, 'Fear and Insecurity: Competing Narratives of the Iran–Israel Relationship', PhD dissertation, SOAS, University of London, 2019.

Maltzahn, Nadia von, *The Syria–Iran Axis: Cultural Diplomacy and International Relations in the Middle East*, London: I.B. Tauris, 2015.

Mannheim, Karl, *Ideology and Utopia: Collected Works of Karl Mannheim*, vol. 1, London: Routledge, 1936.

Marx, Karl, 'Introduction', *A contribution to the critique of Hegel's Philosophy of Right*, 1843. Available at www.marxists.org/archive/marx/works/1843/critique-hpr/intro.htm, accessed 12 December 2013.

Masroori, Cyrus, 'An Islamic language of toleration: Rumi's criticism of religious persecution', *Political Research Quarterly*, Vol. 63, No. 2 (2010), pp. 243–256.

Matin-Asgari, Afshin, 'Iranian postmodernity: the rhetoric of irrationality?', *Critique: Critical Middle Eastern Studies*, Vol. 13, No. 1 (1994), pp. 113–123.

Matthiesen, Toby, *The Other Saudis: Shiism, Dissent and Sectarianism*, Cambridge: Cambridge University Press, 2014.

Mearsheimer, John J., *The Great Delusion: Liberal Dreams and International Realities*, New Haven: Yale University Press, 2018.

Mearsheimer, John and Stephen Walt, 'The Israel lobby', *London Review of Books*, Vol. 28, No. 6, 23 March 2006, available at www.lrb.co.uk/v28/n06/mear01._html, accessed 23 May 2006.

Mehran, Golnar, 'The presentation of the "self" and the "other" in post-revolutionary Iranian school textbooks', in Nikki R. Keddie and Rudi Matthee (eds.), *Iran and the Surrounding World: Interactions in Culture and Cultural Politics*, Seattle: University of Washington Press, 2002, pp. 232–253.

Mirsepassi, Ali, *Transnationalism in Iranian Political Thought: The Life and Times of Ahmad Fardid*, Cambridge: Cambridge University Press, 2017.
   Iran's Quiet Revolution: The Downfall of the Pahlavi State, Cambridge: Cambridge University Press, 2019.

Mirzai, Behnaz A., *A History of Slavery and Emancipation in Iran, 1800–1929*, Austin: University of Texas Press, 2017.

Mohaghegh, Jason Bahbak, *Insurgent, Poet, Mystic, Sectarian: The Four Masks of an Eastern Postmodernism*, New York: State University of New York, 2015.

Mohebi, Melody, *The Formation of Civil Society in Modern Iran: Public Intellectuals and the State*, London: Palgrave, 2014.

Montazeri, Ayatollah Hosseinali, *Khaterat*, Los Angeles: Ketab Corporation, 2001.

Moshirzadeh, Homeira, 'Identity and security in the Middle East', *Iranian Review of Foreign Affairs*, Vol. 4, No. 2 (2013), pp. 5–32.

Mottahedeh, Negar, *Displaced Allegories: Post-revolutionary Iranian Cinema*, London: Duke University Press, 2008.

Nabavi, Negin, 'The changing concept of the "intellectual" in Iran of the 1960s', *Iranian Studies*, Vol. 32, No. 3 (1999), pp. 333–350.

Nakanishi, Hisae, 'The construction of the sanctions regime against Iran: political dimensions of unilateralism', in Ali Z. Marossi and Marisa R. Bassett (eds.), *Economic Sanctions under International Law: Unilateralism, Multilateralism, Legitimacy, and Consequences*, The Hague: Springer, 2015, pp. 23–41.

'Human security and political violence in the Middle East: views from security-development nexus perspective', *Advances in Social Science, Education and Humanities Research (ASSEHR)*, vol. 138, International Conference on Contemporary Social and Political Affairs, 2017.

Nazemi, Nader, 'Sacrifice and authorship: a compendium of the will of Iranian war martyrs', *Iranian Studies*, Vol. 30, Nos. 3–4 (1997), pp. 263–271.

'Netanyahu's speech at AIPAC', *The Times of Israel*, 6 March 2012, available at www.timesofisrael.com/netanyahus-speech-at-aipac-full-text/, accessed 2 February 2019.

Newman, Edward, 'Critical human security studies', *Review of International Studies*, Vol. 36, No. 1 (2010), pp. 77–94.

Nuchu, Joanna Randa, *Everyday Sectarianism in Urban Lebanon: Infrastructures, Public Services, and Power*, Princeton: Princeton University Press, 2016.

Orsi, David, 'Interview – Arshin Adib-Moghaddam', *E-International Relations*, 26 July 2018. Available at www.e-ir.info/2018/07/26/interview-arshin-adib-moghaddam-2/, accessed 24 June 2019.

Parsi, Trita, *Treacherous Alliance: The Secret Dealings of Israel, Iran, and the United States*, London: Yale University Press, 2008.

Patrick, Michael, and David Ryan (eds.), *US Foreign Policy and the Other*, London: Berghahn Books, 2014.

Rahimi, Babak, *Social Media in Iran: Politics and Society after 2009*, New York: State University of New York Press, 2015.

Rahnema, Ali, *The Constitution of Iran: Politics and the State in the Islamic Republic*, trans. John O' Keane, London: I.B. Tauris, 1997.

An Islamic Utopian: A Political Biography of Ali Shariati, London: I.B. Tauris, 2000.

Rajaee, Farhang, *Islamic Values and World View: Khomeyni on Man, the State and International Politics*, vol. 13, London: University Press of America, 1983.

Raji, Mohammad Mehdi (ed.), *Āqā-ye Safir: Goftogu bā Mohammad-Javād Zarif, Safir-e Pishin-e Irān dar Sāzemān-e Mellal-e Mottahed* [Mr Ambassador: A Dialogue with Mohammad Javād Zarif, the Former Ambassador of Iran to the United Nations], Tehran: Nashr-e Ney, 1392 (2013).

Rakel, Eva Patricia, *Power, Islam and Political Elite in Iran: A Study on the Iranian Political Elite from Khomeini to Ahmadinejad*, Leiden: Brill, 2008.

Ram, Haggai, *Iranophobia: The Logic of an Israeli Obsession*, Stanford: Stanford University Press, 2009.

Reber, Dierdra, 'Love as politics: *Amores Perros*, and the emotional aesthetics of neo-liberalism', *Journal of Latin American Cultural Studies*, Vol. 19, No. 3 (2010), pp. 279–298.

Rekabtalaei, Golbarg, *Iranian Cosmopolitanism: A Cinematic History*, Cambridge: Cambridge University Press, 2018.

Ricoeur, Paul, *Time and Narrative*, vol. 1, trans. Kathleen McLaughlin and David Pellauer, Chicago: University of Chicago Press, 1984.

  Lectures on Ideology and Utopia, ed. George H. Taylor, New York: Columbia University Press, 1986.

Ridgeon, Lloyd (ed.), *Religion and Politics in Modern Iran: A Reader*, London: I.B. Tauris, 2005.

Rivetti, Paola, *Political Participation in Iran: From Khatami to the Green Movement*, London: Palgrave, 2020.

Rosenbaum, David (ed.), *The Bustan or Orchard of Sa'di*, trans. E. Hart Edwards, London: Omphaloskepsis Books, 2010.

Rouhani, Hassan, 'Europe should work with Iran to counter US unilateralism', *Financial Times*, 1 November 2018. Available at www.ft.com/con tent/3ecaed5e-dcfc-11e8-b173-ebef6ab1374a, accessed 1 September 2019.

Ryan, David, *Frustrated Empire: US Foreign Policy from 9/11 to Iraq*, London: Pluto, 2007.

Saad, Amal, 'Challenging the sponsor-proxy model: the Iran–Hizbullah relationship', *Global Discourse*, Vol. 9, No. 4 (2019), pp. 627–650.

Saad, Joya Blondel, *The Image of Arabs in Modern Persian Literature*, Lanham, MD: University Press of America, 1996.

Sadeghi-Boroujerdi, Eskandar, *Revolution and Its Discontents: Political Thought and Reform in Iran*, Cambridge: Cambridge University Press, 2019.

Saffari, Siavash, *Beyond Shariati: Modernity, Cosmopolitanism and Islam in Iranian Political Thought*, Cambridge: Cambridge University Press, 2019.

Said, Edward, *Representations of the Intellectual*, London: Vintage 1996.

Saikal, Amin, *Iran Rising: The Survival and Future of the Islamic Republic*, Princeton: Princeton University Press, 2019.

Saleh, Alam, *Ethnic Identity and the State in Iran*, London: Palgrave, 2013.

Saouli, Adham, *Socialisation and Its Tragic Ironies*, Edinburgh: Edinburgh University Press, 2019.

Sarchosh, Niku and Afshin Jahandideh, *Eradeh beh danestan: Michel Fuku*, Tehran: Nashr-e Ney, 1383 (2004).

Schirazi, Asghar, *The Constitution of Iran: Politics and the State in the Islamic Republic*, trans. John O'Kane, London: I.B. Tauris, 1998.

Sefat, Kusha, 'Things and terms: relations between materiality, language, and politics in post-revolutionary Iran', *International Political Sociology*, Vol. 14 No. 2 (2020), pp. 175–95, available at https://doi.org/10.1093/ips/olz031, accessed 14 December 2019.

Seyed-Gohrab, Ali Asghar, *Laylī and Majnūn: Love, Madness and Mystic Longing in Nezāmi's Epic Romance*, Leiden: Brill, 2003.

Seyed-Gohrab, Asghar, *Courtly Riddles: Enigmatic Embellishments in Early Persian Poetry*, West Lafayette, IN: Purdue University Press West, 2008.

Shakuri, Naser, Alireza Emami, Mohammad Ali Bahmani, Fatemeh Rake'i, Parviz Abbasi-Dakani and Reza Esma'ili, 'Elegies for a lost leader: six poems on the death of Khomeini', trans. Paul E. Losensky, *Iranian Studies*, Vol. 30, Nos. 3–4 (1997), pp. 277–289.

Shani, Giorgio, 'Human security as ontological security: a post-colonial approach', *Postcolonial Studies*, Vol. 20, No. 3 (2017), pp. 275–293.

Shariati, Ali, *On the Sociology of Islam: Lectures by Ali Shari'ati*, trans. Hamid Algar, Berkeley: Mizan Press, 1979.

'Arise and bear witness'. Available at www.shariati.com, accessed 24 March 2003.

'Civilisation and modernisation,' in Lloyd Ridgeon (ed.), *Religion and Politics in Modern Iran*, London: I.B. Tauris, 2005, pp. 175–196.

Shaw, Donald L. and Shannon E. Martin, 'The natural, and inevitable, phases of war reporting: historical shadows, new communication in the Persian Gulf', in Robert E. Denton Jr (ed.), *The Media and the Persian Gulf War*, Westport, CT: Praeger, 1993, pp. 43–70.

Shomali Alireza and Mehrzad Boroujerdi, 'On Sa'di's Treatise on Advice to the Kings', in Mehrzad Boroujerdi (ed.), *Mirror for the Muslim Prince: Islam and the Theory of Statecraft*, Syracuse, NY: Syracuse University Press, 2013, pp. 45–81.

Siamdoust, Nahid, *Soundtrack of the Revolution: The Politics of Music in Iran*, Stanford: Stanford University Press, 2017.

Siavoshi, Sussan, *Montazeri: The Life and Thought of Iran's Revolutionary Ayatollah*, Cambridge: Cambridge University Press, 2017.

Sinkaya, Bahram, *The Revolutionary Guards in Iranian Politics: Elites and Shifting Relations*, London: Routledge, 2017.

Smith, Dan, 'The US withdrawal from the Iran deal: one year on', *Stockholm International Peace Research Institute*, 7 May 2019. Available at www.sipri.org/commentary/expert-comment/2019/us-withdrawal-iran-deal-one-year, accessed 13 June 2019.

Soltaninejad, Mohammad, 'Iran and Saudi Arabia: emotionally constructed identities and the question of persistent tensions', *Asian Politics and Policy*, Vol. 11, No. 1 (2019), pp. 104–121.

Soroush, Abdolkarim, *Reason, Freedom & Democracy in Islam: Essential Writings of 'Abdolkarim Soroush*, trans. and ed. Mahmoud Sadri and Ahmad Sadri, Oxford: Oxford University Press, 2000.

'Scientific development, political development', *Kian Monthly Review* Vol. 10, No. 54, Oct.–Nov. 2000. Available at www.drsoroush.com/English/By_DrSoroush/E-CMB-19990500-Seminar_on_Tradition_and_Modernism_held_in_Beheshti_University.html, accessed 8 November 2020.

'Soroush: pedar chande-ye eslah talaban nistam [Soroush: I am not the godfather of the reform movement]', *Shargh*, 29 Mordad 1385 (2006).

Sternfeld, Lior, '"Poland is not lost while we still live": the making of Polish Iran, 1941–45', *Jewish Social Studies*, Vol. 23, No. 3 (2018), pp. 101–127.

Sternfeld, Lior B., *Between Iran and Zion: Jewish Histories of Twentieth Century Iran*, Stanford: Stanford University Press, 2019.

Stoakes, Emanuel, 'War on Iran: America's next catastrophe in the Middle East. An interview with academic and author Dr Arshin Adib-Moghaddam on the consequences of a future war with Iran', *Truthout*, 13 April 2012. Available at https://truthout.org/articles/war-on-iran-americas-next-catastrophe-in-the-middle-east/, accessed 1 May 2012.

Stone, Lucian (ed.), *Iranian Identity and Cosmopolitanism: Spheres of Belonging*, London: Bloomsbury, 2014.

Straw, Jack, *The English Job: Understanding Iran and Why It Distrusts Britain*, London: Biteback Publishing, 2019.

Tavakoli Targhi, Mohammad, *Refashioning Iran: Orientalism, Occidentalism and Historiography*, London: Palgrave, 2001.

Tezcür, Günes Murat, *Muslim Reformers in Iran and Turkey: The Paradox of Modernisation*, Austin: University of Texas Press, 2010.

'"The Nazi origin of Iran's name": another fake news from Bernard-Henri Lévy', *Les Crises*, 4 June 2018, available at www.les-crises.fr/the-nazi-origin-of-irans-name-another-fake-news-from-bernard-henri-levy-bhl/, accessed 26 January 2019.

The Royal Society, 'Knowledge, networks and nations: global scientific collaboration in the 21st century', London, March 2011. Available at http://royalsociety.org/uploadedFiles/Royal_Society_Content/policy/publications/2011/4294976134.pdf, accessed 12 July 2018.

'The Spiritual-Political Will and Testament of the Martyr Major-General Qasem Soleimani', available at https://soleimany-vasiatnameh.com/en, accessed 12 May 2020.

Warnaar, Maaike, *Iranian Foreign Policy during Ahmadinejad: Ideology and Actions*, London: Palgrave Macmillan, 2013.

Wehrey, Frederic, Jerrold D. Green, Brian Nichiporuk, Alireza Nader, Lydia Hansell, Rasool Nafisi and S. R. Bohandy, *The Rise of the Pasdaran: Assessing the Domestic Roles of Iran's Islamic Revolutionary Guards Corps*, Santa Monica: RAND Corporation, 2009.

'West–Eastern Divan Orchestra', available at www.barenboim-said.es/en/west-eastern-divan-orchestra/, accessed 12 September 2019.

Wilkerson, Lawrence, 'Pompeo: the real threat to US national security', *LobeLog*, 19 February 2019. Available at https://lobelog.com/pompeo-the-real-threat-to-u-s-national-security/, accessed 28 March 2019.

Williams, Raymond, *Marxism and Literature*, Oxford: Oxford University Press, 1977.

Xenophon, *The Cyropaedia*, London: Henry G. Bohn, 1885. Available at https://books.google.com.au/books?id=IA4ohkXjeF4C&printsec=frontcover&source=gbs_ge_summary_r&cad=0#v=onepage&q&f=false, accessed 1 September 2019.

Yadgar, Yaacov, *Israel's Jewish Identity Crisis: State and Politics in the Middle East*, Cambridge: Cambridge University Press, 2020.

Zarif, Mohammad Javad, 'Indispensable power: hegemonic tendencies in a globalized world', *Harvard International Review* Vol. 24, No. 4 (Winter 2003), pp. 72–75.

Zarif, Mohammad Javad and Mohammad Reza Alborzi, 'Weapons of mass destruction in Iran's security paradigm: the case of chemical weapons', *Iranian Journal of International Affairs*, Vol. 11, No. 4 (1999–2000), pp. 511–553.

Zia-Ebrahimi, Reza, *The Emergence of Iranian Nationalism: Race and the Politics of Dislocation*, New York: Columbia University Press, 2016.

Zolfaghari, Mahdi, 'Iran's soft power in foreign policy', *International Journal of Management and Applied Science*, Vol. 4, No. 1 (2018), pp. 66–69.

Index

CPSIA information can be obtained
at www.ICGtesting.com
Printed in the USA
LVHW012056080821
694812LV00021B/1864